A Kineño's Journey

ON FAMILY, LEARNING, AND PUBLIC SERVICE

Lauro F. Cavazos, with Gene B. Preuss

Texas Tech University Press

This book is typeset in Mrs Eaves. The paper used in this book meets the minimum
requirements of ANSI/NISO Z39.48-1992 (R1997). ∞

Designed by Kasey McBeath
Cover photograph provided by Lauro F. Cavazos

Library of Congress Cataloging-in-Publication Data
Names: Cavazos, Lauro, author. | Preuss, Gene B., 1966- co-author. | Cavazos, Lau-
ro, Kineño's remembers.
Title: A Kineño's journey : on family, learning, and public service / Lauro F.
Cavazos, with Gene B. Preuss.
Description: Lubbock, Texas : Texas Tech University Press, [2016] | Series: The Gro-
ver E. Murray studies in the American Southwest | Continues: A Kineäno remem-
bers : from the King Ranch to the White House. 2006. | Includes bibliographical
references and index.
Identifiers: LCCN 2016017176 (print) | LCCN 2016025685 (ebook) | ISBN
9780896729681 (hardcover : alkaline paper) | ISBN 9780896729698 (E-book)
Subjects: LCSH: Cavazos, Lauro. | Cavazos, Lauro—Family. | Cavazos, Lauro—
Friends and associates. | Cabinet officers—United States—Biography. | United
States. Department of Education—Officials and employees—Biography. | Mexican
Americans—Biography. | King Ranch (Tex.)—Biography. | Educators—United
States—Biography. | Tufts University. School of Medicine—Biography. | Texas Tech
University—Presidents—Biography.
Classification: LCC E840.8.C385 A3 2016 (print) | LCC E840.8.C385
(ebook) | DDC 370.92 [B] —dc23
LC record available at https://lccn.loc.gov/2016017176

16 17 18 19 20 21 22 23 24 / 9 8 7 6 5 4 3 2 1

Texas Tech University Press
Box 41037 | Lubbock, Texas 79409-1037 USA
800.832.4042 | ttup@ttu.edu | www.ttupress.org

For Peggy, who journeyed with me,
and for our family

~ Lauro F. Cavazos

For Mari, Isabel, and Eugene.
Thanks for your constant encouragement

~ Gene B. Preuss

Contents

Illustrations

Author's Note

In 2006, Texas A&M University Press published my memoir *A Kineño Remembers: From the King Ranch to the White House*. In it I chronicled my early years growing up on the King Ranch and the many life lessons I learned there. I wrote of my father's work as foreman of the Santa Gertrudis division of the ranch and my parents' commitment to educate their children. I told of the Angel of Goliad, heroine of the Texas Revolution. I described aspects of my childhood, my elementary and secondary education, and my subsequent university education. I wrote about the academic institutions I led and of my work as US secretary of education.

I was aware, of course, that I would have to leave out many stories as I wrote and edited that first account. So many stories of people who influenced my academic and personal life in the many roles I played as a student, teacher, medical school dean, university president, and cabinet officer could not fit into that first memoir. Some of them passed through my life rather quickly, while others remained a part of it for many years. So in this book, *A Kineño's Journey*, I try to give voice to those individuals who were previously muted. They were an eclectic lot, religious and profane, university professors and presidents, national leaders and quiet, private men and women. Yet all these people, regardless of their positions or how fleeting the encounters, have left an indelible mark on the fabric of my life, and those experiences molded the person I became. Through these encounters, I learned valuable lessons about life and how to live.

Although I spent many years in academia, I realize that not all of my education happened in classrooms, laboratories, or dissecting rooms. It also came through my travels and encounters and experiences outside educational institutions. I must say, not all of these experiences were positive. I enjoyed my time working in the hectic world of national politics, and saw what government can

With Peggy and Mari Nicholson-Preuss at the Old North Bridge, Concord, MA, June 2013.

accomplish, but I also saw the negative impact it can have on education.

In this book, I also wanted to share more about my time with the love of my life, Peggy. We have spent over sixty years together. I cherish the years we have devoted to each other and fondly recollect how we worked together to raise and educate our ten beautiful and loving children. I trust my love and admiration of her as my spouse and mother to our children shine brightly through my written words. I share many stories about raising and educating our children. Repeatedly, Peggy and I urged them to value education, certain that it would enrich their lives as it had ours. Peggy and I were thankful to be able to raise our children in beautiful Concord, Massachusetts, but we journeyed so our children would understand there is much more to the world.

Gene Preuss's essay "A Kineño's Journey: A Historical Assessment" ends this volume. Gene and I would like to thank our friends and colleagues at the Southwest Collection/Special Collections archives at Texas Tech University, especially Monte Monroe, Bill Tydeman, Janet Neugebauer, Diane Warner, and Tai Kreidler, for their help with the Lauro F. Cavazos Papers housed at the archive. Part of Gene's research was made possible with assistance from a 2006 West Texas Historical Association William Curry Holden Grant for Research and by a Formby Research Fellowship from the Southwest Collection/Special Collections Libraries in 2007. We'd also like to thank Judith Keeling and Joanna Conrad at Texas Tech University Press for their assistance in the publication process; their tireless advice and helpful comments and suggestions are deeply appreciated. Special thanks to Texas historian David Murrah for his help over the years. Thanks to Ben Sargent and the Universal Uclick syndicate for permission to reproduce his delightful cartoon. Finally, we'd like to thank the anonymous reviewers for their insightful and thoughtful comments that helped make this a better book.

My life has been one of learning, teaching, research, and administering educational institutions, and I'm pleased to share some of what I experienced as I journeyed through life with Peggy and our children. Gene and I have tried to be as accurate as possible in our descriptions, but time may have blurred some of the details. Please forgive us for any errors and omissions.

Lauro F. Cavazos
Concord, Massachusetts
2015

A Kineño's Journey

Prologue

Today, an obsidian figure sits on a shelf in our home in Concord, Massachusetts. When I notice it, it reminds me of the person who sold it to me,
an old vendor on top of the Pyramid of the Sun in Teotihuacán who talked to me of patience, optimism in the face of adversity, and acceptance
of one's lot in life. The obsidian figure also takes me back to a time when
my wife, Peggy, and I were introducing our ten children to the grand educational value of travel.

During the summer of 1967, Peggy and I took our children and my
mother to Acapulco, Mexico, and from there to Mexico City. We wanted
our children to visit Latin America to increase their understanding of
other peoples and their culture. Peggy and I also believed that if they
traveled to those countries they would have more insight into their own
Hispanic heritage. Ours is an academic family—I am a professor and Peggy is a nurse—but our income was modest. Still, we managed to raise and
educate our children by example, through schooling them, and by taking
them on extensive travels throughout the United States, Mexico, Central
America, and Europe. We wanted them to understand that the world is
a classroom, and that there is so much one can learn through travel. I
smile when I recall Mark Twain's statement: "Travel is fatal to prejudice,
bigotry, and narrow-mindedness, and many of our people need it sorely
on these accounts. Broad, wholesome, charitable views of men and things
cannot be acquired by vegetating in one little corner of the earth all one's
lifetime." I wholeheartedly agree.

This was the children's first visit to Mexico, and it was clear they enjoyed seeing a new country. In Acapulco we rented a small house located only a short walk from the beach. The children enjoyed walking on the beautiful beaches, wading in the surf, and exploring the city. We were in Acapulco during the rainy season, and so every evening, as the children prepared to go to bed, we reminded them not to leave their shoes on the bedroom floor. The house had windows but no panes. When the daily evening tropical rain came, it poured into the room. In no time at all, there was about an inch of water on the floor. If one of our children forgot and left their shoes on the floor, the next morning they would find them floating in a corner.

From Acapulco, we flew to Mexico City. The effects of the high altitude of Mexico City on Mother and the children concerned me. It is 7,400 feet above sea level. But it had no effect on the children or Peggy, and Mother seemed to adapt to the altitude. I arranged for a guide to drive us about the city in a minibus. For the next two days, we had a grand tour of Mexico City. On the first day the guide explained the history, architecture, and significance of the statues as we traveled about the city. He took pride in showing the children the beauty of Mexico City.

The next day, our guide drove us to Teotihuacán, an archaeological site about twenty-five miles northeast of Mexico City, to see the remains of the largest pre-Columbian city in the Western Hemisphere. It dates back to 400 BC and flourished until AD 700. We walked down the Avenue of the Dead. Ruins of temples flank the broad street, running from the Pyramid of the Sun to the Pyramid of the Moon. Our guide told us the Pyramid of the Sun was constructed between AD 50 and AD 200. He explained that it is two hundred feet high, has about 250 stairs leading to the top, and is aligned with the rising and setting of the sun on a summer solstice. It is one of the largest structures ever built by Native Americans.

It is an impressive sight looking up from the base of the Pyramid of the Sun. Our guide assured us the climb to the top would be worthwhile and the view from there extraordinary. Several of the children asked if they could climb to the top. They pleaded with Peggy and me. Peggy and I talked it over, and she said only the three eldest, Laurie, Sarita, and Rick, could climb to the top with their father. The rest of the children were to stay with her, Mother, and the guide. At the last moment, Sarita decided the pyramid was too high for her, and she stayed on the ground to help with the younger children.

My sons and I started the climb. I told them to watch their step and to take their time; if it were a building, it would be about twenty stories high. We climbed at a steady pace, stopping from time to time to catch our breath and enjoy the magnificent view. We finally reached the top after about thirty-five or forty minutes. From there, we had an imposing view of the Pyramid of the Moon at the end of the Avenue of the Dead. Below, we saw Peggy and the children at the first level of the pyramid. It appeared she had gone as high as she wished them to go and was herding them down the steps.

We saw several tourists climbing the pyramid, and three or four were at the top when Laurie, Rick, and I arrived. Also at the top, seated on a blanket, was a thin, old Mexican man, his wrinkled face bronzed by the sun. He had a large white mustache, and tufts of white hair stuck out from under his sombrero. The old man wore sandals, a white shirt, and loosely fitting white pants. In front of him on a blanket, he displayed his wares. They were obsidian figures of various gods and animals. I decided to buy a figure to remind us of our trip to the top of the pyramid.

I greeted him in Spanish, and he politely returned my greetings. The two of us talked about the view. The old man told me that for years he had climbed the pyramid almost every day to sell a few obsidian figures. Life, he said, was hard, and some days sales were so slow he barely made enough money to feed his family. The old Mexican man told me he had not had many sales that day, but hoped they would get better. He said as he had grown older he had become wiser. He was more patient and optimistic that the harsh conditions he and his family lived under would improve. Most of all, he had finally learned to accept what life had given him.

The old man asked if I would like to buy one of his obsidian figures. He said his prices were reasonable. I pointed to one and asked its price. The old man said it was one of his favorites, an especially fine one. He told me the price, expecting me to bargain with him to lower the price. I thought to myself, this poor man climbed this mountain every day to sell a few obsidian figures, and he asked practically nothing for them. I told him I would buy it. The old man looked at me, appearing somewhat disappointed that I had not bargained with him. He smiled and nodded, and I gave him the money. I descended the pyramid, obsidian figure in hand.

Several years later, another moment from our travels would parallel my encounter with the man on the pyramid. In 1985 Peggy and I visited Big Bend National Park. We drove to Rio Grande Village and went on to the ruins and deserted buildings of Boquillas, Texas. From there, directly across the river, in Mexico, is a small town named Boquillas del Carmen. That day, Peggy and I planned to walk to the banks of the Rio Grande and see Boquillas Canyon. Here the Rio Grande flows through the towering Sierra del Carmen.

It was a hot day and we parked at the base of a high hill and walked up the trail leading to the top. Arriving there, we saw a lone Mexican man, sitting on a big rock. He appeared to be sixty-five or seventy years old. In front of him on a cloth were displayed several fine fluorite mineral specimens. We stopped to look at them. I thought some of them would make fine additions to my mineral collection. I greeted him in Spanish and told him the specimens of fluorite he displayed were exceptional. He said they were from mines in Mexico.

The old man asked if I wanted to buy some of his specimens. He said it had not been a good day for him. He had not sold one item; we were the first persons to come his way all day. I intended to purchase several rocks, but didn't want to appear too eager. In this region of Texas, as in Mexico, frequently one is expected to bargain about the price of items.

I told him I would think about buying something and asked if he would still be there in about thirty minutes when we returned from Boquillas Canyon. He promised he would, assuring me that he was in no hurry as there was no place else he had to be. He urged us to be careful on the path to the river, and to watch for snakes. He warned us that the trail down to the river was not an easy one, but also assured us that the view of the river and the high walls of the canyon were worth the walk. He said the stone walls of the canyon seemed to reach to the sky. The old man said he crossed the river daily and often thought of the patience of the great river to carve out the canyon over millions of years. Peggy and I left the old Mexican man sitting on the rock, under a hot sun and a cloudless sky, a pensive look on his face as he gazed into the distance.

When we returned from the canyon, we found him patiently waiting at the spot where we had left him. I couldn't understand how he withstood the heat of the day without shade. He hoped the two of us had enjoyed the walk to the river and the canyon, and wanted to know if now I wanted

With Peggy on the banks of the Rio Grande at Boquillas Canyon, Big Bend National Park, 1985. Here the Rio Grande flows through the Sierra Del Carmen.

to buy some of his fluorite crystals. He said he would sell them to me at a cheap price because he needed to earn a few dollars that day. Looking down on the minerals, and in a casual tone of voice, I asked their price. The old man said he had taken a liking to my wife and me. For that reason, he would sell two specimens for five dollars and not a penny less, saying at that price the stones would be a bargain. I responded that he was asking far too much and if he sold me four mineral specimens that I selected, I would pay four dollars. With a pained look on his face, the Mexican man said I drove a hard bargain and suggested three stones for five dollars. In English, Peggy asked me to be fair and agree to the original price of five dollars for two stones. She noted that he looked so poor and said it would be a reasonable price. Before I could respond, the Mexican trader said to me in fairly good English that I should listen to my lovely wife. I laughed and shook my head, knowing I had lost the bargain. I handed him a ten-dollar bill and took three stones.

He said he did not want to trouble us, but asked if we had something cold for him to drink. He had run out of water. I told him it would be our privilege and suggested he come down to the car where we had a cooler. As I handed him cold bottles of water and soft drinks, the Mexican trader said he still had a long day in the sun, and he hoped his next customers would be as kind and generous as we had been. He told us not to wait too long before we came back to this beautiful land; he would probably be sitting on the same rock.

The trader walked back up the hill, stopped, turned, smiled, and waved good-bye. As I watched him climb back up the hill, I told Peggy I admired the man's patience and commitment to work. Imagine, I told her, walking miles each day from Mexico, crossing the Rio Grande, and sitting without shade in the sun for hours to sell a few rocks. Peggy said he was a lesson in tranquility and acceptance of one's lot in life. I said there were many lessons in life to be learned, some taught at universities and some by old men sitting on rocks in the hot sun.

From time to time, I find myself thinking about these two old men—one atop the Pyramid of the Sun and the other at Boquillas Canyon—each vending their stone wares, climbing pyramids and hills every day just to sell a few items to tourists who happened by, remaining optimistic that sales would improve. Each spoke of patience and acceptance of what life had given him. I decided these lessons were important ones for me, lessons taught by wise old men. I have not forgotten them.

In some sense, I feel that I have become like those two old men—but instead of looking out after a steep climb, I can now look back with the perspective offered by nearly nine decades. Now, I stand not on the King Ranch hill, named after my father, nor on my beloved Annursnac Hill in Concord, but on a vantage point afforded by the advice and teachings of my parents and so many experiences. A lifetime's journey with my family, from my work as an academic and administrator in higher education to service to my country through leading the national discussion about the importance of education, has provided me a viewpoint that I would like to share with you—a Kineño's journey.

Cavazos home on Lauro's Hill, King Ranch, TX, 2006.

Chapter One :: **The View from Lauro's Hill**

I was born on January 4, 1927, on the King Ranch in South Texas. Some sixty years later, I was appointed to the presidential cabinet as secretary of education. In September 2006, our friends Stephen "Tio" Kleberg and his wife, Janell, hosted a signing at the King Ranch Museum in Kingsville for my first book, *A Kineño Remembers*, organized by ranch archivist Lisa A. Neely. The next day we had a bus tour of the King Ranch. The driver, knowing we had grown up on the ranch, asked my sister Sarita and me to comment on places and memories of our childhood on the King Ranch. When the bus stopped by the house where we were born, we led the group around our home, telling stories about our early childhood there. Our wooden home, built in 1926, stood for many years on one of the highest hills on the King Ranch—known as Lauro's Hill. My father, Lauro F. Cavazos Sr.—known to all on the ranch as "Don Lauro"—was foreman of the ranch's Santa Gertrudis division. Oral history has it that Mrs. King ordered our house built so that it was in sight of the main house.

Neither Mother nor Dad ever had a significant discussion with me about our ancestry or the family history. I did know my grandparents, uncles, aunts, and cousins and frequently saw them. It did not occur to me to ask my parents about our family history, and for some reason they did not think it important to enlighten me. I presume that working most hours of the day to provide for a family during those difficult economic times bought on by the Great Depression was far more important than educating us about ancestors and our history.

In my previous book, I described my efforts to research my family history: In all likelihood, my mother's grandfather, Matías Álvarez, was

Dad and Peggy on the Laurel Ranch with Lauro III (Laurie), who was born earlier that year, 1956.

the son of Francisca Alavéz—the Angel of Goliad—and Telesforo Alavéz, a captain in the Mexican army. Francisca was a heroine of the Texas struggle for independence who, before the Goliad Execution of March 27, 1836, pled for the lives of rebels during the war for Texas independence. At some point, the spelling of the family name changed from Alavéz to Álvarez.

I am also a fourth-generation Kineño—or King's people—villagers from Cruillas, Tamaulipas, Mexico, who came to the Santa Gertrudis ranch in 1854 when Captain Richard King bought cattle from Mexico. King promised them work on his ranch, fair wages, homes, and a school for their children if they would stay to work for him. My mother's family, the Quintanillas, came to the Santa Gertrudis ranch from Cruillas, Tamaulipas. In 1884, Captain King offered Matías Álvarez work on the ranch and suggested he bring his family and mother with him. Matías accepted King's offer, and his mother, Francisca, lived on the King Ranch and worked for Mrs. King for many years.

In about 1876, Rita Álvarez, "Mama Grande Rita," my maternal grandmother, was born in Matamoros to Matías and his wife, Maria Felipa

Mosqueda Álvarez, one of four daughters and eight sons. Mama Grande Rita never became a US citizen, and I remember her anxiety when she saw Immigration and Naturalization Service personnel drive by her home in Kingsville. Even late in life she was convinced that if they discovered her status, she would be detained and deported to Mexico. Mama Grande Rita died in 1944 in Kingsville.

In 1894, Rita Álvarez married Francisco Quintanilla Sr., a vaquero and caporal, on the King Ranch. By the early 1900s Francisco and Rita Quintanilla and their family lived in a small community on the King Ranch known as Radiche. It was in Kleberg County about midway between the towns of Ricardo and Riviera. In 1900, Francisco and Rita had a daughter, Tomasa Álvarez Quintanilla. In 1919, Mrs. King sold the property to Theodore F. Koch, a banker and developer from St. Paul, Minnesota. After the sale, the Álvarez and Quintanilla families moved to Rancho Santa Cruz, north of Riviera. It was also part of the King Ranch.

In 1923, Tomasa Álvarez Quintanilla wed Lauro F. Cavazos in a civil ceremony at Rancho Santa Cruz. A week later, they were married at the Corpus Christi cathedral by the bishop. After their marriage, Mother and Dad moved to headquarters division, the Santa Gertrudis ranch. In 1926, my father became the foreman, a job he held until his death in 1958. Dad was born in 1894 at Laurel Ranch near San Perlita, Texas, a small community in Cameron County. Later, part of the county was split off to create Willacy County. The Laurel Ranch was a small part of the San Juan de Carricitos Spanish land grant. In 1781, the Spanish Crown gave the land to José Narciso Cavazos, one of our ancestors. It was equivalent to approximately five hundred thousand acres.

Peggy and I have always felt it was important to educate our children about our family history. In July 2002, we took our daughter Sarita Schoenstein and her family to the Presidio La Bahia in Goliad, Texas, to learn about our ancestor, the Angel of Goliad. Several years later, on March 28, 2004, we took more of our family to the Presidio to attend the dedication of a large statue of the Angel of Goliad sculpted by Valda Che Rickman. I was the keynote speaker at the ceremony, and gave a brief history of Francisca's life. There were about two hundred people in attendance, many of them also descendants of the Angel. I closed my address with this: "Francisca's charitable work will long be remembered when we read or tell of the Texas struggle for independence. Her role as

With Peggy at the dedication of the Angel of Goliad historical marker that we funded at Presidio La Bahia in Goliad, TX, March 28, 2010.

the Angel of Goliad is written large across the face of Texas history." On March 28, 2010, I gave the keynote address at the Goliad County Historical Commission's dedication of the Angel of Goliad historical marker at the Angel of Goliad Plaza. Peggy and I donated the funds to the Texas Historical Commission for the marker.

In our wooden home on the King Ranch, my mother gave birth to her five children: my sister, Sarita; my three younger brothers, Richard, Robert, Joseph; and me. Captain King made good on his 1854 promise to build a school for the Kineños. My entrance into academic life began four generations later when I started school on the Santa Gertrudis ranch. In the years since, my siblings and I have all grown as individuals. My sister, Sarita, had a long and distinguished career as a public school teacher. My brother Bobby was named all-American at Texas Tech University as a tailback in the 1950s and was a leading scorer nationally. He became a rancher. Joe was in merchandising management for many years and now is in public service. In 1976, Dick became the first Hispanic

Dedication of Angel of Goliad statue, March 2004.

brigadier general in the US Army. In 1982, he became the army's first Hispanic appointed a four-star general. Since that time, there have been a few more Hispanics reaching the rank of brigadier, major, or lieutenant general, but none have been appointed a four-star general.

As for me, in 1980 I became the first alumnus—and the first Hispanic—to serve as president of Texas Tech University and the Texas Tech Health Sciences Center. In August 1988 President Ronald Reagan nominated me to be the US secretary of education, and the next month the Senate confirmed me unanimously. I am honored and proud to have been sworn in as the first Hispanic appointed to the presidential cabinet in the history of the United States. President George H. W. Bush asked me to continue as secretary of education following the November 1988 presidential election. I served in his cabinet until my resignation, December 15, 1990.

Looking back to my years as a child growing up on the King Ranch, although my father was a foreman, there was little to suggest that I would ever leave the ranch. Many children who were raised on the ranch remained in the area for much of their lives; no one dreamed they would become president of a university, much less serve in the cabinets of two US presidents. Yet our parents raised us to work hard and never quit.

On the King Ranch, we learned many lessons about life from our parents. They taught us the value of family, work, integrity, honesty, education, and love of country. The men and women living and working on the ranch reinforced those lessons. This shaped our lives and gave us direction and unrelenting motivation to learn and excel. My father told me when I was a young boy that he had three expectations of me. He said that I was expected to educate myself, serve my country, and never disgrace the Cavazos name. These three simple admonitions formed the bedrock of my future life, the foundation on which my father told me to stand firm.

Through the course of my life, I've seen many changes. As the philosopher Heraclitus said, "Everything changes and nothing stands still." Even the family home where I grew up is no longer there; one of the ranch hands bought it and moved it to a nearby town. I've returned to the ranch and the area where I grew up several times, but now I visit as a tourist. Despite these changes, my father's expectations have always resonated with me.

Chapter Two :: **Secretary of Education, 1988–1990**

On September 20, 1988, Peggy and I sat in the office of George H. W. Bush, the vice president of the United States and the president of the Senate. The Senate was in executive session considering a vote on my nomination to President Ronald W. Reagan's cabinet as the fourth secretary of education. If confirmed, I would become the first Hispanic to ever serve in the US cabinet.

When Robert Tuttle, director of presidential personnel, contacted me in late July of 1988, asking if I had any interest in an appointment to the cabinet as secretary of education, I told him I needed to think about it. A few days later, after Peggy and I had spent substantial time talking and thinking about it, I agreed to be considered for the position. A few days later, I went to Washington to meet with Tuttle in the West Wing of the White House. Peggy went with me. He asked her if she had something to read, because the interview would be at least two hours. Peggy said she was studying for the National Certification Board examination in perioperative nursing, and any office space or a chair in the hall would be fine. The next day I had a number of interviews with the White House staff and met with Vice President George H. W. Bush. Peggy and I flew back home to Lubbock later in the afternoon.

On August 10, 1988, Peggy and I returned to Washington. This time an air force jet picked us up at the Lubbock airport. At the White House, I met with President Ronald Reagan in the Oval Office, where he officially invited me to join his cabinet. When I accepted, he invited Peggy to join us. I will never forget his cheerful and gallant demeanor when he told Peggy I had accepted his invitation. Then he asked her if she had passed the nursing examination she had been studying for during my interview.

Obviously, Tuttle had mentioned this detail to the president, and we were pleased by the president's thoughtfulness in inquiring about it. When Peggy told the president she had passed, he congratulated her. It was these small touching moments—his personal connection with those around him—that made it an honor to serve in the Reagan administration.

On September 20, 1988, all ten of our children, most of their spouses, and one grandson attended my confirmation and swearing in as secretary of education. As chairman of the Senate Committee on Labor and Human Resources, Senator Edward Kennedy reported on my educational background and academic experience. How special it was for Peggy and me to have our children hear the announcement that I had been confirmed unanimously by the Senate. It had been a long and happy journey for us from Kingsville to Lubbock, through Richmond and Concord, back to Lubbock, and now Washington, DC.

That afternoon, as a family, we went to the White House. While President Reagan looked on, Peggy held our family Bible. I was sworn in as secretary by Vice President Bush. At the swearing-in, President Reagan said:

> Of course, September is the month when American education goes back to work, so now seems a perfect time to introduce a new Secretary of Education. Just 2 weeks ago, many American students, teachers and administrators returned to their classrooms and offices in pursuit of knowledge and its matchless rewards. We sometimes take this for granted, but theirs is a high calling, a grand enterprise of individual effort and collective, national purpose. And I'm pleased to say they could not have a finer colleague, advocate, and spokesman than Larry Cavazos, whose own life and career pay eloquent tribute to the ennobling possibilities of good education.[1]

Soon after I took the oath of office, I met with the employees in the Department of Education. In that first meeting, I stated, "We must continue our work as a group of people, colleagues, dedicated to the most important mission that America has, and that's education." I discussed the problems American schools were facing in the late 1980s. "Not all citizens in America today are moving ahead at the same pace toward education. We must see to it, therefore, that every person receives the best possible education that he or she can receive. I am often struck by the problems that we face." I noted the figures for school dropouts:

President Ronald Reagan and cabinet, January 11, 1989. Courtesy Ronald Reagan Library.

About 12 percent of the Anglos will not finish high school, where some-where in the ballpark of about 14 percent of the Black students will not finish high school. For Hispanics, the number is about 30 percent. I find those figures appalling, the fact that even one person would be lost out of our system in America today. We often look at figures like that and we dwell on the figures, but I say to people, think of the lost hu-man potential; amongst these people there could have been the mind that would help solve the riddles of cancer or AIDS. There might have

been those who could lead us to world peace, to help solve problems of
hunger, racism, and hatred we have. The loss of human potential, no
nation can afford that kind of problem. We don't have that to spare. So
therefore, that just again emphasizes how important your job is, how
important our job is in the future. . . .

I concluded, "We can solve those problems, if we are all educated, and
aware of the problems and we care about them." I told the Education Department employees, "let us work together. I will pledge all of my energies
to moving this department ahead. The time perhaps is a little bit short,
but we'll get it done. But always remember that we have but one job, and
that's to facilitate the education of every person in America today."[2]

Looking back on my appointment as secretary, I have often thought about
why President Reagan appointed me. Although I voted regularly as a student at Texas Tech and Iowa State and as a faculty member at two medical
schools, I was not involved in politics at any level. In Concord I was registered as an Independent. In Texas, I was a registered voter and voted for
Republicans and Democrats.

Some commentators have suggested that my appointment was a way
to attract Hispanic voters to vote for Vice President Bush during the upcoming elections. No doubt there was some political motivation behind
my appointment, but I believe there were other important reasons as
well. I did have an excellent record as a teacher and researcher in medical
schools and had gained considerable academic and management experience as dean of the Tufts University School of Medicine and during the
eight years I served as president of Texas Tech University and the Texas
Tech University Health Sciences Center. Perhaps my credentials as the
parent of ten children educated in public schools—the equivalent of 120
PTA years—made an impression in itself. Maybe the president thought
that with that many children in school, I would be quite knowledgeable
about elementary and secondary education, and concerned about higher
education.

In checking my family background, the White House staff must have
recognized my father's excellent record of leadership on the King Ranch.
I'm sure the fact that each of his five children received a college education

Ben Sargent of the *Austin American-Statesman* drew this cartoon soon after the Reagan administration announced my nomination as the first Hispanic to a cabinet position, 1988. Courtesy *Austin American-Statesman*, Universal Uclick.

resonated, and their achievements must have supported my nomination to the cabinet. Those assessing my credentials for appointment saw that in 1985 the Uniformed Services University of the Health Sciences had given me its highest honor, the Distinguished Service Medal.

Another factor that may have contributed to my appointment was that I had met with President Reagan on two occasions. In 1984, he presented me with an Outstanding Leadership in Education award at a ceremony in the Rose Garden. Later the same year, I was part of a small group of Hispanic educators whom then secretary of education Terrel Bell convened at the White House to meet with President Reagan to discuss strategies to improve the quality of education for Hispanics.

* * *

I brought to the Department of Education a lifetime of learning that formed the basis of many of my pronouncements and the programs I instituted as secretary. My parents were my first teachers, and they did a grand job encouraging me to learn. They were the models I had in mind when, as secretary, I stated that parents should be involved in the education of their children. My parents instilled in me a love of learning and reading early in my life. They did this by creating a home environment that supported and extended education; they made me a lifelong learner. Time and time again, my parents raised my expectations that I could be a successful student. Frequently they asked about my progress in school, and by doing so let me know they were interested in and supportive of my education. Even when I went on to high school and to college, my parents were always interested in my schoolwork and progress.

It was important for my mother that all of her children receive a good education. She was functionally illiterate; she could not read or write. As we progressed in school, we children read to her. For her signature, she labored to draw her name. I fondly recall that when I was in elementary school, Mother frequently asked if I had done my homework and urged me to study and do well in school so that someday I could go to college. I told her it cost a lot of money. She said they would find a way to pay, if I made good grades. It is a testimony to her emphasis on the importance of education that all of her children earned at least one college degree. So, when I returned to Texas Tech as president, I exceeded my dream of being on the faculty and made my mother very proud.

Peggy and I had the same attitude as my mother. We became involved in our children's education. We encouraged them to learn, worked with them on their assignments, and let them know we were interested in their education.

My first days in the office as secretary of education were busy, and I needed time to plan my day. For that reason, I instructed my chief of staff not to schedule appointments for me before 9:00 a.m. Usually, I arrived at my office before 8:00 a.m. This gave me an hour to read, write, and think about how to solve problems or develop new initiatives we could utilize to improve specific education problems. I also used the time to call in various senior members of the department to consider program enhancement in their area of responsibility.

After 9:00 a.m., the appointments began, and the day and part of the evening filled with matters relating to my work. My first meeting was with my chief of staff—initially Bill Phillips, and subsequently Chino Chapa—when we discussed my schedule for the day. I was fortunate that I was able to recruit Chino to the Department of Education and subsequently to the job of chief of staff. He was loyal and thoughtful, and provided wise counsel for me on political and education matters.

Most days there were meetings with Deputy Secretary Linus Wright (later, Theodore Sanders replaced him). Early in my role as secretary, the meetings with the deputy secretary were instrumental in keeping me abreast of the problems and programs that I had to face. Almost daily I met with the assistant secretaries for discussions on education matters and possible opportunities, and on occasion I met with other cabinet officers, especially the secretaries of labor and the interior. Frequently, my speechwriters came to my office to review and discuss upcoming talks.

During the day in the office, I took many telephone calls from members of Congress, usually about funding education projects in their district. It wasn't long before I learned that the first priority of many legislators after they were elected was how to get reelected. To that end, if the legislators had large numbers of Hispanics in their district, they invited me to campaign with them for their reelection. This disappointed me because I had wanted to serve as a resource that might help them improve education in their district, not as a Hispanic whose role was to generate Hispanic votes.

As education secretary, I attended cabinet meetings and accompanied President Reagan, and later President Bush, on school or college visits. With the president, I took part in a number of White House meetings with education groups who were proposing ideas for education enhancement or funding for their programs. I especially enjoyed meetings with minority student groups and explaining the role of the Department of Education. I soon learned the Education Department received hundreds of requests per month for the secretary to participate in meetings, to speak at commencements, to visit and take part in school activities, as well as many social invitations. I delighted in meeting with minority groups and participating in their celebrations. I recall two occasions when I especially enjoyed speaking to Hispanic groups during Hispanic Heritage Month. On September 25, 1990, an army helicopter picked us up at a landing site near the Pentagon and flew us to Fort Monroe, Hampton, Virginia, where I was to be the speaker at a Hispanic Heritage Month luncheon. Of course, a large number of Hispanics were in attendance. It was a family occasion, with typical Mexican food served. Men and women in Mexican costumes performed typical dances. In my remarks, I pointed out that education was an important part of our Hispanic heritage and that educational excellence was the key to our future.

Another celebration of Hispanic Heritage Month was at Andrews Air Force Base in Maryland. There I spoke to a large group of Hispanics whose responsibility was to maintain Air Force One, a Boeing C-137C the president used in his travels. I emphasized the importance of education to their job, and to the advancement of Hispanics. After my talk, the 1990 Hispanic Celebrating Committee presented Peggy and me with a 1/100 scale model of the president's airplane. I flew with the president on several occasions, with Peggy accompanying me once, so the model was especially meaningful to us.

Traditionally, the staff in the department's Scheduling Office made the initial decisions about accepting an invitation. Then they discussed them with the chief of staff, and if he decided to accept the invitation, it went on my calendar. But, no one consulted with me about what went on my calendar! I decided to become more involved. I told the chief of staff and the head of the Scheduling Office that I wanted more input on decisions about invitations I accepted. I asked the head of scheduling to prepare packets for me to take home twice a week. I told him I would review them and let him know my decision as to which invitations to accept and which to decline. In the evenings, when I left my office, I took the packets of invitations to our apartment, read them after dinner, and made my decisions. Peggy and I worked as a team; she took notes on my decisions, and the next day I reviewed the invitations with the chief of staff. The system worked well, and I felt I had a bit of control over where I went and with whom I met.

On a daily basis, the Scheduling Office also prepared my briefing book. It contained a minute-by-minute schedule of my activities for the day. It also had brief descriptions of the occasions I attended and people who were involved in the meetings. Peggy asked me if she could have a copy of my briefing book so she would know where I would be that day, and when she could expect me to return to our apartment. So I instructed my chief of staff to prepare a copy for her. As Peggy read the briefing book, she wrote comments along the margins about the individuals on my schedule that day. Some of them were not flattering! After we left Washington, I archived my briefing books and papers at the Southwest Collection/Special Collections Library at Texas Tech. When Peggy realized the briefing books—along with her commentary—were going to the archives, she attempted to erase some notes she had written. Later, Dr. Monte Monroe, archivist at Texas Tech, asked Peggy if she had tried to erase the comments. She admitted that she had. Dr. Monroe told her there was no need to erase them, as they were an important part of the history of my tenure as secretary of education.

Although Peggy and I had gained more control over our social calendar, we soon ran into a social dilemma. Couples were usually assigned to separate tables at dinner parties or banquets. This troubled us. Peggy and I preferred to sit together whenever possible; both of us felt ill at ease dining and conversing with people we had just met before dinner. Some six weeks after we moved to Washington, DC, we were invited to a fund-raising dinner party with about 150 guests at a downtown hotel. Neither of us looked forward to the occasion, but my chief of staff urged me to attend for political reasons. As Peggy and I entered the foyer leading to the dining room we saw that it was packed with people. Peggy and I worked our way through the crowd to the tables with the seating assignments.

When we picked up our cards with our table assignment, we learned that Peggy would be across the dining room from me. I said that I found the system of dinner party seating and separating of couples in Washington appalling. Peggy agreed, saying we were probably country hicks because we wanted to sit and have dinner together. Soon, chimes sounded announcing dinner, and guests started moving into the dining room. People crowded about the doors waiting to enter. I suggested to Peggy we wait, and then as the last of the crowd moved in, I suggested we not go into the dining room. I said there was no need to go in because I was not a speaker or on the program at the dinner. I assured her that there were so many people that we would not be missed. Peggy agreed, and the two of us walked out of the almost empty foyer into the hotel lobby.

We had about an hour and a half to wait before our driver arrived at

our meeting place to take us home. Peggy said escaping the dinner party and all those speeches would be worth the wait. I suggested we have
a leisurely walk about the streets of downtown Washington. We could
window-shop and get some exercise. Peggy agreed, saying exercise would
be far better for us than eating banquet food. Hand in hand, we strolled
about the city until it was time to meet our driver. After we returned to
our apartment, Peggy fixed a light dinner, which we shared sitting side by
side.

The next day, I instructed my chief of staff to see to it that in the future Peggy and I sat together at dinner parties. I asked him to inform the
Scheduling Office that I would not accept invitations if Peggy and I were
to be seated at separate tables. Even if I was at the head table, I wanted
Peggy sitting next to me. He said he understood and would inform the
Scheduling Office of my seating requirements at dinners, but he asked
if this applied also to White House invitations. I said no, of course it did
not; the social secretary of the White House made those decisions.

From then on, Peggy and I sat by or near each other at all of the many
dinners and banquets we attended while in Washington. We liked the
arrangement, even if some of our hosts might have considered us a bit
countrified and backward in our social graces. Much to our surprise,
however, at the subsequent White House dinner we attended, Peggy and
I were placed at the same table and even seated next to each other. As we
took our seats, the wife of one of the other cabinet members wanted to
know how we had arranged to sit together. She said her husband, as usual,
had a seat across the room from her. Peggy and I looked at each other
and smiled. I shrugged my shoulders and said I certainly had nothing to
do with arranging dinner seating at the White House, that perhaps we
were just fortunate. Somehow our seating preference must have become
known to the social secretary of the White House. Although we had never
expected the White House to honor our seating arrangements, we were
pleased.

I do not want to leave readers with the impression that Washington, DC,
was full of disappointment for Peggy and me, or that political differences
and uncomfortable dinner parties ruined my term as secretary of education. On the contrary, it was a pleasure to meet with many legislators. I

especially enjoyed knowing and working with Massachusetts senator Edward M. Kennedy. I had met Senator Kennedy in 1975, soon after my appointment as dean of the Tufts University School of Medicine. During my years in that job, he supported my efforts to strengthen the financial base of the medical school. Repeatedly I emphasized to him the importance of the federal government declaring medical schools a national health resource. I sought Senator Kennedy's support to continue direct federal financial aid to American medical schools.

In 1976, Senator Kennedy invited me to testify before the Committee on Labor and Human Resources on the need for continuing fiscal support of medical schools. I argued before the committee that such support would result in improved health care of the public. My testimony that day, along with that of other deans, must have convinced the committee, because for many years federal funding continued to the medical schools based on their student enrollment.

On April 23, 1976, Senator Kennedy spoke at the Tufts Medical Alumni Association dinner and meeting. His presence made the evening a great success and helped me solidify support from the alumni. Peggy and I took our two eldest children, Laurie and Sarita, to the dinner. Afterward we introduced our children to the senator, who signed the dinner program for them as follows: "To the Cavazos Children. I enjoy knowing and working with your Dad. Ted Kennedy." Later, in 1976, Peggy and I contributed a hundred dollars from our personal funds to his reelection campaign. I forgot about this contribution, but when nominated by President Ronald Reagan to be secretary of education, the contribution became public information. I'm certain some in the Republican administration did not appreciate my financial support of a Democrat. But neither President Reagan nor any member of his administration mentioned the contribution to me.

After my nomination to be secretary, I was summoned to testify before the Committee on Labor and Human Resources, which Senator Kennedy chaired. During my years in Washington, I frequently met with Senator Kennedy on education matters. We sat in his office or mine and resolved our differences on education and discussed the strategies we might employ to improve education. Both of us had the same goals: providing the highest quality education possible for all of America's children, majority or minority. Senator Kennedy and I agreed on most education matters, though he wanted far more funding than I thought I could persuade the Reagan administration to budget for education. Senator Kennedy advised me on how to strengthen the federal student loan program when it came up for reauthorization. He, like I, especially wanted to protect those institutions that educated large numbers of minority students.

I met several times with Eunice Kennedy Shriver, Senator Kennedy's sister. The first meeting with her was in 1990, when she came to my office to talk about the role of values in education. That day, we also discussed her interest in the Special Olympics. As one of the founders of the Special Olympics, she worked diligently to improve opportunities for people with mental disabilities. Soon after our first meeting, at her request, I gave a major speech at the University of Virginia on July 31, 1990, on the importance of ethics and values in education. I spoke of my support for teaching values in education. I said teaching values in our schools prepared young students for the inevitable challenge of decision-making later in life.

Later, Eunice Shriver invited Peggy and me to a dinner at her home. We accepted with some trepidation, as partisanship in DC was growing, and President Bush—who was a moderate Republican—was facing increasing pressure from conservative elements of the party, and within his administration. I worried that some in the administration would not approve if the press drew attention to a cabinet member in a Republican administration having dinner with such noted Democrats as Eunice Kennedy Shriver and Robert Sargent "Sarge" Shriver. He was a former advisor to Lyndon Johnson, and the leading force behind many of the Great Society's War on Poverty programs, including Head Start and Job Corps. I enjoyed meeting him because I admired his leadership in starting up and subsequently directing the Peace Corps during John F. Kennedy's presidency.

After dinner, Mrs. Shriver led Peggy and me on a tour of part of their home. She had one special room with many magnificent large photographs of her brothers John F. Kennedy and Robert Kennedy. In the same room, she proudly showed us large photographs of her daughter, Maria Shriver, a television personality and news anchor who was married to bodybuilder-turned-movie star Arnold Schwarzenegger.

Peggy and I were surprised to be invited to Rose Kennedy's one hundredth birthday celebration in July 1990, at the Kennedy compound in

Hyannis Port, Massachusetts. I felt confident there would not be many members of the Bush administration at the party. Our invitation gave instructions to gather at a parking lot in town. From there, we would be bused to the Kennedy compound. The night before the birthday party, Peggy and I drove from Washington and stayed at our home in Concord. The next morning we went to Hyannis Port. Locating the parking lot, I found the bus that would take us to the Kennedy compound. When we boarded someone called out, "What are you doing here?" I turned my head and saw former Connecticut senator Lowell P. Weicker Jr. I responded, "What are *you* doing here?" He laughed and said he was glad to see us. Weicker had left the Republican Party in 1989. Now he was running for governor of Connecticut as an independent. I had come to know Weicker during my confirmation hearing before the Senate Committee on Labor and Human Resources. At that hearing and subsequently while I was secretary, he asked me to work on improving the education of disabled students. We shared similar views on enhancing the education that minority students receive, and I appreciated his support in that endeavor. He won the election and served as governor of the state from 1991 to 1995.

After we got on the bus, I saw Dr. Robert R. Davila and his wife, Donna, board. In January 1989, I had appointed him assistant secretary for the Office of Special Education and Rehabilitative Services (OSERS). His early childhood was one of adversity, which he overcame through determination and hard work. The son of migrant workers from Mexico, he and his parents and siblings had few financial resources. Still, it was a loving and supportive family that saw to it he learned English and helped him through his early education. Davila had been deaf since the age of ten after a bout of spinal meningitis. He had a PhD and, at the time of his appointment to the Department of Education, was serving as a vice president of Gallaudet University. From my first meeting with Davila, when I was considering him as my assistant secretary for OSERS, and subsequently in many more meetings, I saw parallels in our lives. We are both Hispanic and come from caring and loving families; our parents had limited resources and worked long hours. Davila's parents and mine pushed learning and education and instilled in us a desire to educate ourselves. Both Davila and I earned PhDs and have used our learning to motivate other minority students to educate themselves. During the years we worked together, I found him an excellent administrator and a superb role model for people with disabilities. Davila turned out to be one of the best appointments I made while secretary. I knew I could count on him for thoughtful direction and helpful counsel on education of students with disabilities. In 2006, he became president of Gallaudet. Davila had been invited to the birthday celebration because of his work with Anthony Shriver, the youngest of the five Shriver children and founder of Best Buddies, an organization working to enhance the lives of people with mental retardation.

About 250 attended the reception at the Kennedy compound. There were business leaders, government officials, educators, and current and former political appointees. After the reception, fifty of us moved under a nearby tent for lunch. Senator Kennedy explained that his mother had asked to be excused because she was not feeling well, but she would be observing her party from a window at her home. We were delighted to be there celebrating Rose Kennedy's long life and great achievements. The event was especially meaningful for Peggy. For years she had admired Mrs. Kennedy's devotion to her large family and Catholicism. She appreciated Rose Kennedy's daily attendance at Mass. I worried about how my presence might appear in the press. A cabinet member of a Republican administration associating freely with Democrats might raise some eyebrows, but back in Concord that evening, we were relieved that despite the considerable coverage of Mrs. Kennedy's birthday celebration, we did not appear on TV.

My position in the Reagan and Bush administrations allowed Peggy and me to encounter many interesting people. For example, in 1992, Peggy and I visited with Eunice and Sarge Shriver for the last time at Claudia "Lady Bird" Johnson's eightieth birthday party at the LBJ Library and Museum in Austin, Texas. Lady Bird founded the Texas Wildflower Center (now the Lady Bird Johnson Wildflower Center at the University of Texas), and I had served as a pro bono member of the board of directors of the center for several years. During the reception, I saw former Texas governor John B. Connally standing at the foot of the stairs that led to where Peggy and I stood. We watched the former governor greet each person coming down the stairs as if he were again running for political office. When he saw me, Connally called out my name. He shook my hand and said how pleased he was to see my lovely wife and me at the birthday party. Although we had never met the governor, I was honored that he recognized me.

On another occasion, at the beginning of October 1990, I flew on Air Force One with President George H. W. Bush to attend the president's speech at the United Nations in New York. After his speech, the president would return to Washington, but I was scheduled to attend a dinner sponsored by UNICEF, the United Nations Children's Fund. As I walked into the dining room that evening, David Dinkins, the mayor of New York City, welcomed me. Soon, I was escorted to my table. Looking at the person seated immediately to my right, at the head of the table, I instantly recognized the film actress Audrey Hepburn. I knew of her fine work for UNICEF as a goodwill ambassador. For many years Hepburn traveled the world drawing attention to the plight of children, meeting with presidents, kings, and prime ministers, and urging them to improve the lives of children around the world.

That evening, Audrey Hepburn and I talked about education and her charitable work. She spoke with conviction and emotion of the many needs of children throughout the world. About an hour after we were seated, and following several long speeches, an appetizer was served. I knew we were in for a late evening. There were some more speeches, and still dinner had not been served. A few minutes before I was scheduled to meet my driver at 10:00 p.m., I excused myself, saying good-bye to the other guests at my table. I turned to Audrey Hepburn and said how I had long admired her film work. I had seen many of her films, including *Roman Holiday*, *Sabrina*, *Breakfast at Tiffany's*, and *My Fair Lady*. She smiled amiably and said, "Yes, I have been in films for a long, long time." I could have kicked myself for my faux pas. But Hepburn, ever gracious, smiled and extended her hand and said good-bye to me. I considered her a fine actress, but admired even more her efforts to save children from hunger, ill treatment, and disease. Still, I admit I was a bit starstruck.

On another occasion, as part of the "Year of the Young Reader" programming in 1989, Peggy and I were invited to a Burl Ives concert at the Library of Congress. Ives was one of our favorite performers, so we looked forward to the evening. We were seated in the middle of the first row and had a great view of the stage. When he came out, Ives was escorted and assisted by his wife. Obviously, he had aged quite a bit and did not appear well. Still, he was jovial and requested the audience to excuse him if from time to time he forgot words to a song. If he did, he said, he just hummed.

The hour passed quickly as we listened to Ives strumming his guitar and singing ballads and folksongs. His music and songs as well as his humorous comments and demeanor enthralled Peggy and me. I hummed some of the songs Ives played. Toward the end of the program, he started playing and singing "The Streets of Laredo." I can't remember the first time I heard the sad and mournful ballad, about a young cowboy, "shot in the breast," and his dying request that "six pretty maidens bear up my pall" and "sixteen tall gamblers handle my coffin." Over the years, I have been to Laredo many times to visit my sister, Sarita, and her husband, Albert Ochoa. On visits there, I walked about the historic central plaza of the town, down its colorful streets, admiring the magnificent architectural impact of Hispanic culture on the plaza and the town. As Ives began singing "Streets," I started singing along in a low voice. Peggy nudged me to be quiet. Ives must have heard her quieting me because he said she should let me sing; he had never had a cabinet officer sing along with him. The audience laughed, and Ives and I finished our duet. After the concert, Peggy and I visited briefly with him backstage.

A few years ago, our daughter Alicia and her husband, Randolph Cohen, invited Peggy and me to accompany them and their children on a personally guided tour of Washington, DC. As part of our tour with the Cohen family, we went to the Library of Congress. The guide explained that the papers of elected and appointed officials were stored in the library, and that their writings and speeches were available online. I wanted to show our grandchildren how the library system worked, so I went to a computer and did a search for my name in the electronic files of the Library of Congress. Immediately up came the reference to my memoir, *A Kineño Remembers*. Just above the reference, however, was another to a recording of "The Streets of Laredo," made by Burl Ives and Lauro F. Cavazos. I didn't know the concert would be recorded, but it had been and now it was stored in the Library of Congress. I showed Peggy the reference and she smiled. Later, however, when I asked my grandchildren, "Wasn't it splendid the Library of Congress had a recording of me singing 'The Streets of Laredo' with Burl Ives?" they looked rather quizzically at me. "You do know who Burl Ives was, don't you?" I asked. All three shook their heads. Immediately, I felt the enormous generation gap.

With President-Elect George H. W. Bush at the Teachers Inaugural Experience at Notre Dame, January 18, 1989. Courtesy George Bush Presidential Library and Museum, photo G23607-12.

* * *

When George H. W. Bush became the president-elect in November 1988, he asked me to continue as his secretary of education. Bush had campaigned on a promise to be the "education president." Beginning in January 1988, he told a school group in New Hampshire, "I want to lead a renaissance of quality in our schools." Later that year, in his September 25 debate with Democratic nominee Governor Michael Dukakis, Bush said, "I want to see us do better. We're putting more money per child into education, and we are not performing as we should. We've gotten away from values and the fundamentals. And I would like to urge the school superintendents and the others around the country to stand up and keep us moving forward on a path toward real excellence."

With President George H. W. Bush in the Oval Office, March 29, 1990. Courtesy George Bush Presidential Library and Museum, photo P11339-01.

In late January 1989, I testified before the Senate Committee on Labor and Human Resources. "A new presidency and a new Congress present a rare opportunity to rekindle hopes for a better future: in this case hope for the goal we all share, which is to educate every American to his or her fullest potential." I told the senators that I hoped the administration and the committee would work together to help improve education across the nation:

> In my view that alliance would be a powerful force for the betterment of American education. As George Bush has said, he is absolutely committed to improving education in America. During his campaign, he laid out in detail his future plans for education in a document called "Invest in Our Children." As President Bush has said, "Our children are our future. The way we treat our children reflects our values as a nation and as a people. . . . Children embody our respect for ourselves and for our future." And that is precisely why the president pledged to lead the nation in making a commitment to our children.

I told the senators I would do my part "to expand on what the president's commitment to be 'the education president' means to America." I noted that as secretary of education, my role was to be "the president's chief advocate for education policy, and I will be active both in presenting the president's policies to you and in sharing your concerns with him." The new president would "have hands-on involvement with education policy," I said, "and I will be here to counsel, guide, and especially to carry out our policies. Both of us will need and welcome your help."[3]

I had served as secretary of education in Reagan's administration for four months when Bush asked me to continue in the post during his administration. At that meeting, I urged him to call a national summit to discuss ways to improve education, and he did so. The meeting was extraordinary. It was the third domestic summit in US history with the president and the governors of the states and territories present. The National Governors Association National Education Summit began its two-day meeting in late September 1989 at the University of Virginia in Charlottesville, Thomas Jefferson's university. Jefferson's vision of an educated citizenry inspired by the Enlightenment can be summed up in one of my favorite quotations: "If a nation expects to be ignorant and free in a state of civilization, it expects what never was and never will be. If we are to guard against ignorance and remain free, it is the responsibility of every American to be informed."

The atmosphere at Charlottesville was charged with history and the importance Jefferson placed on education in the early republic. President Bush commented, "Every step we take at this university is truly a walk in Thomas Jefferson's footsteps." And, "Education is our most enduring legacy, vital to everything that we are and can become. And come the next century—just 10 years away—what will be? Will we be the children of the Enlightenment or its orphans?"[4]

As a result of the summit, we developed six national goals to be met by the year 2000:

Goal 1: By the year 2000, all children in America will start school ready to learn.

Goal 2: By the year 2000, the high school graduation rate will increase to at least 90 percent.

Goal 3: By the year 2000, American students will leave grades four, eight, and twelve having demonstrated competency in challenging

With President George H. W. Bush at the National Governors Association National Education Summit at the University of Virginia, flanked by Governors Bill Clinton (Arkansas) and Terry Branstad (Iowa). Courtesy George Bush Presidential Library and Museum, photo P06745-18.

subject matter including English, mathematics, science, history, and geography, and every school in America will ensure that all students learn to use their minds well, so they may be prepared for responsible citizenship, further learning, and productive employment in our modern economy.

Goal 4: By the year 2000, US students will be first in the world in science and mathematics achievement.

Goal 5: By the year 2000, every adult American will be literate and will possess the knowledge and skills necessary to engage in a global economy and exercise the rights and responsibilities of citizenship.

Goal 6: By the year 2000, every school in America will be free of drugs and violence and will offer a disciplined environment conducive to learning.[5]

Although I never expressed it publicly, I believed we might be able to reach goals one through four, but I had my doubts that we would be successful in reaching absolute goals such as universal literacy and completely drug- and violence-free schools by the year 2000. While we have closed the gap in literacy, violence and drugs continue to plague American schools.

In addition to establishing education goals, the National Education Summit urged restructuring of schools. In compliance with the mandate from the summit, as secretary of education I repeatedly urged that schools be restructured to improve the quality of education provided to all students. Restructuring involves fundamental, radical changes in school organizations. The precise nature of these changes depends on local conditions and circumstances, but they have only one purpose: to allow parents, teachers, and administrators to respond to the needs of all students. Restructuring is not a formula, but liberation from the mandates of the educational bureaucracy weighing so heavily on principals and teachers. For teachers, restructuring means the freedom to teach to the best of their abilities, in exchange for a willingness to be held accountable for the results.

In 1993, the governors and the Congress added two additional goals on teacher education and professional development, as well as parental participation.

* By the year 2000 the Nation's teaching force will have access to programs for the continued improvement of their professional skills and the opportunity to acquire the knowledge and skills needed to instruct and prepare all American students for the next century.

* By the year 2000, every school will promote partnerships that will increase parental involvement and participation in promoting the social, emotional, and academic growth of children.[6]

I am disappointed we did not reach any of the education goals. We seem to have forgotten about our national goals, and there has been no significant effort in subsequent administrations to sustain them. Educational reform became politicized. As party control changed in Washington, education policy was used as a weapon to bash the other party. The reforms we set forth at Charlottesville in 1989 emerged as National Standards in the late 1990s and Common Core in the new millennium. Although the nation's governors began the reform movement, within a few decades some politicians began to frame the reform as a federal attempt to wrest control away from the states. I remain, however, the perpetual optimist, and hope someday this nation will renew its efforts to reach those national education goals set so long ago.

Soon after the national goals were agreed upon, as secretary of education I gave numerous speeches about them and proposed strategies to achieve them. For example, I placed considerable emphasis on the need to enhance the education minorities receive. I spoke about the need for our colleges and universities to educate more minority teachers.

Under my direction, the Department of Education developed and published *What Works: Schools without Drugs*. It provided a plan for action regarding what parents, schools, and students can do about eliminating drugs in school.

Teachers' unions and some members of Congress opposed my efforts to give parents more of a choice as to where their children attend school. I urged school districts to utilize school-based management and thereby empower teachers. This was not well received by some in the education bureaucracy.

Those national education goals were more than a set of standards set by a group of politicians. They were what many parents across the nation, including Peggy and I, wanted for their children; they were our own family's educational goals. Long before I got involved in politics, we believed in early childhood education and having our children begin school ready to learn. Most of them attended kindergarten. The others we tutored at home so they were ready to learn when they started first grade. We were also proud that all of our children graduated from high school, met their mathematics and science requirements, and enrolled in challenging subjects. We wanted to prepare them to be lifelong learners, and without exception they continue to read, learn, and stay informed about national and international matters to this day. Without exception, all of our children exercise the rights and responsibilities of citizenship. Fortunately, none of our children had a problem with drugs or violence. Many other parents can make the same claims and are equally as proud of their children. I hope that even as we struggle to improve education and to meet our national education goals, we as Americans will make every effort to give all students the best possible education.

It pains me, however, that many children from economically disadvantaged groups are not reaching their full academic potential. Data suggests that student achievement is directly related to poverty and low family income. A child from a family in the top income quartile is five times more likely to earn a baccalaureate degree by age twenty-four than is a child from the bottom income quartile.

Our education system has the same enormous interdependence found elsewhere in our economy and society. Weaknesses in any part are soon felt throughout the system. The poor elementary and secondary education provided to many minority and economically disadvantaged children is reflected in their low enrollment, retention, and graduation rates at our colleges and universities. For that reason, I wanted education goals not only for elementary and secondary school students but also for colleges and universities. Perhaps the idea of goals for higher education arose from my long experience as a university professor and president. I could not persuade the White House staff that we needed to set such goals. But in 1990, in the Department of Education, I developed and proposed seven goals for higher education.

First, I wanted the gap in degree completion rates between black

Americans, Hispanics, and American Indian students on the one hand, and white and Asian students on the other, to be closed. At that time, about one-half of the black American and Hispanic students entering higher education did not earn a degree, while about one-third of the white and Asian American students failed to graduate.

Second, I called for a substantial increase in foreign language proficiency among baccalaureate degree recipients. Then and now, only 10 percent of current graduates are proficient in a language other than English. I proposed raising the proficiency rate to 50 percent. I believe knowledge of other languages and cultures is important in the growing diversity of our nation. It also helps our nation compete in a global economy.

Third, I recommended all associate and baccalaureate degree recipients become competent in college-level math and science. At the time, less than half of all graduates took more than two science courses, and 20 percent took no mathematics at all.

Fourth, I urged that all graduates be able to write coherently and effectively and have a basic understanding of world history and geography.

Fifth, I asked that we increase the number of college graduates completing doctoral programs in arts and sciences by 25 percent. Further, I sought an increase of 50 percent in the number of women, black Americans, American Indians, and Hispanics earning doctoral degrees.

Sixth, I proposed that all students graduating from postsecondary institutions be able to demonstrate the critical thinking and problem-solving skills needed to productively contribute to the economic and political well-being of this nation.

Finally, I stated that if we hoped to expand educational opportunities for minority students and women, all vestiges of racial, gender, religious, and ethnic discrimination must be eliminated from our nation's college campuses.

To my disappointment, my goals for higher education were ignored by the White House administration, the press, and the politicians. Moreover, they did not get the attention of educators in our colleges and universities. Today, I still believe those higher education goals are valid and important. Perhaps in the future higher education leaders will recall the higher education goals I set in 1990 and decide to use them as benchmarks on how institutions are progressing toward a high-quality education for all students.

As secretary of education, I frequently had to fend off attempts by White House staff to impose their views on national education policy and programs on legislators and the public without prior discussions of their activities with me. In spring 1989, I learned that Richard Darman, director of the Office of Management and Budget, wanted John Chubb as the administration's education czar. Chubb was a political scientist at the Brookings Institute, one of Washington's oldest think tanks. This troubled me greatly because I felt my position as secretary of education was being downgraded. Moreover, I was angry that I learned of Chubb's pending appointment from a newspaper article rather than from Darman or the White House staff. As soon as I found out about this attempt to usurp my job, I met with John Sununu, President Bush's chief of staff. In no uncertain terms I let him know of my disapproval of Chubb's appointment. Sununu assured me that no final decision on Chubb's appointment had been made and that if he received an appointment, it would be in a staff position, not as the education czar. Chubb did not receive the White House appointment.

Early in my tenure as secretary, I experienced the negative impact of partisan politics on the legislative process. In 1989, the Democrats were the majority in the legislative branch of the government, whereas a Republican president headed the executive branch. This could result in political gridlock and limited legislation, so not many bills reached the president's desk for his signature.

On April 5, 1989, less than three months after taking office, President George H. W. Bush submitted his Educational Excellence Act (H.R. 1675). There were a number of important proposals to improve education in the bill. These included: Presidential Merit Schools, Magnet Schools of Excellence, Alternative Certification of Teachers and Principals, Presidential Awards for Excellence in Education, National Science Scholars, Drug-Free Schools, Urban Emergency Grants, and endowment grants for the historically black colleges and universities. As secretary of education, it was my responsibility to move the president's Educational Excellence Act through the House and Senate. After some modification to the bill, it passed the Senate.

I failed, however, to push the bill through the House of Representatives. In April 3, 1990, almost one year after submission of the Educational Excellence Act of 1989, I went again before the Subcommittee on Elementary, Secondary, and Vocational Education to emphasize the importance of H.R. 1675 for achieving the National Education Goals developed at the National Education Summit.

It became clear to me that the Democrats on the subcommittee were not going to allow President Bush, the "education president," success and credit for improving elementary and secondary education. Instead, they countered with their own resolution, H.R. 4379. On April 3, 1990, I testified before the subcommittee. I said I found the bill proposed by the Democrats unrealistically expensive. It lacked vision, and the increased funding authorizations for ongoing education programs would be more appropriately considered during their respective reauthorization process. Furthermore, the Democrats' bill lacked several of the proposals in the president's.

The Democratic members of the subcommittee added amendment after amendment to H.R. 1675, and the price tag on the legislation grew enormously. Finally, recognizing the Democrats were not going to pass H.R. 1675, the executive branch pulled it from consideration. This was my first lesson in partisan Washington politics, and I found the defeat disillusioning.

Improving Minority Education

Predicting the future in our world is difficult because political and economic developments occur rapidly, aided by the technology of the information age. I can, however, forecast one aspect of the future. I believe the greatest challenge we face as a nation is how to provide high-quality education for the increasing racial diversity within our nation's schools.

Our public schools reflect our nation's racial diversity. Whereas ethnic minorities made up a small portion of our schools' students at the opening of the twentieth century, in the early twenty-first century they became the "new majority." In Texas and California, Hispanic students already constitute the majority, and their numbers are increasing. The ten largest school districts in the United States are 70 percent black American or Hispanic American.

A major contributor to this demographic shift is the rapid growth of the Hispanic population. In the late 1970s and early 1980s it was apparent that the Hispanic population of the United States was growing and would soon become the most numerous minority group in the nation. Indeed, by 2010, the estimated Hispanic population was 50.5 million,

National High School Graduation Rates, 1980–2010

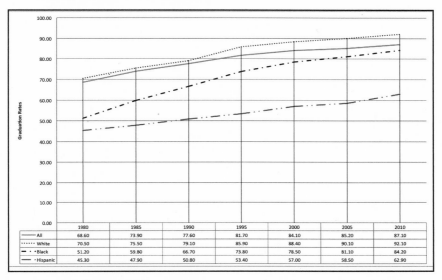

	1980	1985	1990	1995	2000	2005	2010
All	68.60	73.90	77.60	81.70	84.10	85.20	87.10
White	70.50	75.50	79.10	85.90	88.40	90.10	92.10
Black	51.20	59.80	66.70	73.80	78.50	81.10	84.20
Hispanic	45.30	47.90	50.80	53.40	57.00	58.50	62.90

Source: "Percent of People 25 Years and Over Who Have Completed High School or College, by Race, Hispanic Origin, and Sex: Selected Years, 1940 to 2013," US Census Bureau.

13 percent of the total population of the United States, not including the four million residents of the territory of Puerto Rico. The US Hispanic population has grown by 43 percent in the last decade. By 2050, it could be one-third of the US population.

These changes pose unprecedented challenges for our nation and for schools striving to provide the highest caliber education possible to minority students. In my years in higher education administration, as dean of Tufts University School of Medicine and as president of Texas Tech University, I worked to increase educational opportunities for minority students. I knew they were underrepresented in critical fields in our colleges and universities, and many faced tremendous obstacles in pursuing a postsecondary education.

Growing up on the King Ranch, I never saw discrimination against Hispanics or heard derogatory terms used against us because of our Latin American heritage. At home on the ranch, we were Americans—or

Texans—or Kineños. Certainly, however, there were many prejudicial practices against Hispanic and black Americans in Kingsville in the 1930s—as there were throughout Texas and the South in general. Most of these prejudices were institutionalized in local and state laws; others, by misguided tradition.

Of course, the schools in Kingsville were segregated during that period. White children attended the Flato Elementary School, Hispanic children went to Stephen F. Austin grade school in the barrio, and black American children took classes at the Frederick Douglass grade school in their community. The school board in Kingsville gave my parents permission to transfer their children from the Santa Gertrudis School on the King Ranch to Flato Elementary School. Although enrolling Kineño children in Flato was unprecedented, my father was determined that we get the best education possible. As the first Hispanic boy at Flato, I experienced bullying from some of the Anglo boys, and got into several fights. While the teachers and the principal tried to stop the harassment when they saw it, the bullying continued. Fortunately, after a few weeks the attacks stopped. I presume the boys realized I was not much different from them. Many of them became my friends, and some of those friendships have lasted a lifetime.

During World War II when I left Kingsville for the army, no one in the army called me a "spic" or a "chili belly," yet the US military was still racially segregated. Black Americans in the armed forces lived in separate barracks and served only in all-black American units. Segregation in the armed forces didn't end until 1948, when President Truman issued Executive Order 9981, ordering the integration of the armed services.

In college, my minority heritage did not seem to be a problem, but I do remember one instance of prejudice. Driving from Kingsville to Lubbock, I stopped for breakfast in a small town south of San Antonio. At the entrance to the restaurant, I saw, to my dismay, a sign in the window stating that "chili bellies" were not welcome in the café. I ignored the sign and entered. I found a table, sat, and ordered breakfast. I must have not fit the café owner's stereotype of a "chili belly," because I was served breakfast and no one told me to get out. Walking to the counter to pay my bill, I thought of telling the man behind the cash register that they had just served a "chili belly." Wisely, I decided I had quietly won one little battle against discrimination and had best move on to Lubbock and Texas Tech.

Fortunately, Peggy and I never encountered racial discrimination in Richmond, Virginia, during our early years of marriage. No one ever called me a "Mesican" or "spic." During our years there, we were happy and fulfilled. Our children were too young (ages one through eight) to be aware of the racial problems, and they did not experience discrimination in their schools. Thankfully, our eight children were healthy, well adjusted, and a joy to their parents. My academic work at the Medical College of Virginia (MCV) flourished. I obtained considerable support for my research from the National Institutes of Health. I had several graduate students and published a number of research articles every year. In 1960 I was appointed an associate professor of anatomy. Yet, regardless of my academic successes and our home situation, after almost a decade in Richmond, Peggy and I considered moving out of the South. We anticipated there was going to be turmoil, even more racism than already existed in Richmond and problems in the near future over civil rights.

We were disappointed that Richmond, like other southern cities and towns, was segregated. Although we did not experience it personally, we did not want our children to grow up among segregation; we wanted them to learn that all people were equal. We decided that if the right academic opportunity came along outside the South, we would consider leaving Richmond. In 1964, that opportunity came when I took a position at the Tufts University School of Medicine, and we moved to Concord, Massachusetts, a more liberal community with racially integrated schools. Yet, even though it was integrated, minority enrollment at the Tufts medical school was low; so as dean I worked to improve minority enrollment. When I returned to Lubbock as president of Texas Tech, I was concerned about the low number of minority students enrolled there. As president, I did experience two instances where people made derogatory statements about my Hispanic heritage. I ignored them.

School Dropout Rates

When President Reagan appointed me secretary of education, I wanted to continue to use my position to bring national attention to the low enrollment of Hispanics and other minority students in our nation's

High School Dropout Rates, by Race

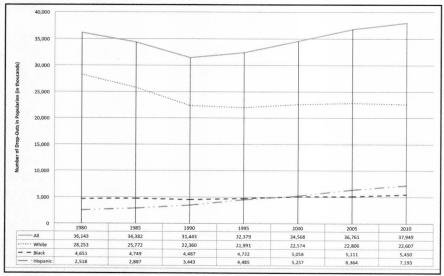

	1980	1985	1990	1995	2000	2005	2010
All	36,143	34,382	31,443	32,379	34,568	36,761	37,949
White	28,253	25,772	22,360	21,991	22,574	22,806	22,607
Black	4,651	4,749	4,487	4,732	5,058	5,111	5,450
Hispanic	2,518	2,887	3,443	4,485	5,237	6,364	7,193

Source: Digest of Educational Statistics, 2013, Table 219.71, "Population 16 through 24 Years Old and Number of 16- to 24-Year-Old High School Dropouts (Status Dropouts), by Sex and Race/Ethnicity: 1970 through 2014," 2015, US Department of Education, Institution for Educational Sciences, National Center for Education Statistics.

institutions of higher education. In 1980, before I came to Texas Tech as president, the National Center for Education Statistics reported in *The Condition of Education for Hispanic Americans* that "it is clear that Hispanic Americans are a large and growing segment of the US population. In recent years, the Congress has become increasingly concerned about ensuring their full participation in the mainstream of American life, particularly in education." The report showed that almost 20 percent of Hispanics lived in poverty, almost double the percentage of the white population. Hispanic high-school dropout rates were double those of the white population, as was the Hispanic unemployment rate.

I have always believed that we, as a nation, must make every effort to give all of our students—not just some of them—the best education possible. Unfortunately, in the growing racial diversity of our nation, the educational attainment of Hispanic, black American, and Native American students has continued to lag significantly behind that of the general population. Education professionals call this difference the "education gap."

At Tufts, as dean, then at Texas Tech as president, I tried to reduce the education gap by increasing our efforts to recruit minority students. Once a minority student enrolled, we made available as much financial aid as possible, provided mentors for them, and, if they needed it, counseling. At Tufts I worked with our minority medical students to recruit minorities when they came on campus for their admissions interviews. Our minority students told these prospective students that Tufts was the medical school to attend because it had an excellent faculty that truly cared about their students. At Texas Tech I frequently went on recruiting trips with staff and explained to prospective minority students and their parents that Tech welcomed diversity on campus. As secretary of education, I wanted to draw attention to the education gap and improve minority graduation rates. Therefore, I initiated two major studies seeking to improve the education of minorities: one for Hispanics and one for Native Americans.

Hispanic Education Initiatives

As secretary of education, I puzzled over the low educational achievements of Hispanics. I was concerned because education has a long tradition in Hispanic culture, going back to when the Spanish settled the New World. They established universities at Lima and Mexico City in 1551. These were the first institutions of higher education in the New World. The Spaniards founded five more even before Harvard opened its doors in 1636. I resolved to seek answers as to why so many Hispanics were minimally educated.

In the summer of 1990, I called for a series of community discussions in five cities around the nation to begin gathering data as part of the national effort to improve the level of Hispanics' educational attainment. At these town hall meetings, we asked students a variety of questions about their educational experience and hopes.

* If left up to you, how would you go about restructuring, or changing, your school?

* What made you stay in school? What advice would you give someone else about staying in school?

* Did you find that your teachers were helpful in preparing you for the world outside of school?

* If it were up to you, how would you change your teachers? Would you change the way they were evaluated about the subject they teach you?

* Have you ever experienced racism on campus?

* Do you think it is important for colleges to make an extra effort to recruit minority students?[7]

The responses we received from students and their parents at these discussions in San Antonio, Chicago, Boston, Miami, and Los Angeles formed the basis for the report that the Task Force on Hispanic Education submitted to President Bush. We provided solid recommendations on ways to enhance education for Hispanic students. The task force suggested the president create a Hispanic education advisory group; have federal departments assess the effects they were having on Hispanic Americans, and seek ways to increase Hispanic participation and involvement in the federal government; strengthen the role of the family in federal education programs; provide financial literacy information to families so that they could plan their children's educational paths beyond high school; encourage states to improve remediation strategies for at-risk students to reduce dropouts; work to improve educational opportunities for migrant students; and increase language development and early English-language proficiency. We also included a recommendation for the president to issue an executive order on improving Hispanic education.

In 1968, Congress established National Hispanic Heritage Week as an annual celebration in mid-September. Twenty years later, Congress expanded the weeklong event into Hispanic Heritage Month. Two years later, on September 24, 1990, President George H. W. Bush signed the White House Initiative on Educational Excellence for Hispanic Americans and proclaimed the theme for that year's Hispanic Heritage Month to be "Education Excellence—Key to Our Future." Bush remarked at the signing: "It was Simon Bolivar who said, 'Nations move toward the pinnacle of their greatness in proportion to their education progress.' We must see that education is the key to our future, of our identity as a nation, and to our very soul as a people." The president continued: "Tragically, too many Hispanic Americans are not getting the kind of first-rate education they need and they deserve. And that must change." He talked about the growing Hispanic population in the nation, and predicted that "in the next century, Hispanics will become the largest ethnic minority of our population." He then came to the heart of the task force's recommendations:

> And this means that youth is the key to the flourishing Hispanic community. Today, though, less than two-thirds of Hispanic young adults earn a high school diploma. We must find new strategies to boost graduation and literacy rates, strategies that really do get the job done, strategies that really work. We must figure out how to help these young people, how to equip them with the tools to enter a nation and a world where technology advances so rapidly that literacy and analytical and technical skills are not luxuries but essentials.

The president concluded by stating he would sign Executive Order 12729, Educational Excellence for Hispanic Americans. In signing the order, he said, "It is my fervent hope that this will ensure that Hispanic education is the priority it must be and will be."[8] Subsequently, Presidents William J. Clinton and George W. Bush continued it. On October 19, 2010, President Barack Obama renewed the Initiative on Educational Excellence for Hispanics by signing Executive Order 13555. This means four presidents have signed the executive order we wrote in 1990 when I was secretary of education. I am pleased that we have seen some improvement in the education of Hispanics. Between 1990 and 2012 the Hispanic dropout rate from high school declined from 32 percent to 13 percent. More Hispanics are graduating from high school. In 2010 the graduation rate for Hispanics from high school was 71 percent, up from 61 percent in 2006. In 2013, 69 percent of Hispanic high school graduates enrolled in college compared to 67 percent of their white counterparts. Still, much needs to be done to enhance the education Hispanics receive.

American Indian Education

Although Native American education is the responsibility of the Bureau of Indian Affairs in the Department of the Interior, as secretary of education, the poor quality of education American Indians received concerned me, and I sought ways to improve it. To that end, I visited several

With Secretary of Interior Manual Lujan and President George H. W. Bush as Bush signs the White House Initiative on Educational Excellence for Hispanics and the Hispanic Heritage Month Proclamation, September 24, 1990. Courtesy George Bush Presidential Library and Museum, photo P15955-07A-09241990.

schools on reservations in New Mexico, California, Washington, Arizona, and Utah.

Early in my administration, I suggested to the secretaries of the interior and defense that American Indian education and schools for military dependents in the United States and overseas be in the Department of Education. However, I was never able to convince either the secretaries, or the White House, to effect such reorganization. I suspect this was largely because of federal bureaucracy's natural opposition to giving up programs, power, and especially funding, not because they thought it was best for a child's education. Nevertheless, as secretary of education I reached out to the Departments of Interior and Defense, to ask that we cooperate as best we could on education matters. Neither department must have felt that such cooperation was a high priority because they did not respond. I had several discussions about American Indian education with Secretary of the Interior Manuel Lujan. I suggested we work together to improve educational opportunities for Native American children. We visited reservations in New Mexico, Utah, and California, but no new programs or efforts resulted. I wanted our departments to work together to develop a study similar to Secretary Terrel H. Bell's famous *A Nation at Risk: The Imperative for Educational Reform*. The report, released early in President Reagan's first term, captured the attention and informed the American public of the poor quality of our educational system and the need to improve it. Bell's study led to numerous efforts to restructure American public education. I told Lujan that perhaps a similar review of American Indian education and recommendations for improvement would lead to similar restructuring of American Indian schools.

On October 8, 1989, Peggy and I left Washington, flying to Anchorage, Alaska, where I was to speak to the Twenty-First National Indian Education Association Convention the next day. While there I was to receive an honorary degree from Alaska Pacific University. Peggy and I decided it would be a good opportunity to visit schools in Bethel, an isolated village of about six thousand people—mostly Native American—on the west coast of Alaska, some 340 miles west of Anchorage. It can be reached only by air or water.

A few days before our flight to Alaska, I received the draft of my speech, written by two of the department's speechwriters. I made some minor suggestions for changes and additions, but the background material, and the historical information on American Indian education, was notable. I told the speechwriters that I was impressed with the draft they had given me and to go ahead and prepare the final version. I felt confident it would be a first-rate speech for the members of the association. When I received the final version of the speech, I read it several times, and although I made some minor changes, I felt I was ready to talk to the educators in Anchorage.

Two hours before our landing in Anchorage, I pulled out the speech for the convention and read it. Peggy was sitting beside me, reading an article by Dennis McDonald, "Stuck in the Horizon: A Special Report on the Education of Native Americans," in the August 2, 1989, edition of *Education Week*. When I finished reviewing the speech, I handed it to Peggy and asked her to peruse it when she finished reading the report. I always liked to get her input on the content and educational quality of my speeches.

After a few minutes of going over the speech, she said, "Oh, no!" and turned back to the article she had been reading. She held the speech against the text of the *Education Week* article and told me to compare them. To my dismay, it was obvious that the speechwriters had used much of the text of the article without quotations or attribution. The more I compared the report with my prepared speech, the more upset I became with them.

Peggy asked what I was going to do. I told her I could not give the prepared speech. It would be dishonest on my part to knowingly give a speech that had been lifted from the *Education Week* article, and a person who heard my talk and had read the article would rightly question my credibility. I told Peggy we would have to write a new speech before the next morning. She agreed, and even before we landed in Anchorage, we had started the revision. Our work continued late into the evening in our hotel room. We did not have a laptop computer and printer, so we made changes on the copy of the original speech with pen and ink. Finally, at midnight, we finished. We had added new material, salvaged some of the text of the prepared speech, but acknowledged quotations from the *Education Week* report. We were exhausted; I reminded Peggy of the time difference between Washington and Anchorage. We had been up continuously for about twenty-one hours.

The next morning, I spoke at the convention. The auditorium was full, with several hundred in attendance. In my opening remarks I said I hoped it was clear to all present of the department's commitment to education of all students, and the special emphasis I put on minority students, especially to improving the quality of education for American Indians, African Americans, Hispanics, the disabled, and the children of migrant workers. I wanted all students brought into the educational mainstream. To me, this was an important step if we were to break the cycle of inadequate education provided to so many of our minority children.

I told the convention participants that a study of high school sophomores by the Department of Education found that from 1980 through 1986, American Indians and Alaska Natives dropped out of school at more than double the rate of other students. Only about 8 percent of American Indians had completed four years of college. Poor-quality education had devastating economic consequences for the American Indian nations. A 1986 Department of the Interior study found that male unemployment on reservations was at 58 percent, with some reservations reporting rates as high as 90 percent.

The members of the National Indian Education Association understood the waste of lives and loss of human potential that resulted from educational failure. They knew American Indian students were more likely than others to be classified by school systems as having learning disabilities. I asked the educators to adopt policies allowing more self-determination, and to strengthen parental control over the education of American Indian children. For the majority of Native American parents whose children attended schools not on the reservation, this meant being able to choose which school their child attended. As one whose parents made the decision to move their children to the best available school, I believed that Native American parents should also be able to choose a school where they believed their child would receive the best education. Although my father didn't know it at the time, he instilled in me the importance of school choice when he insisted that my sister and I attend the Anglo school in Kingsville because he believed we would receive a better education there than at the all-Hispanic school in the barrio.

I told the convention attendees that our national system of education needed to be vastly improved. The historical legacy of Native American education was one of crossed purposes and unfulfilled hopes. I informed them that I planned to appoint a commission made up of American Indian citizens and educators who would analyze the educational problems American Indians faced. Most importantly, I promised their work would not be another government study filed in a bureaucrat's desk drawer and forgotten. Instead, I said it was my hope and expectation that the product of the commission's work would have an impact similar to that of Secretary Bell's landmark study of national education, *A Nation at Risk*. I reminded those in the auditorium how *A Nation at Risk* had shocked the American public and resulted in an education reform movement in many parts of the country. The Native American commission's report, to be titled

Indian Nations at Risk, would lay the groundwork for an interagency task force and a White House conference on Native American education. Such an initiative was already provided for in the amendments to the 1965 Elementary and Secondary Education Act authored by Augustus F. Hawkins and Robert T. Stafford, which President Reagan had authorized in April 1988. I closed my speech by stating, "It will take time, but let us start today, here—in this place. America has waited too long to educate all of her children."

I commissioned the Indian Nations at Risk task force on March 8, 1990. I made the announcement at the historic Shawnee Methodist Mission in Kansas, which had opened in the 1830s as a boarding school for young Shawnee, Delaware, and other Native American students. I appointed fourteen education professionals to the task force, and all but two were Native American: Byron F. Fullerton, an attorney and past dean of the Texas Tech University School of Law, and Terrel H. Bell, former US secretary of education. Secretary Bell and William Demmert, Jr. (Tlingit/Sioux), a former Alaska commissioner of education, served as the cochairs. With the high caliber of education leaders serving on the task force, I was confident the task force would succeed.

They held seven public forums, gathering public testimony about the problems facing Native American education and recommendations for change. They made thirty school site visits and commissioned twenty-one papers from experts on American Indian–Alaska Native education. In August 1991, the task force issued its final report, *Indian Nations at Risk: An Educational Strategy for Action*. In their report, they made many important recommendations, including an emphasis on early childhood education, training for parenthood, and language development. The members called for improving the school environment to be conducive to learning; they urged improvement in the quality of teachers and teaching, and the implementation of challenging and culturally appropriate curriculum; suggested partnerships between schools, parents, social service agencies, business, and industry; and advocated systemic changes in education leadership and increased accountability. The report also included thirteen model programs and successful practices as examples for others to follow. After I resigned, the next education secretary, Lamar Alexander, issued the report. I was disappointed that no one at the Department of Education or the White House thought of sending me a final copy of

Indian Nations at Risk, but not surprised. In the minds of some bureaucrats, when the leadership changes in a department or unit, that person is forgotten. I downloaded a copy from the Library of Congress. I was also disheartened that I was not invited to the White House Conference on Indian Education, which was finally held in late January 1992. The conference explored the feasibility of establishing an independent Board of Indian Education having responsibility for all existing federal programs relating to the education of American Indians. In addition, it sought recommendations for the improvement of education programs relevant to the needs of American Indians. It also advocated for more funds for American Indian education and an increase of support for the language and culture of American Indians and Alaska Native children.

Throughout American history, our educational system has largely ignored American Indian youth, and the consequences have been tragic. While I was secretary of education, I wanted to make sure all our children were educated to their fullest potential. I believed we needed to transform the educational process for American Indian children to give them the same educational opportunities as other children across the nation. Although I had visited with Secretary of the Interior Lujan to discuss Native American education, I did not ask his permission to appoint a commission to study and suggest strategies to improve it. I saw no one addressing the problems in Native American education and decided to appoint the commission on my own. The fact that no one in the Department of the Interior or in the White House ever contacted me to protest or support my efforts is telling. It suggests to me that they did not truly care about improving Indian education or believed that our work was not significant or could not make a difference.

It's been a quarter of a century since I left Washington, and we are still struggling to find ways to improve the education of minority children. While there has been some steady improvement for African Americans and Hispanics over the years, the needle hasn't moved very much for Native American students. When *Indian Nations at Risk* came out, American Indian students had the highest high school dropout rate in the nation. The report stated, "As many as 35 percent, and in some places 50 to 60 percent, of American Indian and Alaska Native students leave school early."[9] As late as 2013, while overall high school completion rates were increasing, Native American student graduation rates remained significantly lower, and in many cases were falling. While the overall graduation rate for all American students is at 75 percent, for Native American students it is only 64 percent nationally. Graduation numbers such as these lead me to wonder why Native American education continues to be largely ignored.

The number of minority students in our public schools continues to increase rapidly. From 1993 to 2003, minorities increased as a percentage of total public school enrollment from 34 percent to 41 percent. In 2003, 65 percent of the students in central-city public schools were minority. Yet only about one-half of Hispanic and black American ninth graders graduate from high school within four years, compared to 79 percent of Asian Americans and 72 percent of non-Hispanic whites. While more than 65 percent of non-Hispanic white high school graduates continued on to college in 2000, only 49 percent of Hispanic high school graduates enrolled in a college or university. It is somewhat encouraging that in the class of 2012, according to the Pew Hispanic Center, a record 69 percent of Hispanic high school graduates enrolled in college. This is two points higher than the 67 percent of white students. Still, Hispanics face many educational disparities as indicated by higher education measures.

Just as important, despite the growing numbers of minority students, the proportion of minority teachers has remained level at about 10 percent for the last fifteen years. As a consequence, many minority students will not be taught by minority teachers nor receive the benefits of exposure to minority teaching professionals. The racial composition of the faculty of community colleges, colleges, and universities needs attention. Minority faculty members not only educate minority students struggling to learn, but serve as role models to help them understand the value of an education. I urge the preparation of more minority faculty, especially in education, mathematics, and the sciences. The faculty in America's colleges and universities is without equal in the world of education and research, but I suspect we have neglected potential teaching and research talent in our society. As a result, there is a significant imbalance between the numbers of minority and majority faculty. According to the National Center for Education Statistics, in 2009, 7 percent of over one million college and university faculty members were black Americans and 4 percent were Hispanic. Higher education institutions must work to promote greater racial diversity among the faculty.

Unfortunately, to date, the number of minorities entering the academic professions has not increased significantly. Still, many educational institutions have made exceptional efforts to recruit minorities by employing assertive programs to recruit minorities who are interested. They provide significant scholarship support and mentoring and tutoring programs.

In a 2006 article, William Demmert, Jr. (who cochaired the commission that produced *Indian Nations at Risk*) described the lasting influence of the report and the later White House Conference on Indian Education:

> These two reports have directly or indirectly influenced all of the following legislation or funding for programs: a) The Native American Languages Act of 1992 (PL 102-524); b) the Native Hawaiian and Alaska Native education amendments of Title VII, Part B and Part C with language supporting the development of programs that meet the special language and cultural needs of Native students; c) the amendment to Title VII, Bilingual Education, Language Enhancement and Language Acquisition Programs (PL 103-382) allowing for the development of Native languages as long as English is one of the priorities; d) the enactment of two Presidential Executive Orders (Clinton, 1998; Bush, 2004) regarding the education of Native Americans and meeting their cultural and linguistic needs; and e) the establishment of a partnership between the Council of Chief State School Officers and the Educational Testing Service to support the development of plans for twelve State Departments of Education, to narrow the achievement gap for Native American students.[10]

I am proud to have initiated studies to address some of the concerns caused by the minority education gap that we were only beginning to discuss in the 1980s and 1990s. I consider those two reports focusing on improving the education of Hispanic and American Indians as among my greatest accomplishments.

Many wise and busy people have devoted considerable time and energy to prepare studies like the two I initiated on minority education. Perhaps it is the nature of Washington politicians and bureaucrats to continue to call for more studies on how to improve the educational attainments of Hispanics, African American, and Native American students. I suggest, however, that we do not need another study on how to improve minority education; we know how, and need to apply what we know in every school in America. I submit that excellence in education starts at home with parents who care about their child's education. I certainly had caring parents as a young person growing up on Lauro's Hill. They repeatedly reminded me of the importance of education and how to achieve it. I utilized the lessons I learned there and applied them the rest of my academic career.

The ideas contained in the reports on Hispanic and Native American education that I commissioned are still relevant today, and can still serve as blueprints to improve the quality of education for minority children. I regret that efforts to improve the educational achievements of minorities have become politicized and, as a result, less effective. These issues will continue to challenge the nation's educators, politicians, and the public.

Presidential Delegations

BOLIVIA

President George H. W. Bush asked me to head the presidential delegation to Bolivia in the summer of 1989 to attend the inauguration of Jaime Paz Zamora scheduled for August 6. There were probably a number of reasons he asked me to go. First, my ability to speak Spanish was an important factor. I also had considerable experience teaching students in several Latin American countries. Most importantly, as secretary of education I initiated several programs to educate parents and teachers about drugs, and I participated in writing the National Education Goals. One of our goals was that by the year 2000, schools would be free of drugs. Bolivia had a significant drug-trafficking problem. Under my leadership the Department of Education published a model curriculum for use by schools to teach about drugs.

In preparation for the trip a State Department officer briefed me about President-Elect Paz Zamora. In 1971 he was exiled from Bolivia to Chile by the dictator Hugo Banzer. While in exile, Paz Zamora cofounded Movimiento de Izquierda Revolucionaria (MIR, Revolutionary Left Movement). It resulted from a merger of the left-wing faction of Bolivia's Christian Democratic Party and the radical student wing of the Revolutionary Nationalist Movement.

I learned of the existing political and economic conditions in Bolivia during the briefing for the trip. The State Department officer asked me to try to persuade Paz Zamora to be forceful in eradicating the drug problem in his country. Drugs from Bolivia flowed to Panama, and subsequently to the United States. According to the briefing officer, Paz Zamora and General Manuel Noriega, the dictator of Panama, were friends. Noriega became dictator in 1983, and still controlled Panama at the time of our visit. The officer wanted me to ask President Paz Zamora to give his moral support to the people of Panama in their struggle to end the Noriega dictatorship and restore democracy.

Several months after our visit to Bolivia, in December 1989, US forces invaded Panama, captured Noriega, and ended his dictatorship. He was indicted for drug trafficking, racketeering, and money laundering and imprisoned at the Federal Correctional Institution in Miami. In 1992 Noriega was convicted of accepting bribes to allow shipments of US-bound cocaine through Panama in 1992. Later, it was revealed Noriega had been on the CIA payroll for years, assisting US interests in Latin America and working as a liaison to Cuban president Fidel Castro. Although Noriega's sentence ended in 2007, he remained in prison pending the outcome of extradition requests by Panama and France. In April 2010 the United States extradited Noriega to France, where he was tried on money laundering and drug-trafficking charges. France sent Noriega to Panama in December 2011. There, he received two twenty-year terms for murdering two of his political opponents in the 1980s.

As we neared the landing in Bolivia, the cabin of the aircraft started to depressurize. The pilot came on the intercom and said that because of the high altitude of the airport, the crew needed to put on oxygen masks. The air force required its pilots to wear oxygen masks above 12,000 feet. We landed at 5:30 p.m. at John F. Kennedy International Airport (later El Alto International Airport) in El Alto, Bolivia, elevation 13,313 feet. It is the highest international airport in the world. It overlooks La Paz, elevation 11,811 feet, known as the "city that touches the clouds."

As we descended, our steward informed us that after we got off the aircraft it would be refueled and flown to a Bolivian airport at a lower altitude because the plane's hydraulic systems would be damaged by low air pressure. The plane would return when it was time for us to return to the United States.

The steward also announced that when we disembarked the passengers would go to a room in the terminal where a cocoa tea would be served to prevent *soroche*, or mountain sickness, and oxygen would be available for those who needed it. As head of the official presidential delegation, however, I would go outside to make my remarks to the reception committee and the press. Before we left for Bolivia, a State Department person had given me a prepared speech to read in Spanish to those meeting us at the airport in Bolivia.

As we disembarked, I told Peggy to lead the way down the stairs. Our ambassador to Bolivia, Robert S. Gelbard, met us at the foot of the stairs and directed Peggy and the delegation to the waiting room. He and I went outside to face the television cameras, radio microphones, a number of reporters, and welcoming dignitaries. I gave my remarks in Spanish. During my talk, I was gasping for breath. I had never been at such a high altitude without oxygen.

I said I was honored to be in La Paz as the US representative for President Paz Zamora's inauguration. President Bush wanted me to extend his greetings to the people of Bolivia. Praising Bolivia's efforts to strengthen democracy, I also noted its remarkable progress with its new economic program. It had established a model for other nations trapped by hyperinflation and weakened by an unstable economy. I pointed out that much remained to do in the battle against drugs, perhaps the most serious problem facing Bolivia. I closed my speech by stating that President Bush was committed to cooperating with the government of President Paz Zamora on matters of equal concern. After my talk, Ambassador Gelbard and I joined Peggy and the rest of the delegation in the terminal waiting room. For some reason I was not given tea or oxygen support. I guess someone decided I didn't need either. A few minutes later, we boarded the cars taking us to La Paz.

We descended to La Paz, which is situated at the bottom of a canyon. The lighted city spread out before us was a spectacular sight. After checking in at the La Paz Hotel, we had an informal dinner and team briefing hosted by the ambassador at his residence. The next morning we left La Paz for the town of Batallas. There we visited the Batallas Education Project and took a tour of a school, which included a briefing on some of the efforts to educate rural children. We then went to Lake Titicaca where we ate lunch at a small restaurant on the shore. This is the second

With Peggy at the Unidad Académica Campesina in Batallas, Bolivia, August 1989.

largest lake in South America, covering an area of 3,200 square miles. At 12,500 feet above sea level, it is the highest lake in the world navigated by steamboats. We saw several *balsas de tortora*, or boats of reed, used by the Indians for fishing.

We went to the Presidential Palace late on the afternoon of August 5. As head of the delegation, it was my responsibility to present our credentials to President Víctor Paz Estenssoro. After we entered the main reception area, a representative from the Foreign Ministry greeted us. He directed the delegation to form two rows of three, with me in the center of the first row next to Ambassador Gelbard in center of the other.

There is a great formality to these occasions. We walked slowly, in unison, toward the front of the ballroom where there was a podium and three chairs. Approaching the podium, we stopped, waiting to be presented. Then, accompanied by Foreign Minister Valentin Abecia, I extended greetings to the president. The foreign minister and I sat on chairs placed to the left of the president. The rest of the delegation and the ambassador took seats along one side of the ballroom. After we were in place, the press came in for photographs for less than a minute. After they were cleared from the room, the president, foreign minister, and I spoke to each other for a few minutes.

When we were finished, the president stood up and bid us farewell. I shook hands with him and the foreign minister, and then, as instructed, backed away from them so that I did not turn my back to the president. The rest of the delegation formed two rows where they stood, and I again took my position in the center of the first row. President Paz Estenssoro bowed from the podium, and we, as a delegation, returned the bow. We moved to the other end of the ballroom. When we reached the door, we turned around to face the president, bowed once more, and proceeded out of the room.

That evening, Peggy and I and the rest of the delegation attended a reception given by the outgoing president at the Presidential Palace. Ambassador Gelbard, Prescott Bush, Jeanie Austin, and I went to the inaugural ceremonies at the Legislative Palace the next day. The president gave a farewell speech, which was followed by the swearing-in ceremony and a speech by incoming president Paz Zamora.

Later, after the inauguration, Ambassador Gelbard and I met briefly with President Paz Zamora. We spoke in Spanish. He greeted us warmly, saying it pleased him that I had been asked to be chief of delegation. He graciously did not mention his disappointment that President Bush could not attend. Most of the Latin American presidents represented their countries. I do not know why President Bush did not attend, nor do I have enough facts to even speculate. Possibly, the inauguration of a Latin American president was not a priority, or perhaps the inauguration dates did not fit his schedule.

I extended President Bush's congratulations on his election as president of Bolivia and his best wishes. (Paz Zamora would serve as president until August 6, 1993.) I said those of us in the United States knew Bolivia would continue to strengthen its democracy under his leadership. We talked about general economic conditions in Bolivia. I urged him to continue Bolivia's economic reform program. Paz Zamora described some of his objectives for his four years as president. He hoped to extend economic reforms and to strengthen democracy in his country. He mentioned the continuing war on the drug trade, although he did not elaborate on how he would stop it. His bringing up the drug trade was my opening to say that President Bush had requested him to be even more vigorous than his predecessors in stemming the drug trade. I acknowledged that Bolivia had made significant strides in this area. Still, I said, much needed to be done, and I asked him to join with us to stop the flow of drugs to the United States.

Paz Zamora listened attentively to my appeal. He looked at me and politely said that if we in the United States could stop people from wanting and using drugs, there would be no demand for them. Without demand, the drug trade would eventually cease to exist. His point was that we had to stop the use of illegal drugs in the United States before he could make significant inroads on halting drug trafficking in Bolivia. At that juncture, I thought it best to drop further discussion of the drug problem, and I did not mention General Noriega.

Peggy and I and the rest of the presidential delegation returned to the airport in El Alto the next morning, August 7, departing at 10:00 a.m. An hour later, we landed at Santa Cruz Airport, Santa Cruz, Bolivia, for refueling, and then left for San Juan, Puerto Rico. We arrived at Andrews Air Force Base late that night.

PERU

On July 27, 1990, Peggy and I flew from Andrews Air Force Base to Jorge Chávez Airport near Lima, Peru, this time to attend the inauguration of Alberto Fujimori as president. Again, I headed the presidential delegation, which included Peggy and the Honorable Charles Untermeyer, assistant to the president and director of presidential personnel. Members of the accompanying delegation included Mr. J. Phillip McLean, deputy assistant secretary for South America; Ms. Agnes Warfield, deputy assistant chief of protocol for visits; and Ms. Catherine Keller, White House liaison.

I presume the president asked me to head the delegation because I had done a good job representing the president in Bolivia. Although honored to represent President Bush once again, I was apprehensive about the safety of Peggy and the rest of the delegation. I knew that two ruthless terrorist groups, the Sendero Luminoso (Shining Path) and the Cuban-inspired Marxist Movimiento Revolucionaria Túpac Amaru (Túpac Amaru Revolutionary Movement), had terrorized Peru for decades. Sendero Luminoso, founded in 1970, was a Maoist breakaway movement from the pro-Russian Peruvian Communist Party. Sendero Luminoso's goal was to destroy existing Peruvian institutions and replace them with a communist peasant revolution regime. Both terrorist groups sought to impose their version of communistic organization by bombings and assassinations. They financed their terror campaign by trafficking in narcotics, kidnapping for ransom, and bank robberies. Peruvian security forces carried out counterinsurgency campaigns against the violence of Sendero Luminoso and Túpac Amaru starting in 1980, and during these campaigns there were violations of legal, societal, health care, and religious rights.

Ambassador Anthony C. E. Quainton and Mrs. Quainton met us at the airport when we arrived in Peru, The Peruvian undersecretary of state at the Ministry of Foreign Affairs, Armando Lecaros de Cossío, also welcomed us to Peru. From there we went directly to Ambassador Quainton's residence for an informal briefing. Since there was the possibility of an attack by one of the terrorist organizations, we were housed in the ambassador's residence instead of a hotel.

Our delegation, accompanied by the ambassador, left the ambassador's residence for the Cathedral of Lima the next morning. We attended the Te Deum Mass at the cathedral, which lasted about an hour and a half. After the Mass, we went to the National Congress building. As head of delegation, I had a seat on the House floor. Peggy and the ambassador were taken to the Galleria Diplomatica, while the rest of the delegation sat in the Senate Chamber.

Shortly after we arrived, the installation of the National Congress and transfer of presidential powers began. Outgoing president Alan García Pérez delivered his farewell address to the Congress and the nation. President-Elect Alberto Kenyo Fujimori arrived thirty minutes later. After his swearing-in, transfer of the presidential sash, and the singing of the national anthem, President Fujimori addressed the Congress and the nation. As decreed in its constitution, Peru had two vice presidents. At that time they were Maximo San Roman and Carlos Garcia. They too were sworn in.

Later, our delegation, accompanied by the ambassador, went to the Government Palace. There, President Fujimori and Foreign Minister Luis Marchand Stens greeted all of the delegations. Our delegation went into the Salon Dorado where the director of general protocol announced me as chief of delegation. I presented a letter to President Fujimori from

President Bush. I was not privy to its contents. Afterward, we moved to the Gran Comedor for a toast of honor, which concluded the ceremonies.

That evening Ambassador Quainton and I attended a reception and dinner at the Government Palace, or the House of Pizarro. This is the residence of the presidents, located on the main square of Lima, La Plaza de Armas. The Government Palace stands on the site that Francisco Pizarro, the Spanish conquistador, selected from which to govern Peru.

During the drive to the Government Palace, Quainton briefed me on the protocol for the reception and dinner with President Fujimori. Near the conclusion of the dinner, he explained, President Fujimori would make a toast at dessert, and Chilean president Patricio Aylwin, the senior president in attendance, would respond on behalf of the chiefs of the foreign delegations. After the toast and response, we were to move to the Salon de Honor for coffee and after-dinner drinks. The ambassador informed me that it would be impolite to leave before the senior delegate departed, but after President Aylwin left, it would be appropriate for the rest of the delegates to individually ask President Fujimori to be excused.

The ambassador told me that because of the real possibility of an attack by Sendero Luminoso, Peggy and the rest of the delegation would stay at the US Embassy. As the time neared for departure to the United States, heavily armed police would escort them to the airport, board our airplane, and wait for me to arrive.

We arrived at the Government Palace and were promptly admitted. At the entrance to the reception area, Quainton pointed out where he would meet me when the dinner was over. From there I would be rushed to the airport with appropriate police protection. As soon as I was on board, the pilots would taxi out and take off for the United States.

I found the gathering a pleasant one, and on behalf of President Bush congratulated President Fujimori on his inauguration. Subsequently, I worked the room, greeting the chiefs of delegation. I knew that in Latin America dinners usually started late in the evening and could go on well past midnight. About 11:00 p.m., we left the reception room and moved to a large dining room where dinner was served. It went on for over an hour. Following dinner, Fujimori made a toast, and Aylwin responded on our behalf. Then we moved to the Salon de Honor for coffee and drinks.

I kept an eye on President Aylwin and my watch, hoping that soon he would ask to be excused. I thought the reception would never end and

I would be seeing the sunrise over Lima. Finally, at about 12:30 a.m., I saw Aylwin thanking the president for his hospitality and asking to be excused. When I saw Fujimori nod and shake his hand, I knew it was time for me to make my move. I approached the president and thanked him for the wonderful dinner and wished him all success during his term of office. I asked to be excused; the president nodded and thanked me for coming to his inauguration.

I was disappointed that Peggy and I did not have an opportunity to tour Lima and the nearby countryside. I had planned to visit schools and talk to teachers and students and their parents as I had done when I represented President Bush in Bolivia, but the State Department limited the amount of time (less than forty-eight hours) the delegation would be in Peru and restricted our activities because of the possibility of terrorist attacks.

Quainton and several security people met me when I came out the door of the reception area. As I entered the ambassador's waiting automobile, I saw a police car behind our car and one in front. As we sped away from the Presidential Palace, we were joined by several more police cars. I counted four in front of our car and could see three behind us. As fast as we were traveling through the streets of Lima and then the countryside on the way to the airport, I thought the drive might be more dangerous to my health than the Sendero Luminoso.

But we arrived at the airport safely and without incident. Our air force jet was on the tarmac, engines idling. Ambassador Quainton walked me from his car to the jet stairs. I thanked him for his support and all of his efforts on our behalf. He had done an outstanding job. There was no exchange of any official substance. I presume this was because of concern by Peruvian security forces or our security personnel of an attack by Sendero Luminoso. As soon as I stepped on board, to my relief I saw Peggy waiting for me in our forward compartment. I took my seat beside her, the cabin door closed, and almost immediately we started our taxi to the runway. In a few moments we were airborne, headed home.

Higher Education Act Reauthorization

In 1988, I worked on improving the student loan program, covered under the Higher Education Act, which would be up for reauthorization in 1991. Having spent my entire professional career in higher education, I relished the opportunity to work on the reauthorization and attendant reshaping of the act. The Congress and the Department of Education were rightly concerned about the soaring student loan default rates. Defaults were costing the federal government about two billion dollars annually.

Before my appointment as secretary, the Department of Education and the Congress sought new rules allowing them to eliminate institutions from the student loan program if their default rate exceeded a certain amount. I considered the levels proposed as not realistic and far too low. I knew several institutions educating large numbers of minority students would surpass the proposed low default rates. This meant their students would not be eligible to participate in the federal student loan programs. This troubled me, so I increased the proposed default rate. Working with key members of the Congress, we achieved the needed reform of the programs. As a result, most of the minority-serving institutions remained qualified to participate. I also asked administrators of higher education institutions to control and limit tuition increases.

On September 26, 1990, in Washington, DC, I spoke to the presidents of the historically black colleges and universities (HBCUs) and to those of the Hispanic-serving institutions (HSIs). I had emphasized to the Department of Education the importance of working with these two groups of presidents because of their crucial roles in educating large numbers of black Americans and Hispanic Americans.

I called the meeting with the university leaders to give them a preview of the Department's Higher Education Act (HEA) Reauthorization proposals. The Higher Education Act initially passed in 1965 as part of President Lyndon B. Johnson's Great Society domestic agenda. The HEA focused on strengthening the educational resources of colleges and universities, and providing financial assistance for students in postsecondary and higher education. It increased the amounts of federal monies going to colleges and universities, created scholarships, gave low-interest loans to students, and established a National Teacher Corps. The 1965 Higher Education Act had been reauthorized several times with many amendments, and I wanted the Department of Education to have a major role in writing the upcoming reauthorization. If we did not, the Congress would again take the lead, as it had done with the 1986 reauthorization. I, therefore, appointed an HEA Reauthorization Task Force to suggest strategies.

I told the university presidents that the Department of Education had formed a University Consortium for Research and Development with the assistance of the White House Initiative on Historically Black Colleges and Universities. This coalition brought together fourteen HBCUs with seven research universities in the Midwest in order to strengthen the HBCU's research base and to provide research opportunities for their faculty and students. I told the university presidents that it reflected President Bush's efforts to increase support for HBCUs. I also informed them that the president had signed an executive order on Educational Excellence for Hispanic Americans that sought to increase Hispanic participation in federal education programs. I told the presidents that the task force had finished its deliberations in June 1990 and submitted our proposals to the Office of Management and Budget in early September.

Then I moved on to describe the department's reauthorization proposals. They were along the lines of the four themes of our education policy. First, they rewarded excellence and success in education by providing incentives for educational achievement. Second, we wanted to target federal monies to help individuals, institutions, and programs most in need of federal funding. The third premise promoted school choice for individuals and flexibility in the delivery systems of existing programs. The fourth theme sought greater accountability for student loan defaults and for disclosing more information about the performance of the loans.

The Reauthorization Task Force recommended significant changes to the Higher Education Act. In our proposal, the Department of Education sought to increase the efficiency and cost-effectiveness of the loan program in order to curb rising default rates. I informed the presidents that I wanted to increase the amount that needy students received from the Pell program. The Pell Grant, named after Rhode Island senator Claiborne Pell (D), provided need-based grants to low-income undergraduate and some postbaccalaureate students that do not need to be repaid. I wanted to use the Pell Grants as incentive and reward for student high achievement.

I reminded the college and university presidents of our recently established National Education Goals and the need to improve the quality of elementary and secondary education. I suggested they develop new programs for effective teaching in America's culturally and ethnically diverse classrooms. I said we needed to enhance parental involvement, promote early childhood education, and remove barriers to success in education and work to help students achieve their potential at all educational levels.

I asked the HBCUs and HSIs to establish collaborative relationships giving high school students the opportunity to take college-level math and science courses. I suggested they open their computer and science facilities for use by local schools lacking these critical teaching tools. I also urged the HBCUs and the HSIs to initiate mentoring and counseling programs to improve student performance in our elementary and secondary schools.

I noted that the growing racial and ethnic diversity of the American classroom had greatly outstripped the availability of minority teachers. While minorities constitute 30 percent of our elementary and secondary students, they currently make up only 10 percent of our teaching force. I stated that in addition to providing valuable teaching talent, minority teachers often served as critical role models for minority and disadvantaged students from communities in which education may not be valued as much as it should. I said a shared background might help a teacher communicate the importance of learning to students who otherwise would see little purpose in attending school.

I reminded them of my higher education goals. One was to increase significantly the number of undergraduate and graduate students, especially women and minorities, who earn degrees in mathematics, science, and engineering. By encouraging students to specialize in these fields, HBCUs and HSIs could make an enormous contribution to American education and to our competitiveness in the world economy. Although I emphasized these education issues in many speeches, I especially welcomed the opportunity to talk directly to the presidents of the HBCUs and HSIs. Their leadership placed them in the vanguard working to improve the education of minority students, which was why I wanted to demonstrate that they had the full support of the Department of Education.

Chapter Three :: **After Washington**

Resignation

Early in December, President Bush instructed John Sununu to ask for my resignation and to offer me an appointment as ambassador to either the Dominican Republic or Costa Rica. His request caught me by surprise. I had completed or had under way a number of important initiatives to improve the quality of education. Years after leaving the job as secretary of education, I still wonder why I was asked to resign. The president never discussed the quality of job I was doing as secretary. His chief of staff, John Sununu, never expressed any concerns that my leadership in the Department of Education was lacking. Neither ever suggested that I could have done a better job. I can only conclude President Bush wanted a secretary of education with solid Republican credentials. It is possible that the president's White House aides and advisors persuaded him to replace me. I do not think that John Sununu wanted me replaced. He was always friendly to me, and in addition to educational matters, we sometimes spoke of our days at Tufts University where he was dean of engineering and I dean of the medical school. The fact that I did not let politics influence decisions I made may have gotten me on the administration's radar. Perhaps I should have been more forceful in keeping the education agenda in front of the president. Maybe I didn't speak to the American people forcefully and loudly enough about how to improve America's schools. When making decisions about educational matters, I always wanted discussion and reasoned debate on the issues.

Recently, Peggy and I were reflecting on our days of service in Washington. She told me of a discussion with a staff member in my outer office where she was waiting for me. They were talking about a story that had appeared in the press that day that was highly critical of my leadership of the Department of Education. The staff member suggested Peggy urge me to be more forceful and to "go after" the press, media, and those politicians who complained about my "low key" leadership of the department. Peggy told her that bombastic language and dais-thumping were not my style. Frequently, when she expressed anger about a negative story published that day, I would tell her to ignore them and not waste her energy on uninformed comments by the media. Peggy told the staff person that she had come to Washington with a gentleman who had good manners and knew she was going to leave Washington with the same gentleman, unchanged by the media and politicians.

From time to time, I have reflected on my leadership at the Department of Education, my successes and failures as secretary. I was successful in persuading President Bush to convene a national summit focusing on educational improvement, which resulted in the development of the National Education Goals and the commitment to restructure schools to provide higher-quality education. I was prudent to push academic choice in public schools from the beginning, too. Today, choice is a widely used strategy to improve education and restructure schools. I am pleased that I was able to reduce defaults in the federal student loan programs. I commissioned two major studies on improving Hispanic and American Indian education, and we secured President Bush's executive order on Hispanic education. It created an office for the White House Initiative on Educational Excellence for Hispanics in the Department of Education, which still exists today.

Yet, as secretary of education, I did face some setbacks. The nation did not meet any of the National Education Goals approved at the National Education Summit. Further, I failed to move the president's Education Excellence Act through the legislature, and colleges and universities, and the Bush administration, ignored the higher education goals I wrote. Another failure was that, for the most part, the reports I initiated on improving the education of Hispanic and American Indian students have been ignored or only partially implemented.

The evening after John Sununu asked me for my resignation and I had met with the president regarding that, Peggy and I talked about our future. I said I did not want to be an ambassador; I had had my fill of Washington, politics, and politicians. I would not accept a political appointment in Washington again. I told her I looked forward to returning to the academic world. Peggy was pleased. She missed patient care and would be happy to go back to hospital work. We decided to leave Washington the next day, after I telephoned the president. When I called President Bush the next day, our conversation lasted only a few minutes. I told him my resignation letter, effective December 15, 1990, would be on his desk late that morning. I chose the date because of a commitment to give an address at one of the historically black colleges and universities on December 14, 1990. I thought it fitting I end my Washington career as a cabinet officer speaking at an institution committed to educating minority students. I also informed the president that I would not accept an appointment as an ambassador.

Although I was happy to be leaving, Peggy and I were disappointed in the comments on my service by some in the Bush administration. Some said I was too passive. Others intimated that I took advantage of my position and provided special benefits to Peggy, but investigations into those allegations concluded they were unfounded. We went to our home in Port Aransas, Texas. There we had quiet time to reflect on the quality of the job I had done in Washington, and think about our plans for the future. I assured Peggy that although I would no longer have a federal appointment, I wanted to continue working to improve public elementary and secondary education. Later that year, I was pleased to rejoin the faculty at the Tufts University School of Medicine. This time, my appointment was in the Department of Public Health and Community Medicine. I retain my faculty appointment at Tufts to this day. My teaching and administrative duties are limited, which allows me to continue my efforts at the national level to enhance the education of minorities. I assist several foundations committed to improving minority education. I've stayed busy.

As a consultant, I advise senior colleges and universities on strategies to attract more minority students to their campuses. Also, for several years I worked on the board of directors for the National Alliance on Hispanic Health and the National Assembly on School-Based Health Care.

During the time I was secretary of education, the news media frequently criticized my leadership. I do not agree with their evaluation. I believe I did a fine job, under the circumstances. In the end, it will not

In regalia for graduation ceremony at Tufts University School of Medicine, 1990.

be the popular media that evaluate my performance as secretary of education. The programs and initiatives I started as secretary, such as minority initiatives, choice, school restructuring, and parental involvement in their children's education, continue to be successful. I am confident that when historians examine the work I did as secretary, they will conclude that I moved a number of new initiatives forward that improved the quality of American education.

The overarching strategies to better education are not complex. It requires the will and commitment of people who care about learning, dedicating themselves to work vigorously, thoughtfully, and together to advance education. Secretary Bell's study, *A Nation at Risk*, warned about our education deficits. Secretary Bennett vigorously pushed education improvement. Although my record was mixed in terms of successes, I too sought educational reform and believe some of those efforts reap rewards today.

Now I believe that it is far easier to make inroads on improving education place by place as a consultant. I know that I can be more effective improving education outside of the federal government. In Washington, DC, there are so many political considerations and stakeholders that have to be appeased before any real discussion about improving the educational situation for the students begins. Politics colors and influences all cases for reform. As a consultant, however, these limitations do not dominate the discussion, and I can offer my honest opinion about how to best benefit American children. Under these conditions, I am pleased that students, not politicians, become my constituents.

Five secretaries of education have followed me, yet the same questions about how to improve education are being debated, with no solution or significant changes in sight. We must vigorously pursue improvement of our education system for all of our children because it is the nurturing foundation for the freedoms and economic circumstances we benefit from as a nation. The role of the federal government in education is, and should be, limited. The statutory authority of the US Department of Education is confined to research on the improvement of teaching programs, gathering data on education, and administering funds for those in need of financial support to pay for their education. About 9 percent of the expenditures for education in this nation comes from Washington. By far, the majority of the funding is generated from state and local governments. US schools are governed by almost fifteen thousand independent school boards. Authority for education is vested by the Constitution in the states and at the local level. There is no mention of a federal role in education in the Constitution.

Partnerships

As secretary of education, I stressed creating partnerships between teachers, administrators, and parents. I never forgot how in Kingsville, Ruby Gustavson, principal of the school my siblings and I attended, would visit with Mother from time to time. Mother appreciated her taking time to come to our home; it was as if the parish priest had come for a visit. She would invite Ms. Gustavson into our living room, serve her coffee, and would tell her how she was grateful to hear about our educational progress. Although I did not know then about education partnerships, looking back on those visits I see that my mother and the principal were establishing a partnership to work to improve our education.

I urged K–12 schools, community colleges, universities, and professional schools to form partnerships to improve education, especially that of minority and educationally disadvantaged children. The Health Professions Partnership Initiative (HPPI), which enhanced diversity and learning opportunities for minority and disadvantaged students wanting to enter the health professions, is one example. The Robert Wood Johnson and the W. K. Kellogg Foundations funded it, and I served as a member and chair from 1995 to 2005. One of its major strategies was to create partnerships between the health profession schools and K–12 school systems, undergraduate colleges and universities, and community-based organizations. Evaluation by the national program staff of HPPI reported that it "contributed approximately 2000 minority students to the pool that subsequently applied to enter the health professions." I am pleased that many of the programs developed by the HPPI partners have been institutionalized and their efforts continued. As we move forward, perhaps we'll better understand how to overcome the obstacles that impede the entrance of minority students into the health professions.

Education Leadership Summit

As secretary of education, I repeatedly emphasized the importance of accountability by demonstrating to parents and the community the quality of education students were receiving. The educational community rarely reported on the quality of education provided in terms of dollars spent. As a result, communities and parents had little information on this. In the 1970s and early 1980s, accountability was not a focus of many educators. In 1984, however, the Department of Education published the first of what became an annual state education performance assessment, known as the "wall chart." It gave state-by-state comparisons of student academic performance. It provided educators, community leaders, and parents the data needed to compare student performance. Such intense focus on how individual states were doing raised considerable opposition from local politicians who wanted to demonstrate to their constituents that their local schools were doing a good job; so the Department of Education discontinued the chart. To replace it, the states and federal government turned to enhanced testing of students at the state and local level, and this has become the major method used today to measure educational success.

This strategy of depending on high-stakes testing troubles me. I agree we must measure the success and outcomes of our educational efforts, but high-stakes tests alone do not improve education. As many have complained, too much testing eats into time that should be spent on learning, and results in teachers "teaching to the test." Tests should measure a student's comprehension of concepts. With more and more states and schools relying on high-stakes testing, the general public has echoed the same concerns that I saw: the focus of public schools shifted from what students should learn to how to take tests.

On February 20, 2002, Duke University convened the Education Leadership Summit in celebration of the 150th anniversary of teacher education at Duke. The then secretary of education, Roderick Paige, participated. All of the former secretaries, William Bennett, Lamar Alexander, Richard W. Riley, and I, with the exception of Terrel Bell who died in 1996, and Shirley M. Hufstedler, took part in the summit. Secretary Hufstedler intended to participate but became ill just before the meeting; however, she submitted an excellent essay that was published in the education journal *Phi Delta Kappan*. The former governor of North Carolina, James B. Hunt Jr., did a masterful job moderating the three-hour discussion on education.

A few days before my arrival at Duke, I asked the organizers of the summit to arrange a school visit for me. I wanted to go to a school in Durham with a large minority enrollment. The morning before the summit began, I toured one of the kindergarten classes. Most of the students were minority. I enjoyed my visit with them. They were bright, engaged, alert, and eager to learn and show off their drawings and letter charts to me. As an educator I have spent years evaluating teachers. In that classroom I could see the teachers were committed to providing the best education possible for their students because they were patient with the students, encouraged them to ask questions, and were involved in the discussions that followed. When a child asked a question, they answered it and made sure the child had understood the answer. To me, it was apparent that the teachers loved their jobs and wanted their students to learn to the best of their abilities.

After the visit to the kindergarten classroom, I left to read to fourth and fifth grade students in the library. Walking down the hall with my escort, we came upon a teacher and two young boys. They were about nine or ten years old. "Good morning!" I said, and asked the children if they enjoyed school. The teacher accompanying them told me the students did not speak or understand English. They were recent immigrants to this country and were part of an English as a second language (ESL) class. Then I spoke to the students in Spanish. It pleased me to see the students' eyes light up and the smile on their faces. They politely answered my queries in Spanish. I could sense the teacher was dedicated to helping these children learn English as soon as possible. I told the children "good day" and wished the teacher success in teaching her students. Those two students were fortunate to have parents who insisted they learn English, recognizing that it was vital to their educational success and the key to becoming a productive citizen of the United States. I hoped that their parents also would enroll in English classes so they could speak both English and Spanish in their home, as my parents had when I was growing up.

In the library there were about twelve students sitting on the floor, facing a chair. It was obvious they were excited about my visit. All of the children were either black Americans or Hispanic. The librarian handed me two children's books, one in English and the other in Spanish. She invited me to take a seat and read to the children. The librarian said they were eager to meet me, and that she had given them some background information on me.

I opened the book written in Spanish and started reading to the children. They were an attentive group. After a few sentences, I translated what I had read for the English-speaking children. Next I read to the group in English and then told the story in Spanish.

That afternoon, before the start of the Education Leadership Summit, we former secretaries, Secretary Paige, and Governor Hunt met in a room for photographs and private discussion time. Four of us, Bennett, Alexander, myself, and Paige, had been appointed by Republican presidents. A Democratic president had appointed Riley. Almost immediately, the discussion shifted to the recently passed No Child Left Behind Act (NCLB), a bipartisan effort that President George W. Bush signed a month before our meeting at Duke. In the privacy of the room, I told my fellow former secretaries and Governor Hunt that I had many reservations about NCLB. I worried that the emphasis in schools would shift from learning to testing. As we left the room to start the Education Leadership Summit, I realized that I was the only former education secretary present who did not support NCLB.

The summit topics included accountability, character education, the teacher shortage, the minority achievement gap, and global education. Governor Hunt moved the agenda along and kept us on topic. There must have been four hundred people in the audience. Many were teachers; others were school administrators, parents, university students, and community leaders.

The first summit topic, accountability, sparked a lively discussion. Almost immediately, the No Child Left Behind Act came up. All of the other secretaries praised the legislation and were confident it was a major step in improving education in America. I, however, said I did not agree with my colleagues. I put forward the notion that there were ways to evaluate a student's educational achievement other than high-stakes tests. I gave examples such as courses taken and grades received, as well as graduation rates and college attendance of school graduates. I stated these parameters, and several others, and gave some measurement information on student progress in learning

At the conference, I described my brief conversation at the Durham school with two young boys who could not speak English. I told the audience that under No Child Left Behind, those two children were expected to do as well on a test as the young students who had been speaking English all of their life. The audience burst into applause in support of my remarks.

The conveners at Duke University asked me to give my vision for the future of education in an essay. Published two months later in *Phi Delta Kappan* (May 2002), that essay explained that we "need to examine critically the assessment tools we use and work to identify measures that are reliable and that recognize and reward excellence." I wrote:

> I sense a remarkable consensus on the kinds of changes needed. Schools of the future will involve parents, will empower principals and teachers, will emphasize early childhood education, and will strengthen curricula in mathematics and sciences, English, foreign languages, the social sciences. Most of all, the schools of the future will have more sensitivity to the differing needs of an increasingly diverse population.[11]

Congress debated the reauthorization of NCLB, formally known as the Elementary and Secondary Education Act, from 2009 to 2011. President Barack Obama proposed revision in 2010, but as of late 2014

Congress had not moved on the issue. Although NCLB was useful in extending accountability in schools, there are shortcomings at the state level. Notably, NCLB set standards only for math and reading, without considering other academic subjects such as social studies and history. Obviously, this tends to constrict the curriculum in schools. President Obama announced an executive order in September 2011 that allowed states waivers from participation in NCLB education law because of a variety of concerns. In return, states were required to develop and implement their own set of education standards by 2014.

According to then education secretary Arne Duncan, NCLB was too punitive and prescriptive. Speaking to a US Senate committee in early February 2013, he explained:

> NCLB unintentionally encouraged States to lower their standards so that more students would appear to be proficient, even though they weren't—and many States did. NCLB also labeled every school that missed a single target as failing, including some that were making progress in educating disadvantaged students and closing achievement gaps. It mandated one-size-fits-all interventions, regardless of a school's needs, preventing critical resources from being targeted where they could do the most good for kids. The exclusive focus on tests, and disregard for other important measures of success, forced teachers to teach to the test. And, subjects such as history and the arts were pushed out.[12]

By the summer of 2014, over forty states had received waivers from the NCLB guidelines from the Department of Education to design their own ways of assessing student learning and enhance teacher effectiveness. Finally, in December 2015, Congress passed and President Obama signed a replacement for the NCLB act, called the "Every Student Succeeds Act." The new legislation will allow states to play a greater role in setting their own standards instead of a "one-size-fits-all" model. We can only hope that having the states determine a competent method of evaluating their own schools accurately and effectively will improve our children's education. I regret that we have allowed politics to halt the necessary reforms to legislation for which we have waited so long.

Chapter Four :: **President of Texas Tech**

Many of the goals I set as secretary of education had formed in my mind during the years I was a student, faculty member, medical school dean, and college administrator. Of course, as a student, I was occupied with my studies and graduating. I never dreamed that I would one day become a university president. As a graduate student, I did harbor thoughts of coming back to Tech as a faculty member. I knew, though, there were many years of graduate study ahead before a faculty appointment would be possible.

In fact, I had already come a long way to get to college at Texas Tech. In 1933, I was six years old and began my formal education at the Santa Gertrudis School on the King Ranch with seven or eight other children. About fifty children, all of them Hispanic, attended grades one through seven at the two-room schoolhouse about a mile from our house. It was during the Great Depression nationwide, and vast economic hardships were making it difficult for parents to provide for their family's basic needs, much less give their children's education priority. Elsewhere in South Texas, it was common for Hispanic parents to insist that when their children reached fifteen or sixteen years of age, they quit school so they could work to help support the family. On the King Ranch, however, we were fortunate. The ranch management, starting with Captain and Mrs. King, cared about its people, the Kineños. In those difficult economic times, the ranch leadership provided housing, schooling for the children, and health care for the entire family. The older children stayed in school, but worked on the ranch or at part-time jobs in town.

Our parents frequently reminded us that we were going to stay in school and that we would go to college. My mother was determined her children would be educated, and she pushed us to learn. She insisted we do our homework, and although she had limited English skills, she met with our teachers and monitored our education progress. Mother drove us to the ranch school, and after my parents transferred my sister and me to the Flato School in Kingsville, either she or Maxcimilíano "Vallejo" Garcia, a ranch hand who worked at our house, drove us to school.

In late summer 1979, Peggy and I learned of the search for a new president for Texas Tech University and the Texas Tech Health Sciences Center. We were confident that I had the management skills to lead a large university. I knew the Texas legislature provided Texas Tech with enough resources to support its academic offerings and a quality faculty. Although it had recently emerged from a one-year probation imposed by the Liaison Committee on Medical Education, the medical school still needed substantial work. With my considerable experience in medical and health education, I believed I could improve the academic program at the Tech medical school. After deliberation about the opportunity the position would hold and what it would mean to remove our children from their schools and friends to a new environment, we decided that I would submit an application for the position. In early February 1980, after the search process was complete and I was informed I was the candidate selected, I resigned as dean of the Tufts University School of Medicine.

My friend Murray Blair took over upon my resignation. His administrative skills and knowledge of medical education were impressive. He had a PhD in pharmacology from Tufts. We met at the Medical College of Virginia where he was the associate dean of the medical school. After I left Virginia to chair the Department of Anatomy at Tufts, Blair became director of research for Astra Pharmaceuticals, in Worcester, Massachusetts. Some months after my arrival at Tufts, Blair asked me to be a part-time scientific consultant to Astra. I agreed, and I worked as a consultant at Astra for several years. In 1977, I persuaded Blair to join my administration at Tufts as associate dean. I was pleased when he was named interim dean after my departure.

I moved into the president's home near the Tech campus in February 1980, although my inauguration would not be until April. Peggy and the children not in college remained in Concord until the end of the school

With Peggy at a luncheon following my inauguration as president of Texas Tech University and the Texas Tech Health Sciences Center, April 1, 1980.

year. That summer, after school was over for our four youngest children, we prepared to move to Lubbock. It was an enormous effort moving our children, three dogs, three cats, and household furniture and belongings from Concord to Lubbock.

Instead of selling the home in Concord, we decided to rent it. Housing prices were depressed, even in Concord, because of the financial recession of the early 1980s. More importantly, however, Peggy and I did not want to part with our lovely home on Annursnac Hill Road. We had lived there for fifteen years. We raised ten children there, and it seemed every corner of our home had a happy memory. We were sure the decision not to sell the Concord home also made the children feel a bit better about the move to Lubbock.

It was a cheerless moment for Peggy and me as I closed and locked the door to our home for the last time. Afterward, I told her I should have carved "GTT" on the door. In the aftermath of the Civil War, many Southerners left their farms and homes and moved to Texas. Some of them carved "GTT"—"Gone to Texas"—on their door to let their neighbors know their whereabouts.

It turned out to be a relatively smooth transition from New England to West Texas. In the fall the youngest children started public school in Lubbock and quickly adapted to their surroundings. We were delighted to be back in the beautiful West Texas area and among the friendly people of Lubbock where I had spent years in undergraduate and graduate school, and so near where Peggy had grown up. They made Peggy and I feel welcome. Shortly after our move, Peggy remarked that she had forgotten how people in Lubbock want to tell you their life's story soon after meeting you. They share stories about their family, their education, and problems in their daily lives. I agreed with Peggy's generalization about the people of West Texas. It was one of the things I liked and hoped would never change. Peggy said she found it a welcome change from the reserved New England attitude of not speaking to a stranger. She reminded me how irritated I got when I greeted people on our walks in Concord and they failed to respond—not even with a nod—or ignored us altogether. Still, if a person needed aid or assistance in Concord, or Boston, someone always stepped up and lent a hand.

A few days later, as we drove through the countryside, Peggy said the open spaces of West Texas explained why people were willing to tell you their life story. She pointed at the landscape—where there was nothing to block the view—and insisted that West Texas people must have decided they might as well tell everything about themselves even to a stranger, because there was no place to hide. We laughed and agreed that we were happy to be home.

It was great to be back on the Tech campus. As the president of both the university and the Health Sciences Center, I wanted to be visible. So I frequently walked about the campuses and talked to students and faculty. Instead of "management by objectives," I called it "management by walking around." I arranged a monthly session with the students, inviting them to come to the Student Center to have coffee with the president and discuss problems and give me suggestions on how to improve their university.

On one of my walks a few weeks into the position, I entered a large amphitheater in the Biology Department. A first-year biology class was in session, and I took a seat in the back of the room. Then I recognized the lecturer. It was Polly Cook! In 1948 she was a graduate student when I was a senior undergraduate at Tech. After I graduated in 1949, I enrolled in the master's degree program in zoology at Tech, so I had considerable interaction with Polly. We became friends and colleagues. She did not notice me at the back of the amphitheater, but after her lecture I walked down to the lectern and greeted her as the students filed out of the class. She told me how pleased she was about my appointment as the university president. We talked for a while, reminiscing about our student days at Tech, each of us asking about fellow students and professors from that time.

Now she was a faculty member in the Department of Biology. In addition to the first-year biology course, Polly taught the histology course to third- and fourth-year undergraduate students. She asked if I would like to give a lecture in the histology course. I told her I would be delighted, and about two weeks later I lectured on the microscopic anatomy and function of the pituitary gland; she invited me back every year to lecture to her class. While I was president, I also lectured in the gross anatomy and the neuroanatomy courses for the first-year medical students. I hoped the lectures to the undergraduate and medical students were not simply symbolic but contributed to the education of students. I wanted to be seen by the faculty and students as a teacher, not just an administrator.

When I arrived as president, I was deeply concerned about the low minority student enrollment at the university. I knew major changes on college campuses required leadership from the top, and I went to work on increasing our minority enrollment and retention. I wanted a campus that welcomed and valued diversity. Several times as president, I traveled to San Antonio, Houston, and the Rio Grande Valley and towns around West Texas to promote recruitment of minority students and enhance the diversity of the institution I led. I talked to prospective minority students about coming to Tech and met with their parents, assuring them that their child would receive an excellent education. By the end of my presidency, minority enrollment had increased from 2 percent when I arrived to 8 percent; although it was a small improvement, it was a start in the right direction. Some of the strategies I put forward were successful and continued after I left. I was pleased that a 2013 report in the magazine *Diverse Issues in Higher Education* recognized Texas Tech as one of the nation's top fifty Hispanic baccalaureate producers. It was also ranked forty-seventh for baccalaureate degrees given to American Indian students in the 2010–11 academic year.

Cooperation between the city and the university had been strained at times. When I arrived at Tech in 1980, some people in town believed the university administration had isolated itself from the city. As president, I wanted to greatly improve this relationship. I got involved in a number of town activities, and it was not long before I became quite visible to the citizens of Lubbock. I served on the Lubbock Chamber of Commerce board and successfully led United Way campaigns at the university. I served on a number of town committees focusing on education and dropout prevention. The first year I was president of Tech, Professor Eileen Johnson invited me to tour the Yellow House Draw and the Lubbock Lake area. I was astonished and delighted to see this archaeological site that contains artifacts from some of the area's earliest animals and human inhabitants, dating back over twelve thousand years. I sought funding from the legislature to preserve and enhance the site. Eventually the state approved the funding, though not until I left the presidency. Today, the Lubbock Lake Landmark contains some 336 acres and is a protected state and federal landmark administered by the Museum of Texas Tech University. It is a great archaeological teaching laboratory at the edge of the Tech campus, preserved because of the wisdom and commitment of Professor Eileen Johnson and other Tech faculty as well as Lubbock citizens and members of the legislature. I am pleased I had a small part in its preservation.

During my years at Tech as president, I oversaw many improvements and the expansion of the campus and construction of several academic buildings. I worked with the staff and board of the National Ranching Heritage Center, a museum of ranching history on the Tech campus, to improve and expand this excellent historical site. I was especially proud to participate in the dedication of the Cattle Shipping Complex, which included Caesar's Pens. The King Ranch gave the center a portion of these pens for their railroad exhibit. Named after Caesar Kleberg, the pens had been part of the largest cattle shipping enclosure in the world when they were built. On September 17, 1983, the cattle shipping pen complex opened to the public. That day, I spoke at the dedication and said I could still see my father, foreman of the Santa Gertrudis Division of the King Ranch, perched on the fence of the shipping pens as he directed the cow-hands in the cattle-loading operation. Dad counted the cattle as they went through the chute and into the cattle cars.

As a university president, I was also expected to take an active role promoting Lubbock and Reese Air Force Base. The Texas Tech Rodeo Association, affiliated with the National Intercollegiate Rodeo Association (NIRA), has a history of sixty years as a student organization. They sponsor the Annual Texas Tech NIRA Rodeo every fall. My first year as president, the officers of the rodeo association asked me to lead the parade, and I agreed. I presume that because of my ranching background, they thought I should be able to ride a horse from downtown Lubbock to the university. The day of the parade they saddled a horse for me—a large one. Although I hadn't ridden in years, I mounted the horse and managed to stay in the saddle during the parade. I led a rodeo parade from downtown Lubbock to the Tech campus. At the end of the parade, we entered the Memorial Coliseum parking lot. I dismounted and, with some relief, handed the reins of my horse to a young man who led him away. I must have been a sight: the university president wearing western clothes, a big white Stetson hat, and boots waving to the crowd astride a horse in downtown Lubbock.

Later that fall, I directed the Texas Tech marching band as it played the national anthem at a football game. I climbed a ladder and pretended I controlled a large marching band. I feared I might fall off of the ladder, but managed to keep my balance. Somehow, we got through "The Star-Spangled Banner," and I stopped waving my arms at the same time the band quit playing. The fifty thousand football fans in the stadium seemed pleased by my band directing; they applauded. Later Peggy told me the fans were applauding the band and not me.

Perhaps my favorite extracurricular activity as president during my first year was flying in a T38 supersonic jet trainer. Reese Air Force Base, six miles west of Lubbock, traditionally invited the newly appointed Tech president for a flight in one of its trainer jets. Before takeoff, I was given a thorough briefing on how to parachute out of the airplane in case of trouble, and then the pilot and I climbed into the cockpit. The two seats were in tandem. The pilot sat in the front seat and I in the back. The

Flying over the Texas Tech campus in a T38 supersonic jet trainer, 1980. I'm in the rear seat.

ground crew strapped me in, hooked up the intercom between the pilot and me, and showed me how to use the oxygen mask. Most of our flight would be well above twelve thousand feet, so I needed oxygen most of the time.

The pilot taxied our aircraft onto the runway, and soon we were flying north toward Amarillo, 120 miles away. It seemed only a few minutes, and I could see the city ahead of us. When we were over Amarillo, the pilot turned the jet south toward Lubbock. We were accompanied on our flight by another T38 jet. Repeatedly, the pilot asked if I felt all right. I said I felt fine and was having a grand ride. When he determined that I was not going to be airsick, he asked if I wanted to see how they practiced tactical flying. I said I would, and soon our airplane and the accompanying jet were maneuvering and climbing up and then down through the sky. After a few minutes, the pilot asked if I wanted to fly the jet. I was surprised that he would ask, but told him I would. I "flew" the plane for only a few minutes before he took over the controls and said we were going to have our picture taken. I wondered to myself how someone would take a photograph of our flight, but it soon became obvious. As we approached

Lubbock, the pilot began to slow down, and as we flew over the Tech campus the crew in the accompanying jet photographed our airplane. It remains a treasured memory of my time as Texas Tech president.

One of the benefits of being back in West Texas was that when Peggy and I wanted a break from the pressures of work at Tech or the hospital, we could drive to Big Bend National Park for a long weekend. These trips allowed us the private time that we cherished. On these drives, we talked about how our children were doing in school and how work was going for her at the hospital, and we reflected on my leadership of Tech and the Health Sciences Center. There were no interruptions, phone calls, or meetings; we could simply enjoy each other's company as the beautiful West Texas landscape rolled by.

Spanish explorers called the Big Bend area *despoblado*, or uninhabited, and even in the 1980s only about thirteen thousand people lived there, most either in Marfa, Alpine, or Marathon. Peggy and I found the isolation of the Big Bend country appealing and our visits relaxing. Usually, from Lubbock we drove to Odessa, past Pecos, and went south through the small town of Saragosa, in Reeves County. In late May 1987, a tornado had struck Saragosa, killing some thirty people and injuring over one hundred more. As we drove through a few weeks later, we saw the devastation. Only a few houses still stood. We were shocked. Nearly all of the trees were uprooted or stripped of limbs. Twenty-two people were killed when the tornado shattered the Catholic Hall of Our Lady of Guadalupe Church, where a ceremony for kindergarten students was taking place. The incident was one of the deadliest tornados in the state, and we were saddened by the devastation and the loss of life.

From Saragosa we usually drove south through Balmorhea to Fort Davis in Jeff Davis County. On several occasions we took some time to tour the old fort at the edge of town. It was built in 1854 to help protect the road between San Antonio and El Paso. Soldiers at the post were charged with stopping Apache and Comanche Indians from raiding cattle, travelers, freight, and the mail. From Fort Davis we went to Alpine.

We have always found Alpine interesting and inviting. We never tired of walking about the town and stopping and browsing at several of the small shops. Peggy especially liked the architecture of the buildings and houses, the cool and comfortable falls and summers, and the beautiful mountains nearby. The isolation and solitude of the town always appeal to her. In fact, she said she could live there, and on several trips she tried to persuade me to buy a house in Alpine, or in one of the nearby mountains. I always agreed that it would be a great place to live, but a long commute to Lubbock. Still, even now, with fewer demands on our time, its lure remains.

On our 1983 trip to Big Bend, we spent the night in Alpine at a small hotel on the edge of town, across the highway from Sul Ross State University. Later in the evening, we attended a lecture by the noted Latino writer Richard Rodriguez, author of the 1982 autobiographical *Hunger of Memory: The Education of Richard Rodriguez*. I read Rodriguez's book soon after it was published and found it interesting and thought provoking. Rodriguez wrote of the importance of a solid education and the need to learn to speak and write English well. I certainly concur with his viewpoint; in many speeches to Hispanic audiences, I have stressed the importance of education and English proficiency. Although Rodriguez is critical of bilingual education and affirmative action, I believe both are important for enhancing the education of minority children. I took my copy of his book along. After his talk, I asked him to sign it for me. I appreciated his inscription, and his recognition of me as a fellow educator. He wrote: "To Lauro, my brother and my teacher."

From Alpine we drove south to Big Bend National Park, stopping along the edge of the highway to watch numerous herds of antelope. It is eighty miles from Alpine to the park entrance. It was springtime as we entered the park, and we saw a variety of wild flowers just opening, including bluebonnets, Indian paintbrushes, and Indian blankets. The blooming yucca and ocotillo and the many varieties of flowering cacti added color to the Chihuahuan Desert. The summer tourist season had not started, so there were not many cars in the park and only a few visitors. On that trip and subsequent ones, Peggy and I took time to stop by the roadside and enjoy the beauty of the flowers and cacti.

On our initial visit to the park we returned north along state highway 118 toward Alpine. I wanted to visit the Woodward Ranch, a rock hunter's paradise near the base of the massive Cathedral Mountain. Many varieties of agates, including red plume and pom pom, as well as amethysts, opals, and crystal labradorite, are found on the ranch. It was established in 1883 as a cattle ranch, and although there are still cattle, it is known nationally among lapidaries—rock and gem cutters—as a great place to buy and hunt for gemstones.

The ranch was then operated by J. Frank (Trey) Woodward, III, and his wife, Jan—the third generation of Woodwards to manage the ranch. The first time we arrived at the rock shop, the Woodwards greeted us. I said we wanted to buy some of their agates, and they directed us to "Grandpa's agate pile," where for many years the first J. Frank Woodward heaped agates picked up on the ranch. I selected some excellent specimens from the mound. Afterward the Woodwards took Peggy and me into their home, next door to the rock shop, and showed us "Grandpa's fireplace." It was impressive. The entire front of the massive fireplace is covered by magnificent agates and geodes, some cut and polished. There are numerous mineral crystal specimens as well. Each time we visit the Woodward Ranch we ask to see the fireplace.

On another trip to Big Bend, Peggy and I drove west to the ghost town of Terlingua. There, cinnabar and quicksilver (mercury) mining started in 1884. By the late 1960s mining for mercury had ceased. We saw a couple of small shops open and a few people moving about, but for the most part the town had been abandoned. From Terlingua, we followed the Rio Grande north, through Lajitas. This was a ghost town being revitalized, and there were a number of shops there. From Lajitas we continued on to Presidio. We passed through Presidio and drove to the warm springs a few miles west of town. A small lodge sat at the spring site, and warm water had been channeled through the single-story rooms. One could rent a room for the night and in the morning bathe in the spring. I tried to persuade Peggy to spend the night, but she refused. She wanted to go to Marfa for a clean, comfortable room. She was afraid if we stayed at the warm springs lodge, we would have to chase a rattlesnake out of our bed before morning.

Peggy and I have returned almost annually to Big Bend National Park. We always find the drive interesting and see many things we somehow missed on prior trips. Each time I leave the park, I hope it is not my last visit. If our good health continues, we plan to go there many more times.

The years at Tech passed quickly; our youngest children, Rachel, Veronica, Tom, and Daniel, graduated from high school in Lubbock. It was a milestone when Daniel, our tenth child, graduated from high school.

With Peggy and our two youngest sons, Tom (left) and Dan, after their graduation from Texas Tech, June 1988.

Now, all ten of our children had a high school diploma, and several received degrees at Tech. Sarita, our eldest daughter, earned an MBA degree. Lisa graduated with BS and MD degrees. Victoria got a BS degree in interior design from the College of Arts and Sciences, Rob earned a BS degree in agricultural engineering, Veronica got a baccalaureate and a master of education degree, Tom and Daniel got bachelor of arts degrees in English. With so many children enrolled at Tech, it was not surprising that at a halftime ceremony during a football game in 1985, I tied for an award given by the Dad's Association for having the most children enrolled at Tech at one time—five.

I believe university administrators should know when it is time to leave the job. After many academic battles it is best for the institution and the

Peggy with author James A. Michener at Casa del Sol, Crosbyton, TX, October 21, 1984. Michener was visiting the Texas Tech campus to gather background material for his novel *Texas*.

administrator to part at the right time. There is a natural tendency to stay on a little longer than is best. I believed I had done my share and paid back Tech for my education as a student, and for educating Peggy and many of our children. I announced my decision to resign effective on July 1, 1989, and planned to return to teaching and research in the Department of Anatomy at the medical school. I wanted to give the board of regents ample time to select the next president.

As president of Tech from 1980 to 1988, I worked almost seven days a week. Only Grover Murray, who was president for ten years, had served longer. Although I was in good health, the work was tiring. In 1988 Peggy told me it was a good time for a change. She reminded me that my hair had been dark when I took the job at Tech, but now she could see quite a bit of gray. In my later years as president, there was some tension between the board of regents and me. A few board members tried to micromanage and tell me how to do my job. It seemed to me that some members, as soon as they were appointed to the board, became education experts and now could tell me how to administer the university or the Health Sciences Center. I didn't always agree with their suggestions. I had recommended

Stepping off a trolley with Peggy in San Francisco, 1983.

to the board that they create a system that would unify the two institutions under one administration. But that did not happen. I continued doing the job of three people. After I left, the board did replace me with three people: a chancellor, a president at the university, and a president at the Health Sciences Center.

I was deeply honored when the Lauro Cavazos Elementary School was dedicated in Odessa in 1989. A few years later the Lubbock school district opened the Lauro Cavazos Junior High School. I like to think that this demonstrates the close connection I was able to forge between Texas Tech and the West Texas community, as well as recognition of my commitment to educating children.

Chapter Five :: **Educating Myself**

In 1940, I began my freshman year in Henrietta M. King High School in Kingsville. Besides taking the requisite courses in English, mathematics, Spanish, social studies, journalism, and history, for four years I played clarinet in the band. I also took a typing class and worked on the high school newspaper—the first year as a reporter and the second as editor. Somehow, I found time to be on the school football team and run track. Halfway through my sophomore year, following the Japanese attack on Pearl Harbor, the United States entered World War II. In 1944, during my senior year in high school, I enlisted in the army reserve. I was seventeen years old, and the war was still raging. After I graduated from high school in 1944, I was called to active duty when I turned eighteen years of age. In January 1945, I went through infantry basic training at Camp Hood, Texas, after which I was transferred to Fort Robinson, Nebraska, where I became an infantry scout dog handler. Following the Nazi surrender in May 1945, the United States prepared for an invasion of Japan. At Fort Robinson we were being trained for duty in the Pacific.

The war came to an end when the Japanese surrendered in September 1945. Our unit, the 50th Infantry Scout Dog Platoon, was sent to Fort Lewis, Washington, where we continued our training. On several occasions we were sent out with our dog scouts to search the nearby woods for German prisoners of war or American soldiers who had escaped from the post stockade. Although I was on a number of patrols, I never captured an escaped prisoner. The next year, I was honorably discharged from the army at Fort Lewis. I returned to Kingsville, glad to be home.

In my Kingsville track sweater, 1944. Photograph by "Dac" Crossley.

Undergraduate Studies

Two weeks later I began my college career at Texas A&I College (now Texas A&M University–Kingsville) determined to major in journalism-English. My best friend from high school, D. Ashton "Dac" Crossley, and I had aspirations to be journalists or perhaps write novels. But a first-year biology course taught by Dr. James C. Cross changed our minds. Dac and I found his course so interesting that by the end of the first year, we had changed our major to zoology. When I met with Dr. Cross, he advised me to pursue a bachelor of arts degree because the former required two years of foreign language. When I asked him if I should minor in chemistry for my undergraduate degree, he said I would take a lot of chemistry as an undergraduate and graduate student, and recommended I minor in English. I followed his suggestion.

Two years later, Dac and I followed Dr. Cross to Lubbock when he became chair of biology at Texas Technological College in Lubbock. In 1949, I completed my bachelor's degree, and in the fall I entered Tech's graduate program in zoology with a minor in botany. The department

hired me as a laboratory instructor in biology. I received a stipend of
a hundred dollars per month for teaching several zoology, botany, and
bacteriology (microbiology) laboratories to undergraduates.

I shared office space with three other graduate students on the second
floor of the Chemistry Building. I did my laboratory research work in
the room next door. There I had the supplies and equipment for making
slides and studying them under the microscope. For my master's thesis I
was examining the testicular tissue of the horned lizard, *Phrynosoma cornutum*—popularly called the "horned toad." I wanted to describe sperm for-
mation and determine the number of chromosomes in the species. When
not in class or teaching a laboratory exercise to undergraduates, I focused
on my graduate courses and research. Most days I arrived early to the laboratory and left late at night. I was usually there six or seven days a week.

One of my favorite professors at Tech was Dr. Russell Strandtmann,
who taught a number of undergraduate and graduate courses in biology
and entomology. In the graduate office, our desks were just outside of
Strandtmann's office. This made him readily available to graduate students if they needed advice or had questions about a research protocol
or problem. In the student area, he kept terrariums and an aquarium.
These housed lizards, skinks, salamanders, and fish. One terrarium had
a large rattlesnake.

One afternoon, Strandtmann walked out of his office into the graduate student area where three of us were at our desks busily studying or
reading slides. He got our attention when he asked if any of us knew how
to milk venom from a rattlesnake. None of us had ever tried, and quite
frankly none of us seemed enthusiastic about learning how. He insisted
that as biologists we should know how and he would teach us. He directed one of us to get a large beaker and to place a rubber glove over
the opening, creating a diaphragm. He uncovered the terrarium housing
the rattlesnake; as soon as he lifted the lid, the snake coiled and started
rattling. Using a long rod with two prongs, he pinned down the snake's
head. It continued its loud and rapid rattling. No doubt, if it could have,
it would have struck at its captor. We graduate students moved away from
the terrarium, giving him plenty of space in which to deal with the snake.

Keeping the snake's head pinned down with the rod, Strandtmann
reached in and grasped it by its neck with his other hand. Then he lifted
it out of the terrarium and, with his now free hand, kept the snake from

wrapping itself around his arm. He held the snake's head close to the beaker and rubbed its nose and mouth on the diaphragm. Almost immediately the snake struck it, and soon we saw venom flowing from the fangs and dripping into the beaker. At last, when no more venom came from the fangs, he calmly returned the rattler to the terrarium and fastened the lid. He turned and asked us if any of us wanted to try to extract venom, but we all declined his invitation. I have not forgotten that demonstration over sixty years ago. I have never attempted milking venom from a snake, and I don't expect I ever will.

The same year I began graduate studies, my brother Dick transferred to Texas Tech from North Texas Agricultural College (now, the University of Texas at Arlington), which he attended on a football scholarship that paid for his tuition and room and board. He also had some financial support from the Reserve Officer Training Corps. At Tech Dick majored in geology, which was also housed on the second floor of the Chemistry Building; so frequently I ran into him. One day while we were talking, Strandtmann walked out of his office, and I introduced him to my brother. He suggested perhaps we could help him with a research problem. He needed some pigeons because recently he had collected a few nasal mites in a couple of birds he examined and thought they might be a new species. When we asked where we might find his pigeons, he said there were lots of them on the roof of the Chemistry Building. He admitted he had tried to trap some of the birds and failed, but reasoned that because we were farm boys we would know how.

Dick let him know we had grown up on a ranch, not a farm, but I assured him we could catch some pigeons. Strandtmann told us to be careful, to not fall from the Chemistry Building roof, and to not get caught trapping pigeons by the campus police. We assured him we would be cautious, and said that perhaps we might have some pigeons for him by morning. After he left, Dick laid out a plan. He said pigeons roosted at twilight, so that was the time to go after them. I suggested we get a couple of insect-collecting nets and a gunnysack.

That evening, Dick and I returned to the Chemistry Building, which during my student years was never locked, as graduate students frequently returned in the evening to do research or to study. We climbed the stairs to the second floor in the Biology Department and entered the microscopic anatomy laboratory where windows opened onto the roof over the entrance to the building. Carrying our nets and gunnysack, we scaled the decorative columns leading to the building's main roof. Once there, we moved carefully on the ceramic Spanish tiles to keep from slipping and falling. We could hear the pigeons cooing. Dick whispered that he saw a number of pigeons asleep under one of the eaves and suggested we try to net those. Within a few minutes Dick and I bagged four. Fortunately, we climbed down without getting caught by the campus police or hurting ourselves. The next morning Strandtmann was amazed and most grateful when we presented him with the birds for his study.

Later, when I was a candidate to be Tech's president, after the interview with the board of regents and the search committee, I decided to walk about the central campus before returning to my hotel. As I walked past the Chemistry Building, I thought of the night Dick and I caught the pigeons for Strandtmann. How fortunate it was that we did not get caught. If we had been, I'm confident that Dr. Strandtmann would have come to our rescue and convinced the dean of students that we were only helping him on a science project. I doubt that as president of Tech I myself would have expelled two young men who were brave and ingenious enough to catch birds for one of their professors. I would have called them to my office and congratulated them for their commitment to the advancement of science. Then I would promise them that I would kick them out of Tech if they ever again climbed one of our buildings looking for pigeons or any other bird.

Graduate Studies

In January 1951, I started my PhD graduate study in physiology at Iowa State University in Ames. A few months before, Dr. Robert M. Melampy, a well-respected physiologist at Iowa State, had offered me a research fellowship in his laboratory. With a research stipend of a hundred dollars per month and tuition waived, I somehow met my expenses and even saved a few dollars every month. The time I spent studying and working with Melampy was the most formative period of my entire academic career. He had a national and international reputation for his outstanding research on reproductive physiology. Under his direction, I conducted research on the physiology of the male reproductive tract. He advised me on which courses to take and started me on my research program the first day I worked in his laboratory.

During those first weeks in his laboratory, Melampy told me to start preparing to meet my language requirements. Graduate students were required to be proficient in three languages in order to receive a graduate degree: English, of course, and a working knowledge of scientific French and German. I took the English proficiency examination the first quarter I was at Iowa State. I and the other first-year graduate students were assembled in an amphitheater. Within a time limit, we were to write a theme of several hundred words on one of three or four topics listed on a board. Subsequently, the themes were evaluated by the English Department. I don't remember the topic, but I passed the examination on my initial attempt. That summer at Iowa State I enrolled in a scientific French course. When the course ended, I believed I was ready to take the examination. I took a book in French on reproductive physiology to a designated faculty member of the French Department. She selected a page and told me I had thirty minutes to compose an English translation. I passed the examination on my first effort. Proficiency in scientific German, however, did not come as easily. I took three quarters of scientific German before I felt qualified to sit for the examination. The chair of the German Department selected several paragraphs of a chapter from a book on cell organelles and gave me thirty minutes to translate it. Fortunately, I passed on my first attempt.

Melampy had high expectations of me, as he did of all of his graduate students. When not in class, I worked in his research laboratory. Almost daily, he and I met to discuss the experiments and possible next steps. When we finished the experiments, I wrote the first drafts for publication of the results and gave them to Melampy to review. I was disappointed when he returned my writing efforts with extensive edits and rewrites. I realized I had a lot to learn. I saw this as a challenge to improve my scientific writing skills, and resolved to try to make every day a learning day. If I was going to succeed in my graduate education, I had to learn from my failures as well as my successes.

About a month after I started working in Melampy's laboratory, he suggested I prepare my Texas Tech master's thesis for publication. Given his critique of my first paper, this suggestion caught me by surprise. But he told me my master's thesis was excellent, and he directed and edited

Studying slides in the lab at Iowa State University, 1953.

my revisions. The paper, "Spermatogenesis of the Horned Lizard *Phryno-soma cornutum*," was accepted for publication without further revisions by *American Naturalist*. When I received my copy of the journal and saw my first major publication, I was delighted and proud of my introduction into the science profession.

Growing up on the King Ranch, I clearly remember my father work-ing seven days a week from dawn until dark. There were no days off for him, except for Christmas and Thanksgiving. As a child, I thought work-days like those were the norm. Now I realized that Melampy's work sched-ule and his high expectations of me were not that different from what my father was trying to teach his son about commitment to work. During the three and a half years I was his graduate student, Melampy instilled in me a work ethic that continues to this day. During my academic career, I published over fifty scientific articles, review chapters, and abstracts on the reproductive tract. In addition to those publications, I wrote about forty-five papers on renal tumors, studies on the ovary, medical education, and general education.

In 1954, while working alone in my laboratory at Iowa State, I had a visitor. It must have been around 11:00 p.m. and Melampy had already left for home. While looking down the twin barrels of my microscope studying a slide, I heard the laboratory door open. A man's voice called out asking if he could come in. Startled, I looked up and immediately recognized my guest. Standing before me was Henry A. Wallace, who had been vice president of the United States during President Franklin D. Roosevelt's third term. I said "Of course, you're welcome! Please come in." Wallace had a national and international status as an agriculturist, humanitarian, and statesman, and was also known for his social liberalism and introspective manner.

Wallace had graduated from Iowa State College (later Iowa State University) in 1910, and served in Roosevelt's cabinet as secretary of agriculture. His father, Henry Cantwell Wallace, also had attended Iowa State College and been agriculture secretary for Presidents Harding and Coolidge. In 1940, Franklin Roosevelt picked the younger Wallace as his running mate. He served as vice president for four years but lost the nomination for another term in 1944 to Harry Truman. He then served as secretary of commerce from 1945 until 1946. Then, in 1948, Wallace ran unsuccessfully as the Progressive Party presidential candidate.

He stepped into my laboratory and introduced himself. He told me he had attended an evening program at the Student Union. Afterward, he decided to walk about the campus. He had noticed the lights in my laboratory and decided to stop by to see who was working so late. I said I knew of his political career and was honored that he had stopped by. He asked how my studies were progressing, and I told him this was my last year of graduate study toward my PhD in physiology. When I told him I had grown up on a ranch in South Texas, he asked if I spoke Spanish. When I replied, in Spanish, Wallace surprised me by continuing in fluent, if not perfectly enunciated Spanish. He said he had long been troubled about the treatment of the Mexican American agricultural workers in the Rio Grande Valley. He knew they had been exploited and taken advantage of by the big farm owners in the state who viewed them as nothing more than cheap labor. As Wallace spoke about the plight of migrant laborers,

I thought about those I had seen in the South Texas fields near Kingsville. The men, women, and children—usually Hispanic—arrived at the fields at dawn, and picked cotton, harvested vegetables, and pulled fruit until dark. When the harvest was complete, they boarded their old trucks and drove to fields farther north. We would not see them until the next harvest. They traveled a circuit known as the "big swing," following the harvest across the state, sometimes even farther north. I don't remember children of migrant workers in our school. Surely some attended, but most received little or no education because their families traveled about following the crops. I told him that the only way migrant workers could escape their harsh, troubled lives and minimally paying jobs would be through educating themselves and their children. Wallace agreed. For the rest of my life, as an academic administrator and as secretary of education, I remembered this conversation. I still believe that education is one of the important ways of escaping the endless cycle of poverty that faces so many migrant workers and Hispanics.

As he departed, he told me not to work too late, shook my hand, wished me success in my studies, and bade me "good night." Wallace's demeanor and thoughtful comments about Mexicans and Mexican Americans impressed me. I appreciated a person of Wallace's prominence caring about how farmworkers were treated by the landowners.

Chapter Six :: **Peggy, the Model of Perseverance**

A Whirlwind Courtship

Peggy and I met in 1948 while we were students at Texas Tech. Both of us attended Mass at St. Elizabeth Catholic Church. The church sponsored a Newman Club for Catholic students on campus. It was a center for Catholic ministries, addressed the spiritual needs of Catholic students, and provided social events for them. Peggy and I participated in many Newman Club meetings and social activities during our first year at Tech, and it was at one of those activities that we first met. In the course of the evening, we talked about our interests and background. Peggy told me she was a convert to the Catholic Church and had recently been baptized. Our friendship grew. Toward the close of the spring semester, the Newman Club sponsored a formal dance. I asked Peggy to go with me. She agreed, and I ordered a corsage of a single gardenia. It was a grand evening, and we both enjoyed being together. Years later, long after we were married, she showed me the flower from the corsage, pressed into a keepsake book.

During my senior year, Peggy and I drove with six other members of the Newman Club to Kingsville to attend a conference of Texas Newman Clubs sponsored by Texas A&I College. We took two cars. One belonged to a fellow student, while the other was a parish car loaned to us by Father Harold Powers, the priest who coordinated Newman Club activities. Upon arrival, we went to my family's home on West Ella Street. Mother had invited us to stay there during the conference. When we returned from the conference the next day, Mother surprised us with a barbecue dinner. My youngest brother, Joe, was there helping our ranch hand Vallejo barbecue the steaks. Mother cooked pinto beans and Mexican rice and made a salad. Just before dinner, Dad stopped by and entertained us with many stories about the King Ranch, raising Santa Gertrudis cattle, training quarter horses, catching game poachers, and fighting bandits. My college student friends were pleased to meet and listen to a real cowboy tell stories about his life. Dad was very charismatic.

Mother and Dad were impressed with Peggy. Before we left, both told me she was a nice person and advised me that if I had romantic interests in her, I should tell her. Mother warned me there were probably a lot of boys who would like to court her.

One day in 1952, while Dr. Melampy and I were working in the laboratory at Iowa State University, he suggested I take a few days off and visit my parents in Texas. I said I couldn't go anywhere because I had several experiments under way, but he insisted. Dr. Melampy replied he knew better than I did when I should take time off; he could take care of my experiments. I agreed to take ten days and go to Texas. Once I arrived in Kingsville, I realized I had needed the time away and was happy to visit with Mother and Dad. I drove about town, went to the barrio, and saw several of my aunts, uncles, and cousins. I drove out to the King Ranch and had a visit with more of my uncles and aunts. I decided to go to San Antonio and stop by Santa Rosa Hospital where Peggy was in nursing school. I wanted to bring her to Kingsville for the weekend. I telephoned her, and after some hesitation, she agreed. I told her I would arrive at Santa Rosa Hospital that Friday afternoon and have her back in San Antonio by Sunday afternoon.

Peggy was packed and ready to go when I arrived at her dormitory, but she still needed permission from the nuns for a two-day leave. We went to the office where she introduced me to the nun in charge of the dormitory. Peggy assured her I was a nice Catholic boy and that she would be safe with me. She explained that we had known each other for four years and she knew my parents. Not once did the nun smile, and I began to doubt she would give Peggy permission to leave. The nun said she was hesitant to send one of her charges out for the weekend with a tall, skinny young man she had just met that afternoon. Peggy persisted, and the nun reluctantly agreed to the weekend pass. But in a stern voice, she told me I was to have Peggy back at the hospital by Sunday afternoon at 3:00 p.m. For emphasis, she added, "and not a minute later, do you hear me?" I told her I did. As we turned to leave, the nun again said, "Young man, remember, no later than 3:00 p.m. Sunday."

We had a great weekend in Kingsville, and Peggy renewed her acquaintance with Mother, Dad, and my brother Joe. On Sunday, I drove Peggy to San Antonio. I was worried we might be delayed by some unseen circumstance, so I allowed extra time. To my relief, I made the deadline. The nun was pleased to see us and told me that she knew I would return Peggy early.

On December 28, 1954, Peggy and I wed at St. Elizabeth Catholic Church near the Tech campus. For over sixty years we've shared the good times and faced the challenges hand in hand, and we're incredibly proud of the ten children we raised together. People are often amazed that we had such a large family, but we planned it from the start.

Earlier that summer, in June, my parents and brother Joe and Peggy came to Ames to attend my graduation from Iowa State University. We had a fine visit. I gave them tours of the beautiful campus, some of our facilities, and my laboratory, and we visited with several of my professors. The evening before my graduation, Peggy accompanied me to my laboratory. I told her I needed to stop by to take care of some animals we were using for research. Peggy helped me, and afterward I suggested we go for a walk on the campus toward the bell tower. It was a beautiful evening, warm and quiet. When we arrived at the campanile, I told Peggy that a six-year courtship was long enough, and asked if she would she marry me. Peggy was surprised but accepted. Then she told me she hoped I wouldn't take back my proposal, but there was a condition: she wanted ten children. I've often said that as a young man in love, I couldn't disagree with my intended's wishes. So began our first major commitment to each other, one that we've never regretted.

We've often been asked why Peggy wanted to have ten children. She had several thoughtful reasons. First of all, Peggy said, as Catholics, we had an obligation to have a large family. Also, Peggy and I both came from relatively large families; we each had four siblings, so with ten children, it was as if we were matching our two families. Peggy also said she had observed that large families appeared to be happier and more loving and had less conflict among the children. Just as importantly, she believed children in large families tended to look after one another. Peggy told me that

With Peggy walking on the Iowa State University campus on the afternoon before my graduation, June 11, 1954. I am carrying my academic regalia.

with our education, our strong work ethic, and the help of the Lord, we should be able to educate and support ten children. I agreed with her, but anyone who knows Peggy would say that it's hard to refuse her. Once she sets her mind to do something, for example to have ten children, she finds a way to accomplish it. It was a personality characteristic she developed as a young woman in West Texas.

Grit and Determination

Peggy was born in the West Texas town of Plainview on August 20, 1930, the third child of Gertrude and Jessie L. Murdock. A few months after Peggy's birth, her parents relocated the family to her maternal grandfather's farm in Ellis County, Texas, where they lived for about a year before they rented a house in Waxahachie, Texas. The rental house was a step up from her grandparents' home because it had indoor plumbing.

A year later, the Murdocks moved to a farm near Buena Vista, Texas. There were only two buildings in Buena Vista, a church and a school. Their Buena Vista farm home did not have indoor plumbing, and the family used a privy instead. When she was six, Peggy started school in Buena Vista. In 1942, the family moved to Littlefield, Texas. Peggy remembered her home there as a lovely place to live. But a few months after moving to Littlefield, Peggy's parents separated and her mother took the children to her grandparents' farm in Ellis County.

The move and separation interrupted her schooling, and Peggy didn't finish the sixth grade in Littlefield. Soon after the return to Ellis County, she started school in nearby Ferris. After finishing grade school, she attended Ferris High School until midway through her junior year. That year, when Peggy was fourteen, her parents divorced. Her mother sent Peggy and her two youngest sisters to live with their father in Littlefield.

Peggy finished her junior year in high school in Littlefield. Near the end of the year, her father bought the Flynn Hotel, which he renamed the "Murdock Hotel." The hotel was across the highway from the railroad depot. It was small, with only fifteen guest rooms, but was still the largest hotel in town. Peggy became manager of the hotel when she was fifteen. She was also the maid, housekeeper, clerk, and custodian. Somehow she found time to cook for and look after her two youngest sisters. Her day started by preparing breakfast for her sisters and sending them to school. In spite of all of her responsibilities, Peggy persisted in her education and started her senior year in high school.

Her father was a cotton buyer and traveled throughout West Texas, purchasing cotton from gins and compresses. Frequently, his business travel took him away from town for several days. When her father was gone, Peggy operated the Murdock Hotel. On school days, before leaving for high school, she placed a note for registered guests on the hotel front desk. It read: "Please leave your room key on the desk and put the money you owe for lodging in the cigar box. Thanks." To this day, Peggy insists not one hotel guest skipped out without paying his bill.

On Christmas day, 1946, her father telephoned the hotel. Peggy's brother answered the telephone. His father informed him that he had married a woman named Kathryn Cook and was bringing his new bride to the hotel later that day. They planned to be in Littlefield for only one night, and then would be leaving on a trip.

When Peggy learned about the visit, she knew she had a problem. Two days before, her mother, Gertrude, had unexpectedly arrived in Littlefield to visit her children. Peggy put her in a bedroom on the second floor. Peggy was determined to avoid a confrontation by keeping her mother's presence a secret.

Peggy went to her mother's room and warned her about her father's expected arrival at the hotel with his new bride. Peggy persuaded her to stay in her room until the couple left the next day. Peggy said she would bring her meals. She urged her brother and sisters not to say anything to their father and his new wife. To her relief, Jesse Murdock and his new wife left the next day, never the wiser, and Gertrude departed a few days later. It was not the first time Peggy had to be strong and cunning while running her father's hotel.

During the 1947 Littlefield rodeo all the hotel rooms were booked. The hotel was noisy with rowdy cowboys going up and down the stairs. Others were in the lobby boisterously telling stories of their rodeo feats. Late one night, Peggy's father and Kathryn had a raucous quarrel. He stormed out of their rooms and sat in a rocking chair in the lobby, muttering to himself about his terrible-tempered and unreasonable wife. A young cowboy came stomping into the lobby demanding to use the pay telephone. Peggy's father thundered for him to be quiet or get out of the hotel. The cowboy said, "Make me be quiet, old man."

Peggy and her sisters were in their bedroom, which opened into the lobby. They heard a thud, commotion, shouting, and the sounds of people fighting. Peggy jumped out of bed and ran into the lobby. She saw her father and the cowboy wrestling on the floor. Still in her pajamas, she grabbed each of them by their collars and told them to quit fighting and to get up. She said they should be ashamed of themselves for brawling like two little boys. Her father told Peggy to mind her own business, but the cowboy mumbled an apology and left the hotel. Jumping in between two fighting men shows that even as a young woman, Peggy had the grit that carried her so far in her later life.

Peggy graduated from Littlefield High School that spring and in the fall enrolled at Texas Tech. She attended for three years, during the fall, winter, and summer semesters. Because there was not much financial support or encouragement from her father and his wife, during the last semester of her first year at Tech she took a job at Lubbock Memorial Hospital as a nurse's aide to help meet her college and living expenses. Throughout the first part of her second year there, Peggy worked full-time, on the 3:00 p.m. to 11:00 p.m. shift. Not surprisingly, frequently she was tired and sleepy in class and had trouble concentrating on her coursework. She decided she wanted a baccalaureate degree in nursing, so in 1949 she transferred to Incarnate Word College in San Antonio, Texas. It was one of the few academic institutions in the nation at that time offering a degree in nursing. During her first year there, she learned her father had divorced Kathryn and remarried. Peggy also was disappointed to find out that her mother had divorced her second husband and also had married again. Even with all of this turmoil in her family life, Peggy was determined to complete her studies. And in 1952 she graduated with a BS in nursing. The next year she took the Texas Board of Nursing examination and became a registered nurse.

Chapter Seven :: **Virginia and Tufts**

Beginning Our Family

The year 1954 was a momentous one for me. I received a PhD in physiology, got married, and began my academic career as an instructor at the Medical College of Virginia (MCV) in Richmond. I decided to pursue an academic career in anatomy, while my research continued to be on the physiology of the male reproductive tract. As I neared completion of my degree, I began searching for an appointment at a medical school. An appointment there would allow me to teach and have adequate time for research. I applied for a faculty position at four medical schools and received three invitations for interviews.

At my interview at MCV in Richmond, one of the professors said it would be the place to start my academic career. Alton D. Brashear said the department emphasized faculty development, did first-rate teaching, and had several top-quality research programs under way. He made a positive impression on me; his friendly persona and his commitment to education were apparent. The chair of the Anatomy Department, Erling S. Hegre, and Brashear provided the senior leadership for the department. Both had a positive attitude about excellence in education. After my three interviews, I ranked MCV as my first choice for an appointment. Hegre said if he hired me, I would have to be able to instruct medical and dental students in any of the anatomy courses the department offered. I was confident I could teach gross anatomy, embryology, and histology, but not neuroanatomy. I told Dr. Hegre that if teaching neuroanatomy was a requirement for an appointment, then I would enroll in a summer

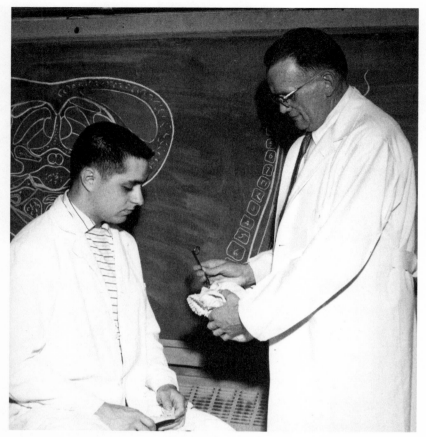

Dr. Alton D. Brashear explaining the foramina of the skull to medical student Burt Moss at the Medical College of Virginia, 1958.

course at the University of Michigan School of Medicine. With this commitment, he offered me a job as an instructor at MCV with an annual salary of $4,800. I accepted the appointment, and a few days after graduating from Iowa State I left for Ann Arbor.

Dr. Elizabeth C. Crosby, whose research on the nervous system made her world renowned, taught the neuroanatomy course. She was a gifted teacher, among the best I've known, and I can still picture her as she lectured to the class. She was less than five feet tall, quite thin, with gray hair, and she usually had a smile. When she lectured, she would lean against the chalkboard, her elbows on the tray. Dr. Crosby used no notes, and when she taught, although she was soft-spoken, she had the attention of the entire class. On one occasion, Dr. Crosby lectured on the olfactory system of the brain. Her lecture was complex, and I took many notes. That night as I sat studying, however, I found I needed clarification of some of the details. I went to the library and looked for information on the material in her lecture. After considerable searching I still had some questions about the neural connections she had described. The next day, I asked her about two or three points and told her how I had been unable to find any information either in textbooks or neuroscience journals. She smiled and said the information was not in the literature yet. She had lectured on some of her research findings on the topic, and they would be published shortly. Dr. Crosby remained active in teaching and scientific research until her death at age ninety-four.

During the last week of the course I was in the laboratory studying slides when Dr. Crosby handed me a telegram. It informed me that I had been awarded a one-year postdoctoral National Institutes of Health research fellowship to work and study in New York City with one of the most distinguished reproductive physiologists in the United States. I had applied for the fellowship with Dr. Melampy's encouragement and submitted it shortly before graduation, but had heard nothing until I received the telegram. I showed it to Dr. Crosby, and she congratulated me. I told her I had already accepted a job in anatomy at the Medical College of Virginia. Dr. Crosby said I had some decisions to make. After much deliberation, I decided to decline the fellowship. I wanted to begin my career as a teacher and researcher. Dr. Crosby's neuroanatomy course gave me confidence I could do the job, so as soon as the course ended I left Ann Arbor and went to Lubbock where Peggy had taken a job at one of the hospitals after finishing her nursing degree in San Antonio. Peggy and I made wedding plans, and the next day I took a bus from Lubbock to Kingsville to spend a few days with my family. Then I left for Richmond.

My salary at MCV was competitive with those offered by other medical schools where I had interviewed. As a graduate student, I had lived on a research stipend of $1,200 per year, so $4,800 seemed like a lot of money to me. I honestly believed that I would be able to support Peggy and myself on that. At MCV the faculty and staff welcomed me as a colleague. They eased my transition from graduate student to faculty member. That first year I taught gross anatomy, but also assisted, part-time, in histology

Giving a lecture to medical
students on the anatomy of the
skull at the Medical College of
Virginia, 1958.

and neuroanatomy. Before the first semester ended, my research program was under way, and I submitted my first application for a research
grant to the National Institutes of Health (NIH) to do a cytological study
on the effects of vitamin C deficiency on the reproductive tract of the
male guinea pig. I was later awarded the grant.

In 1954, after years of living in an apartment, Dr. Brashear bought
a house. He suggested I sublet his third-floor, one-bedroom, walk-up
apartment, and near the end of my first semester at MCV I moved in.
Peggy and I married at the end of the year in Lubbock, then took five days
to drive to Richmond. The going was slow because most of the highways
were just two lanes in those days. We finally arrived in Richmond just as it
was getting dark. As we carried our luggage up the three flights of stairs,
I warned Peggy that our apartment was small, but I hoped she would not
be disappointed. I promised that someday soon we would be able to move
into a more spacious one.

When we walked in, we found flowers and gifts on the dining room table from my colleagues in the Anatomy Department. These included a bottle of champagne, champagne glasses, plates with snacks, a small cake, and a used waffle iron. We got fifty years out of the waffle iron before it stopped working. Even then, Peggy was reluctant to throw it out. She said it had served our family so well. It did not take Peggy long to transform our small apartment into a livable place. We stayed there until just before our first child, Laurie, was born in 1956. Then we rented a small two-bedroom house for sixty-five dollars a month, the same amount we had been paying for the apartment.

I worked closely at MCV with Brashear, who became my mentor. I do not remember anyone calling him "Alton"; he was "Brash" or "Dr. Brashear." He directed the gross anatomy course for the first-year dental students. He was born in Fort Smith, Arkansas, in 1906. He earned a DDS at Ohio State University in 1932 and a master's degree in anatomy from the University of Rochester. He joined the department at MCV in 1938. His life revolved around teaching anatomy and photography. He was an accomplished photographer and a member of the Richmond Camera Club. He won many prizes for his work. Still, there is no doubt that his greatest accomplishment was preparing thousands of students for a career in dentistry. I assisted Brash in the dental gross anatomy course.

I helped Brash teach his postgraduate course on the anatomy of the head and neck. All of the students were dentists, most oral surgeons. I thought I knew the anatomy of the head and neck, but when I listened to Brash explain anatomical structures on a cadaver, I knew I still had much to learn. After the lectures, we went to the laboratory where Brash and I assisted the dentists in their dissection. He took time to enhance my knowledge of human anatomy and how to teach it. The postgraduate program in the anatomy of the head and neck that Brash initiated so long ago continues to this day at MCV. It is a five-day course in anatomy named in memory of him.

Brash was usually in his office when I arrived around 7:30 in the morning. He would invite me in to have a cup of coffee, and we'd talk about how to improve the anatomy courses we taught. He was one of the people who nurtured my lifelong passion for education and learning. Brash also encouraged my research, and although he did not have a bench research program of his own, he published several papers on the clinical anatomy of the head and neck. In 1954 Brash started writing a history of the 45th General Hospital unit, in which he had served in World War II. The unit was primarily made up of the clinical staff of the MCV. Brash was chief of dental services for the 45th General Hospital and reached the rank of colonel. I remember seeing him work in his office on his manuscript, writing on a tablet with a sturdy pencil. Then the pages were typed in the department office. This was before computers, and I don't believe Brash could type. His book, entitled *From Lee to Bari: The History of the Forty-Fifth General Hospital, 1940–1945,* was published in 1957. Frequently, when I was in his office, he read to me a few paragraphs from his manuscript and asked for my reaction and comments. I had only a few changes to suggest, for Brash was a superb writer.

Within three years at MCV, I directed the gross anatomy course for medical students, and I had increased funding from the National Institutes of Health. Three graduate students worked toward advanced degrees under my direction. My active research program resulted in several scientific publications each year. In time, I became secretary of the Graduate Council, and a key member of the committee charged with designing a new curriculum for the first two years of medical school. After its implementation, I was appointed curriculum coordinator for the first phase of medical education.

Two years after I started as an instructor in anatomy, I was promoted to assistant professor. The senior faculty in the department, my colleagues, increased my knowledge of the anatomical subjects. Erling Hegre, the chair, was my other mentor at MCV. He was a masterful teacher and spent hours with me discussing the fine points of gross anatomy and embryology. He and other faculty made positive suggestions on how to improve my teaching and ways to better my communication skills in the classroom. They also took time to acquaint me with the fundamentals and traditions of a life in education. Sidney R. Cunningham, a colleague in the anatomy department at MCV, was one of the faculty so generous in that regard. My research continued to be on the physiology, histology, and histochemistry of the male reproductive tract. Although my major teaching responsibility was gross anatomy, the faculty member directing the histology course for medical students, Dr. John W. Kelly, annually invited me to give the lectures on the microscopic anatomy of the male reproductive tract. Just before one of these lectures, Dr. Cunningham approached me to ask my permission to sit in. I told him of course I welcomed his presence. I said there was no need for an eminent senior anatomist and professor to ask permission to hear a lecture given by an assistant professor. He smiled and said at Johns Hopkins School of Medicine, as a matter of academic courtesy, a senior faculty member always asked permission to sit in on a lecture given by a junior faculty member. Afterward he told me I had given the finest, most informative lecture he had ever heard on the topic. I have never forgotten my elation over such grand praise from a colleague I held in high esteem, nor his lesson in graciousness and courtesy. In later years if I wanted to attend a lecture given by a junior faculty member, I always asked permission. Then I told the lecturer of the lesson in academic courtesy taught to me by Cunningham.

Dr. Cunningham had retired to Richmond after a distinguished scholastic career in medical education and research. After many years in the Anatomy Department at Johns Hopkins School of Medicine, he became chair of anatomy at Vanderbilt School of Medicine and later dean of medicine at Albany. He volunteered as a faculty member in our anatomy department teaching histology. I hope the medical students appreciated the fact that they were being educated by one of the most renowned teachers of microscopic anatomy in the nation.

Shortly after Peggy and I married, she told me she was ready to look for a nursing job at one of the local hospitals. I said I would ask Brash if he had any ideas where she might apply. When I asked him the next day, he thought for a moment, then picked up the telephone and called the executive director of the Pine Camp Tuberculosis Hospital. After he hung up the telephone, Brash told me to take Peggy to Pine Camp Hospital for an interview. She got the job. Brash seemed to know everyone important in health care in Richmond.

By 1959 we had three children, Lauro III, Sarita Maria, and Ricardo, whose ages ranged from one to three. But we were running out of bed space for our children in our rental home, and Peggy was pregnant with our fourth child, Alicia Maria. From the time that our first child was born until our tenth child was six months old, she stayed home with the children. They never spent a day in day care. Peggy kept up her nursing registration and read her nursing journals. She took continuing education courses in nursing by correspondence because she planned to return to nursing when the children were in school. Then she worked as a nurse part-time in the evenings, 6:30 until 11:30, for five years. By 6:00 p.m.

From left to right: Laurie, Rick, and Sarita share a popcorn feast. This photograph was taken by my mentor Dr. Alton Brashear at our home on Park Lane in Richmond, VA, 1958.

I was home from work and took care of the children. In 1975, when I became dean at Tufts University School of Medicine, Peggy worked full-time on a medical/surgical floor in the hospital from 7:00 a.m. to 3:00 p.m. This schedule allowed her to accompany me on my evening alumni and academic commitments as dean. When Daniel, our youngest child, started school, Peggy went to work full-time at Emerson Hospital on a medical/surgical floor. Subsequently she worked in the operating room until we left Concord for Texas Tech.

Just before Alicia Maria was born, we began looking to buy a house. We bought our first home for $18,500. Although we were a bit apprehensive taking on such a large debt, and did not have much money left at the end of each month, we knew we could handle the house payments.

The day I went to the Realtor's office to close the purchase of our new home I was worried that I would not have enough money for the closing costs. Before I left the department I told Brash about my concern. He told me not to worry. Together, we did some estimates on the closing costs and he wrote me a check for fifty dollars just in case I needed some

Laurie views a painting of his grandfather, Lauro Sr. Photograph by Dr. Alton Brashear.

extra money. If I used it, I could spread the payback of the debt, and if I didn't I could return the check. To my relief, I had just enough money for the closing costs. Peggy and I have never forgotten my colleague's generosity to two young people buying their first home.

Brash never married, but he enjoyed visits to our home. Often he stopped by on Saturday afternoons, bringing chocolate-covered raisins for the children. On some of those visits, Brash photographed our children as they moved about the room or sat watching three adults talk. Peggy and I still treasure the great photographs he took of the children.

Teaching Residents

Although I had a full-time academic appointment, as our family increased in number, I looked for ways to augment my income. I earned an extra forty dollars per month teaching gross and surgical anatomy reviews two evenings a month to residents from the MCV hospital. Surgeons, preparing for the anatomical portion of their surgical boards, came to our department for a review. For a half day tutoring them, I made sixty-five dollars.

In 1961, I began teaching surgical residents at the navy hospital in Portsmouth at the request of the hospital commandant. Twice a month I drove about sixty miles to the hospital for a two-hour session and earned sixty-five dollars. There were two embalmed cadavers in the morgue, and the surgical residents dissected them between my visits. At the beginning of the anatomy session, one or two of the resident physicians gave a presentation to the others on the dissection they had done since my last visit. I commented on the accuracy of their presentation and indicated the anatomical relationships I considered important. The chief surgical resident then reviewed the dissection, pointing out important surgical relations the residents should remember. Following his talk, we moved to a lecture hall in the hospital where I gave a formal lecture. These additional teaching opportunities improved my teaching skills and understanding of anatomy, and, as a result, advanced my academic career. These sessions at the naval hospital enhanced the anatomical knowledge of the students, making them better surgeons. This, in turn, resulted in better patient care at the naval hospital. The honorarium I earned also supplemented our family income.

Dr. Hegre gave me permission to take anatomical specimens to the naval hospital to teach the residents, and frequently I did so. Afterward, I returned the specimens to our anatomical morgue. If I needed anatomical material, and none in the morgue met my needs for teaching the residents, I dissected a specimen prior to my trip to the naval hospital. With the dissected material I could show the surgical residents the anatomical relationships of nerves, blood vessels, tendons, and muscles. After I dissected the demonstration specimen, I wrapped it in plastic sheeting for the drive to Portsmouth. I always drove carefully, following all driving regulations, because I did not want to risk being stopped by a highway patrolman. It would be awkward to explain the body parts in my car.

On pleasant spring days, Peggy and the children went with me to Portsmouth. We flattened the seats in the back of our station wagon and placed pillows and blankets for the children to nap on while we drove. Peggy packed sandwiches and cold drinks. One afternoon in 1963, I invited Peggy to go with me to Portsmouth. We had eight children; Laurie was eight years old, and the others ranged in age from seven years to Ve-

ronica, the youngest, who was only a few months old. Before we got on
the road to Portsmouth, I had to stop at the medical school to pick up a
cadaver inferior extremity that I had dissected for the anatomy session
with the naval residents. Peggy was reluctant to have the children share the
back of our station wagon with an embalmed body part. I assured her that
I had tightly wrapped it in plastic sheeting so embalming fluid would not
leak out and that it would fit beneath the flattened car seats so the children wouldn't know what I had bundled to take to Portsmouth.

Inside the morgue, I located the dissected part. I checked to be certain
it was not leaking embalming fluid, and just to be sure, wrapped it in
several additional layers of plastic sheeting. As soon as I arrived at the car,
Sarita, our second child, saw the bundle and asked what it was. I replied it
was some teaching materials I needed. Asking the children to move to the
rear of the station wagon, I raised the seat and carefully put the bundle
under it. I covered it with more plastic sheets. The older children watched
intently as I worked. Suddenly, Sarita announced it was a "leg" and it
smelled "yucky." Laurie agreed. As I got behind the wheel and started the
station wagon, I assured them the smell would not hurt them, and that
once we were on our way they would not notice it. Peggy said I needed to
be prepared to answer more questions when I unloaded the extremity at
Portsmouth.

We had a pleasant and scenic drive to the naval hospital. We enjoyed
seeing the spring flowers carpeting the pastures. The children seemed to
forget about the dissected body part underneath the seat they played on.
When we arrived, I asked the children again to move to the back of the
station wagon so that I could remove the bundle from beneath the seats.
As Peggy predicted, the children started asking questions. I told them it
contained an anatomical specimen known as an inferior extremity and
that it had three parts: a thigh, a leg, and a foot. Feeling satisfied that I
had taught the elder children some anatomy, I picked up the anatomical
specimen and left for my class with the surgical residents.

Looking back on those sessions with the students that I taught in my
anatomy courses at MCV, Portsmouth Naval Hospital, and Tufts, I see
similarities between teaching students and raising our family. I cannot
help thinking that my life could have been very different had I made different decisions as a young man. I learned something new every day from
our ten children, just as I did from my students. Further, our children

taught me to be loving, patient, and forgiving of their mistakes and child-ish wrongdoings, and to enjoy being with them every day. Our children's natural curiosity revealed how eager they were to learn. Asking about the inferior extremity was natural. The woods near our home were a constant source of questions for Peggy and me to answer. When they were very young they asked why trees lost their leaves, or where the birds went in the winter, and when the wild flowers would bloom again.

Life at Tufts Medical School

In February 1964, I went to Boston to interview for a position as profes-sor and chair of the Department of Anatomy at Tufts University School of Medicine. Earlier in the year—without my knowledge—Brash had learned of the opening and nominated me as a candidate for the job. Dean Hay-man and I talked on the telephone about the position, and he invited me to come to Boston for an interview. I agreed to the visit but considered it a remote possibility that I would be selected for the position.

I met with Dean Hayman in his office. After he described his plans, I decided I could work for him. Although he was brusque in his conver-sation, I liked his no-nonsense manner and his frank answers. He had a clear commitment to first-rate medical education and a determination to build anatomy at Tufts into a superior basic science department. After lunch, I spent the rest of the afternoon touring the Anatomy Department and talking to some of the faculty. Quickly, I recognized that the depart-ment lacked modern scientific equipment and had only a semblance of research pursuits. Teaching medical and dental students was the depart-ment's main activity; it did not have a graduate program. Later that day, I had interviews with the basic science department chairs.

Hayman invited me to dinner at a private club, St. Botolph's, on Commonwealth Avenue. He told me members of the anatomy search committee would also attend the dinner. This, he said, would provide me with a chance to question them about the medical school and their departments. Also, it would give the search committee an opportunity to interview me. He arranged for the chair of the committee, Dr. Alan Callow, to give me a ride. He suggested that because Callow was a surgeon, the two of us should get along fine. And he said that although St. Bo-tolph's served good food, the drinks were even better.

At the club, we were escorted into a spacious sitting room illuminated by several large chandeliers and many lamps. There were hefty drapes about the windows, and the floor was covered by a lush carpet. The room had dark wood-paneled walls adorned with a number of large paintings. There were numerous oversized chairs, a couple of couches, and a huge fireplace with glowing logs—a truly elegant setting. I was directed to a big chair next to the dean, facing the members of the search committee. Soon, a waiter appeared to take our drink orders. The waiter asked Hayman if he wanted his usual martini. He said yes, then changed his mind and asked the waiter to bring him two martinis. He explained the martinis were the best in Boston, and suggested I try one.

I soon suspected everyone ordered two martinis at the same time every evening. When I started to decline two drinks, the dean said he usually ordered two because that way he didn't have to wait for the waiter to come back so that he could order another. He said it saved time because the martinis were really quite small. That seemed reasonable.

As soon as the waiter left with our drink order, the conversation turned to my assessment of the anatomy department and the potential for building it into a modern one with substantial research activity and graduate teaching. I proceeded to share my vision for the department, including the need for scientific equipment, hiring additional faculty, the importance of starting a graduate program, and the need of extensive renovation and updating of the teaching and research facilities. As I finished my analysis of the department, the waiter returned and placed the drinks on the side table for me. When I looked at them, I saw the glasses were two tumblers—not martini glasses—almost filled with gin, each with two olives and no ice. I began to worry that if I finished both drinks, I would not be able to walk out of the club, much less make sense about the anatomy position. I managed to sip my way through the cocktail hour, but didn't touch the second drink. Fortunately, dinner was announced, and we moved to the dining room where the interview continued.

When I returned to Richmond I told Peggy I wanted the appointment at Tufts. The medical school had an excellent national reputation and an outstanding faculty. The other basic science departments all had numerous graduate students, postdoctoral fellows, and active, well-funded research programs. Further, the medical students were educationally excellent, many coming from Tufts University and the rest from other highly selective colleges and universities in the nation. Furthermore, the administration, from the dean to the university president, shared a commitment to enhance the excellence of the Anatomy Department. If they offered me the position and if Peggy agreed to a move to Boston, I would accept it.

Soon, a letter from Tufts arrived. Dean Hayman offered me the position. The appointment came with tenure, and the salary offered was almost double what I made at MCV. I showed Peggy the letter. It was a bittersweet moment. We were thankful for Brash's unsolicited nomination for a position that allowed me to take a giant step forward in my academic career. Unfortunately, Brash would never know I got the position. He had died of a brain tumor on June 30, 1963. He was only fifty-seven years old.

When appointed professor and chair of the Anatomy Department at Tufts, I was thirty-seven years old. I had advanced from instructor to full professor in only ten years. My goal when I became an academician was to be a full professor, but I never expected I would reach it so early in my career. Clearly, the opportunity placed our family in a better economic and more secure situation. It also gave me the chance to build a department almost from the ground up, as Hayman committed to several additional academic positions and to renovation of the departmental facilities.

I resigned from the Anatomy Department at MCV and started working at Tufts in late spring 1964. At Tufts, I was organizing the anatomy courses, teaching, and directing the physical renovation of the Anatomy Department. The department occupied the fifth floor of the Medical-Dental Building, about fifteen thousand square feet. In the center was a large laboratory where histology, embryology, and neuroanatomy were taught. On the periphery of the departmental space were the gross anatomy laboratory, a morgue where bodies used in the teaching program were embalmed and stored, and an anatomical museum. There were four small offices and laboratories for the faculty. The renewal called for moving the morgue and the gross anatomy laboratory to newly renovated space in the basement and repurposing the fifth-floor area into research laboratories and offices for the faculty.

When I took the job at Tufts, there were only four faculty members in the Anatomy Department. I started hiring additional ones. I expected them to devote half of their academic time to teaching and the rest to research. I chose to direct and teach the medical gross anatomy course. This meant I spent almost four hundred hours in the gross anatomy laboratory with students. Two faculty members assisted me. In addition to teaching, I administered the department and carried on an active research program. Still, I continued the mentoring tradition instilled in me by senior faculty at MCV. I taught my faculty about setting goals for their teaching programs, how to improve the delivery of their lectures, how to improve their testing programs, and the importance of fully responding to student questions.

Soon after my appointment as chair, I took a telephone call from Dr. Alice Ettinger, chair of the Department of Radiology at Tufts medical school. Ettinger asked if she could come to my office to discuss a possible teaching collaboration. We met later that day and talked about the use of radiology in teaching gross anatomy. She planned to assign some of her faculty to lecture in the gross anatomy course and to assist in the laboratory. Dr. Ettinger asked me to have X-ray view boxes installed in the anatomy laboratory, so as medical students dissected cadavers, they could review X-ray films of the area being studied. The anatomy-radiology program that Dr. Ettinger started in 1964 continues to this day.

After I became dean of the School of Medicine, Ettinger helped me raise funds from our alumni. She frequently attended alumni receptions with Peggy and me, and her former students were pleased to see their great teacher again. On one occasion, Peggy wore a green pantsuit purchased at Marshall's, a discount clothing store. As we prepared to leave home for the meeting, Peggy told me she hoped no one would know her pantsuit came from the bargain basement. I assured her no one would and I'd never tell. Later, on our way back home, Peggy told me that Ettinger had walked in to the alumni gathering wearing a dress of the same color and fabric as the green pantsuit she had on. Alice approached Peggy, looked at her pantsuit, greeted her with a smile, and said, "My dear, I do believe the two of us have excellent taste in clothing."

Ettinger was one of the most highly regarded teachers in the medical school and hospital, as well as one of the most distinguished teachers of radiology in the nation. Thirteen Tufts graduating classes gave her the outstanding teaching award. The year after I came to Tufts, she resigned as chair of radiology but continued as a radiologist and teacher until her retirement in 1985 at the age of eighty-six.

I frequently spoke at committee and faculty meetings of the need to attract more minority students. In 1967, the dean of the dental school, Louis Calisti, asked me to chair an equal education opportunity committee. I was glad to do so. Its charge was to develop strategies to increase the number of minority students entering dentistry at Tufts. We were moderately successful. Years later, as dean, I was determined to increase the number of minorities in the medical school. Before I left Tufts, I managed to increase minority enrollment from approximately 2 percent to about 10 percent of the student body. I used a number of strategies to do so. I convinced the faculty, and most importantly, the medical school admissions committee, of the need to attract minority students. Although we always needed more funding for our programs, I allocated funds to provide more scholarship support to our minority students. Our minority medical students started an organization, Progressive Alliance of Minority Students. Members became our best recruiters for convincing minority applicants that this was the school to attend because the faculty truly cared about educating them.

I enjoyed teaching gross anatomy. Over the years, I became quite knowledgeable about the subject. Sometimes, students asked if I was bored teaching anatomy because I knew it so well. I told them I was not because I learned something new almost each time I entered the anatomy laboratory. Sometimes I saw an anatomical variation I had never observed before. Each academic year as I started a new entering class in anatomy, my students asked why they were spending so many hours dissecting a human body. I explained anatomy was the basis for much of the language of medicine. I told the students that by systematic dissection, as we were doing in the laboratory, they learned how the human body was structured. When students were unable to identify an anatomical structure they were to dissect that day, they asked for assistance. When I arrived at the dissection table, they explained their problem. Usually, I reached into the cadaver with my probe and exposed the structure they couldn't find. The students were often dismayed that I had located the structure so quickly. I told them not to be concerned; I had taught anatomy for over a decade.

One of the aspects of teaching gross anatomy I found most rewarding was the contact with the students. I came to know each of the first-year medical students during the first few weeks of the semester. In addition to the anatomy lessons, the students and I discussed their expectations in medicine. We talked about problems and opportunities in the medical profession. In our dialogue at the dissecting table, I told students they must give their cadaver the same respect they would have for any patient, and reminded them that at one time the cadaver had been a doctor's patient. In fact, I told the students to think of it as their first patient. Sometimes we talked about domestic and foreign problems as well as civil rights and political matters. These discussions at the dissecting table established a rapport and friendship between us; some students asked me to be their mentor. I had an open-door policy, so students frequently came to my office for counseling on a personal problem.

At the end of the gross anatomy course, we prepared the bodies for burial in a marked grave at a cemetery maintained by the three Boston medical schools, or for returning it to their next of kin. Frequently, as they left the gross anatomy laboratory for the last time, students thanked me for giving them an excellent course in anatomy and for my friendship and guidance during their first year of medical school.

When I assumed the job at Tufts in 1964, the United States was heavily committed in the Vietnam War. By fall 1967, after years of war, many people in the United States protested against it. Calls for leaving Vietnam were frequent and strident, especially on college campuses. Throughout the country, students led the protests and urged peace. For the most part, the medical students at Tufts remained focused on their studies. From time to time, however, some participated in protests calling for an end to the war. In 1967 we evacuated the medical school buildings at least three times because of telephoned bomb threats, which fortunately turned out to be false alarms. Two of the bomb threats, however, were on mornings a gross anatomy practical examination was scheduled.

In these examinations, students move from cadaver to cadaver identifying structures tagged on the body. The tagged item, for example, might be an artery, a vein, a nerve, a muscle, or a tendon. In addition, they answered questions posed on cards. When the timer buzzed, they moved to the next table. Preparing a practical examination in anatomy entails considerable faculty effort. We had to be in the laboratory at least two hours before the start of the test to tag the anatomical structures and place cards with questions. The bomb threats disrupted and delayed scheduled examinations. For the most part, we managed to keep the anatomy course on schedule.

That same year, 1967, a massive rally of health care workers and college students from throughout the nation was organized to march on Washington, DC, to protest US involvement in the Vietnam conflict. Several of the first-year students at Tufts wanted to participate in the march, even though I had a gross anatomy practical examination scheduled for the day. A number of students came to me to ask for a postponement of the examination. Other students, however, asked me to hold the examination as scheduled. I talked to the class about the upcoming examination and the protest march. I told them that the examination would be given as scheduled and the faculty would be in the gross anatomy laboratory to administer it. I said that if there was a picket line outside the medical school building blocking access to the examination, protestors would have to contend with me, as I would be there to make sure students wanting to enter the medical school building could do so. If anyone was going to attend the march in Washington, that was up to them. All citizens have the right to dissent, I said, but they must do so in a responsible and lawful manner. If they did oppose the decisions of the administration in Washington, I reminded them, they had to be willing to accept the consequences of their actions.

The day of the anatomy examination there was not a picket line outside of the medical school, and every student, with one exception, took the practical examination. That student had gone to Washington. When he returned, the student came to my office, and we talked about his experience and the message he wanted to deliver to politicians. That afternoon I gave him a makeup examination in anatomy. When the class of 1971 graduated, they labeled me a "strikebreaker" in their yearbook. Still they gave me an outstanding teacher award at their graduation ceremony.

I refrained from discussing the Vietnam War and my feelings about it with the medical students. One morning in 1967, however, one of the students approached me in the gross anatomy laboratory and asked if I had a brother in Vietnam. His question surprised me because I had never mentioned my brother Dick. I told him I had a brother there who was an army lieutenant colonel and commanded an infantry battalion. I asked the student how he knew about him. He told me he had seen my brother interviewed on television the night before and that it had been reported that my brother's men killed many Vietcong. The student thought it terrible what the army had done to the Vietcong. I gently reminded him they had been trying to kill our troops. I said I was proud of my brother's leadership, his commitment to duty and service to our country. With this, our discussion ended and the student shook his head, turned, and walked away. He did not mention the Vietnam War again to me. That evening, I saw the television interview with my brother in Vietnam. The news report was about a battle near Loc Ninh where his battalion came under heavy fire from Vietcong. Dick personally led his soldiers on assaults with such determination that they overran the Vietcong trenches, resulting in a considerable number of enemy casualties and forcing their retreat. On December 17, 1967, for his extraordinary heroism, Dick was awarded his second Distinguished Service Cross (First Oak Leaf Cluster). This is the army's second-highest medal for heroism and bravery in combat and devotion to duty. Dick received his first Distinguished Service Cross for actions as an infantry first lieutenant in the vicinity of Sagimak, Korea, on June 14, 1953. There he was wounded and also given a Purple Heart.

Over the years, five medical school graduating classes named me one of their best teachers in their years at Tufts. I appreciated their thoughtfulness and generosity. Although I have received many honors during my academic and public service career, those given to me by medical students in recognition of my teaching ability were especially meaningful to me.

Chapter Eight :: **Our Family Life**

Investing in an Education

We enjoyed ten years in Richmond. Peggy and I had eight children while living there. After we moved to Concord, Massachusetts, we had two more, for a total of ten, five boys and five girls. Between the eldest child and the youngest one there is a ten-year span. Our commitment to each other the night of my proposal had been met. We were blessed with ten healthy children. Their only illnesses were the usual childhood mumps, measles, and chickenpox.

We began early investing and preparing for our children's education. St. Bridget Catholic Church in Richmond did not have a kindergarten class, so Laurie started parochial school in the first grade in 1962. The next year, we enrolled Sarita, born in 1957, in parochial school. Rick, our third child, born in 1958, did not start school until we moved to Concord. We knew when our ten children began college the costs would be considerable. We promised them that if they stayed in high school, and were accepted to college, we would pay their tuition and support them. We were wise to prepare for tuition and other expenses. Because they were so close in age, seven of our children were enrolled in undergraduate, graduate, and medical school at the same time. Peggy and I saw nine of our children get at least one college degree, and four of them an advanced degree, while one became a licensed vocational nurse. Although it was a struggle, by the early 1990s we had managed to pay off their student loans.

While Peggy worked in a hospital before our first child was born, she did not during the subsequent years in Richmond. During those Richmond years, money was in short supply. Peggy found many ways to save on food and clothing, which helped with our rapidly growing family. We never missed a meal, but clothes were passed down. Yet none of our children ever asked why they could not have new clothes.

Family Life in Concord

When I accepted the position of chair of anatomy at Tufts in 1964, I knew that the move to Boston would require much planning. We decided to build rather than buy a home because, as Peggy reminded me, although we only had eight children, we had to plan for ten. We purchased a one-and-a-half-acre lot in the woods of Concord, about twenty miles from Tufts medical school. Our land bordered a small pond.

I started to work at Tufts in late spring 1964. Peggy and the children stayed in Richmond until Laurie and Sarita finished the school year. I returned several times to Richmond to help Peggy pack, and we were pleased that our home sold promptly. In August, while construction on the home in Concord continued, we moved from Richmond to a small cottage I rented on White Horse Beach, near Plymouth. The cottage had two bedrooms, a sleeping porch, a kitchen, dining room, and sitting room. Although it was small, the children never complained about living in such cramped quarters. Peggy and I took one bedroom and placed cribs in it for Rachel and Veronica. Laurie, Rick, and Rob shared the sleeping porch. Sarita, Lisa, and Victoria used the other bedroom. Meals were served in the dining room and sitting room.

In September, we enrolled our older children in school. Eventually, all of our children attended the Concord public schools. Laurie, Sarita, Ricardo, Alicia, Victoria, and Roberto graduated from Concord High School. Rachel, Veronica, Tomas, and Daniel would graduate from Lubbock ISD's Coronado High School.

Construction of our house was completed in late September, and we were pleased with it. A few days later, our furniture arrived, and we moved into our new home near the foot of Annursnac Hill, the tallest hill in Concord. "Annursnac" means "place to pick strawberries" in the Algonquin language. The area that is now the town center of Concord, or the Mill Dam, once was the site of an Algonquin village. We learned that indeed there were wild strawberries growing on the hill.

Peggy and I wanted a modern home that gave us a view of the woods and the pond. During construction, Peggy reminded the architect and the contractor they were building a home for ten children. They said they understood and suggested several modifications to the plan that would result in more efficient space utilization. Peggy listened to their ideas, accepted most, and proposed some changes of her own.

Our home had three bedrooms on the first floor for the children. Eventually, one accommodated the three eldest girls, and adjacent to it was a bedroom for the two youngest girls. Centrally, there was a large playroom, into which the bedrooms opened. The bathrooms were modified and connected so that one room had two sinks, one enclosed a shower and bath, and the other contained a sink and toilet. Peggy's arrangement for the bathrooms ensured that one child could not create a logjam during the morning rush-hour preparation for school. The boys shared one large bedroom with built-in bunk beds. A couple of years later, we built a small bathroom for the boys by taking space from the storage room.

Peggy's plans for the bedrooms and bathrooms worked well. Still, when all the children were getting ready to go to school, the situation was busy and somewhat chaotic. As soon as they dressed, they went upstairs for a full breakfast. Peggy baked the bread and rolls the day before, and had juice, cereal, and eggs ready when they sat down. During those early years, she baked all of the bread and rolls for our meals. It was rare to have a loaf of "store bought" bread in our home. After breakfast, books and tablets were packed, and Peggy sent the children off to meet the school bus. It picked them up less than a block from our home.

Peggy's foresight in planning our home was probably most evident in the dining room that eventually accommodated all twelve of us. Soon after our move to Concord, Peggy purchased a long pine table with two benches and bought four chairs. All of the years they were home each child sat in the same chair or in the same position on one of the benches. Peggy timed serving dinner, waiting for me to arrive home from work. The eldest girls helped serve. Then, all twelve of us gathered to eat. Today, we still use the pine table, benches, and chairs.

All through those early years in Concord, the discussions at the dinner table were lively. Some of the children shared their activities of the day, or their disappointments and good happenings at school. Others commented on their brothers' and sisters' recounting of their day. Peggy used the dinner table gatherings to teach the children manners. She said good manners were "safety first." Peggy also told the children they needed good table manners because some day they might eat at the White House. None of the children seemed convinced they would dine in Washington.

Peggy and I have always been early risers. Even now, although our children have left our Concord home and we are alone, we're still up at dawn. Both of us take pleasure in the stillness of the morning and in first light as the sun rises and the dawn breaks. We see squirrels, chipmunks, and birds as we sit in our living room enjoying coffee and observing the beauty of the woods and the pond. On occasion, we spot wild turkeys at the edge of the pond, or catch a glimpse of one or two deer watering and feeding. At morning coffee, Peggy and I talk about the day before us—our expectations and what we hope to achieve. If either of us is troubled, worried, apprehensive, or disappointed, we talk about it and work through the problem together. Our morning coffee session ends with a kiss and mutual affirmation of our love.

Our home sits on a heavily wooded lot that ends at a pond. On the banks of the pond are many blueberry bushes, which our children enjoyed picking and eating from. Some Sunday mornings, they would pick a cup of them and ask me to cook blueberry pancakes for breakfast. I must admit they were delicious and that none were ever left over. The pond is about three acres in size and approximately twelve to fourteen feet deep, spring fed with only a small amount of runoff from the hill. Originally, the pond was a cranberry bog. As the area developed for housing, the cranberry bushes were removed and the bog deepened, thereby creating the pond. In time, it filled with water. In the newly formed pond there were no fish and only limited aquatic fauna, but still it became the focal point for many of our children's activities.

The first year after we moved there, Laurie, Rick, and I caught fish on the Concord River and transferred them to the pond. As a result, it was soon stocked with bass, blue gill, and chain pickerel. The children fished from the shore, using small hooks baited with bologna or a piece of hot dog. When they caught a fish, it was always promptly and carefully released back into the pond. As a result, the children came to know some of the fish by their distinguishing features or scale patterns, such as one they named "Old Split Tail." That summer Old Split Tail was caught and released several times.

Knowing how tempting water could be to a young child, Peggy and I resolved to teach our children to swim. Time and time again we lectured the children not to go to the pond alone; they were not permitted to go swimming unless Peggy and I were there watching them from the beach. We staked out buoys so the children would know the acceptable limits.

In 1965, the first summer after we moved to Annursnac Hill, we had a tragic occurrence. One midafternoon the housekeeper from next door ran to our home. She pounded on our door until Peggy opened it. The housekeeper breathlessly gasped for Peggy to call the police and fire departments. She said a boy had run to their house and told her he thought a child had drowned in the pond. The children playing at the pond saw him jump into the water, but they couldn't find him. The housekeeper told Peggy she didn't know what to do and was so frightened she couldn't dial the telephone. Peggy said she would telephone the police, but the housekeeper should go to the pond's common beach and see if she could help. Peggy made the call, then ran to the pond. Within a few moments, numerous emergency vehicles arrived across the pond; later, divers brought up a ten-year-old boy.

Peggy told me about the tragedy when I came home from work that evening. She said she was so scared that she didn't think to ask the housekeeper who drowned. When the housekeeper asked for help, Peggy realized she didn't know the whereabouts of all of our children. Although they were not supposed to be at the pond, Peggy feared one of them might have slipped away to go swimming without permission. It had been a sad, frightful, and tragic day. We renewed our efforts to teach all of our children how to swim, and in time they all became excellent swimmers.

Tomas Martin, our ninth child, was born in January 1965. The next year, Daniel Nicolas, our tenth child, was born. Now our family was complete. On occasion, when someone asked when we were going to have the next baby, we told them there wouldn't be any more. Peggy and I found Concord to be a great place to raise children. The town had approximately sixteen thousand residents, and the public schools were excellent. The train service to Boston was of high quality, so I usually commuted by train to Boston and went by subway to Tufts medical school. If I had to drive to the city, it took about forty-five minutes.

Concord had also been the home of four great authors: Henry David Thoreau, Ralph Waldo Emerson, Louisa May Alcott, and Nathaniel Hawthorne. The area is also rich in landmarks of historical significance. One

Our family, Concord 1968. Front row, left to right: Tomas, Roberto, Ricardo, me, Nickels, Lauro III (Laurie), and Daniel. Back row, left to right: Sarita Maria, Alicia Maria, Victoria Maria, Rachel Maria, Veronica Maria, and Peggy.

of them is the Old North Bridge, which is not far from our home. There, on April 19, 1775, according to Emerson's "Concord Hymn," "embattled farmers" fired "the shot heard round the world," beginning the American Revolution.

During the years we lived in Concord, we made a number of trips to nearby Walden Pond where we'd hike in the woods, fish, or swim. Our first trip was one beautiful fall day in 1965, when we visited the site of Thoreau's cabin. As we walked through the woods, I told the children the story of Henry David Thoreau's two years, two months, and two days' stay at Walden. I explained he was a writer and philosopher who wanted to isolate himself from society to gain a more objective understanding of it. His friend and mentor Ralph Waldo Emerson owned land at one end of the pond and permitted Thoreau to build his cabin on it and live there starting in the summer of 1845.

When we arrived at the cabin site we saw a large mound of stones. Judging from its size, it must have stood there for many years. I asked another visitor if he knew its significance. He explained it was a cairn to mark what was thought to be the site of Thoreau's original cabin. Peggy and I told the children to look around for a stone to add to the mound, but there were no stones nearby because over the years so many visitors had placed them on the cairn. We learned, however, that in 1945 archaeologists determined that the site of the cabin was not where the mound was located. Today, near the cairn, stone posts mark the cabin site, but the stone cairn was left in place, and visitors continue to add stones to it. I called the children's attention to a nearby sign inscribed with one of my favorite passages from *Walden*. "I went to the woods because I wished to live deliberately, to front only the essential facts of life, and see if I could not learn what it had to teach and not, when I came to die, discover I had not lived." On subsequent visits to Thoreau's cabin, as we entered the woods of Walden, I reminded the children to pick up a stone to add to the cairn.

During those early Concord years, we frequently took the children to Sleepy Hollow Cemetery. There, we always walked to Authors Ridge, where Thoreau, Emerson, Alcott, and Hawthorne are buried. We commonly saw gifts left by visitors on Thoreau's grave. I remember a blue jay's feather, and the blue shell of a robin's egg. Sometimes pine cones and pretty stones were placed on his grave. Once we saw a note someone had left for Thoreau. I wanted to read it, but Peggy told me not to meddle with Thoreau's mail. Looking back, I think of the wonderful learning sessions we had with our children as we explored the area, and the educational opportunity available not far from our front door.

Winters in New England can be difficult and seem exceptionally long. As southerners, we did our best to adapt to its abundant snow and ice. I left work so many times in the rain only to arrive home to snow that I came to believe a snowline bordered our Concord neighborhood. A typical winter storm produced ten to twenty inches of snow; so commuting between Concord and Boston was a major challenge for me. If it snowed during the night before I had an early morning class, I awakened our two eldest boys, Laurie and Rick, and asked them to get up, dress warmly, and come help their mother and me shovel snow from our driveway. We did not have a garage, so our car was a mound of snow. The boys knew it was part of their job to sweep the snow off of it. Invariably, one of them would ask why I didn't get the elder girls to help shovel. But they knew I would if there was considerable snow. Sarita and Lisa always listened to the radio to learn if the schools were closed. If they heard "no school in Concord," the children cheered, and then groaned when I would tell Sarita and Lisa to dress warmly and come help us shovel. I reminded them they might not have school that day, but I still had to go to work.

Rob, our third son, always helpful, clearing an enormous icicle hanging from the roof of our Concord home, winter 2015.

In front of our home, there is a fire hydrant to one side of the drive-way. At the top of the hydrant is an iron pole, about three feet long, with a small metallic flag at the tip. It is there to warn snowplow operators of the fire hydrant. When we shoveled snow from our drive, I told the boys to clear a path from the drive to and around the hydrant. I explained that this gave the firemen better access to the fire hydrant in an emergency.

Sometimes Sarita or Lisa asked why we didn't hire someone to plow our driveway. Almost every other family in our neighborhood used a plow service. I always explained that most of the plow drivers left too much snow on the drive. When it melted and froze, our driveway would become a skating rink. I added that doing our own shoveling saved money.

When Laurie and Rick started shoveling that first winter in Concord, I told them to throw the snow as far as they could from the drive. If they did not, before winter was over, we would have considerable snow stacked along the driveway. If this happened, they would not be able to fling the snow over the top of the banks along the drive. When I was nine years old we had a dusting of snow on the ranch—about an inch. It was the first time I had seen snow. We children tried to gather enough to make a small snowman, but there was not enough. That first year in Concord, as I shoveled snow, I thought of snowless South Texas and how I missed those warm winter days on the ranch.

The older boys, Laurie, Rick, and Rob, put considerable energy into keeping a skating rink shoveled on the pond. But they had no response when I asked them why they weren't as happy shoveling our drive. As soon as the pond was frozen to a safe depth, our boys and seven or eight others from the neighborhood went to work building a rink. They enjoyed ice hockey and were superb skaters. On weekends, after breakfast, the eldest boys went to the pond to work on the rink. Frequently the evening before, just before dinner, the boys would cut a hole in the ice, borrow a pump, and flood the rink, which created a smooth layer of ice when the water froze during the night. Doing this, our boys got wet, the water froze on their clothes, and they came home in the evening covered with icicles.

The rules for skating were straightforward. They must let us know when they were going to the pond to skate, and they had to wear a helmet and a mouth guard. We had spent a lot of money on orthodontic care for each of them, and we didn't want their teeth broken and stitches around their mouth. The youngest boys in the neighborhood knew they were not to skate on the rink. The older boys skated very fast and usually had a hockey game going. There were a number of other rinks maintained by the younger boys and the girls. This was safer for everyone.

Tom, our ninth child, wanted to learn how to skate when he was four, but I convinced him to wait until he was a bit older. Finally, on his fifth birthday I decided it was time to buy him a pair of skates. I took him to the

Peggy shoveling snow from our driveway in Concord, MA, 1994.

local sporting goods store in Concord Center. I had never been on a pair of skates, so I asked the clerk to pick out the equipment Tom needed to ice skate and play hockey. As soon as we were home, Tom wanted to try out his skates. I told him we could go to the pond. Although I did not know how to skate, I thought I could at least get him started.

At the edge of the pond on our beach is a massive boulder. From soon after we moved to Concord until the time we returned to Texas, the children sat on it to lace their ice skates, or simply rest and watch activity on the pond. I lifted Tom and placed him on the big rock. I said he was going to fall numerous times while learning to skate, but not to be discouraged. If he kept at it he would be able to stand up and skate a little in a few days.

Tom said he was ready for me to put him on the ice. I held him up until he told me to let go. Using the hockey stick for balance, he skated away from me. He made a couple of turns on the ice and, as his confidence built, started working the puck with his hockey stick. That afternoon, he was invited by the big boys to skate on their hockey rink. They were careful not to knock him off his feet or to hurt him. They encouraged him, gave him pointers about hockey, and soon he moved the puck around as if he had been skating for years.

On Thin Ice

Usually ice formed on our pond during the first days of cold weather, but we never allowed our children to skate before there had been at least ten days of below freezing temperatures. Area dogs, however, did not follow the same restrictions and sometimes ran out on the thin ice and fell through. When someone spotted a dog struggling to get back on the ice, he or she called the fire department to launch a rescue boat.

One winter day in 1976, two of our daughters, Victoria and Rachel, hurried into our studio where Peggy and I were having coffee. They said one of the neighbor's dogs had fallen though the ice and he was going to try to rescue it. Our daughters were worried that he and the dog would not survive in the frigid pond water if he fell through as well. The neighbors were close friends of ours. They had built their home a year before we moved to Concord and were great neighbors. Their children and the dog were frequent visitors to our home.

I quickly picked up the telephone and dialed the Concord fire department. I told them a dog had fallen through the ice on our pond. I gave them its location. They said they would be there as soon as possible. Peggy and I pulled on our coats and hurried to our beach. We found our neighbor donning a wetsuit and preparing to enter the water. Peggy and I couldn't believe he would try to reach his dog with the ice so thin and black. We were certain he would fall through it into the cold water before he reached his dog.

I told our neighbor to wait because I had called the Fire Department. I tried to convince him that even in a wet suit he might suffer hypothermia if he fell through the ice and couldn't climb out. The neighbor said it would be too long before the Fire Department arrived and his dog might not last much longer in the freezing water. Realizing he was determined to rescue his dog, I suggested tying a rope around his waist so if he fell through the ice or got in trouble, Peggy and I could pull him out. He agreed. Fortunately, I didn't have to search for a rope. Soon after we moved into our Concord home, I had attached a rope to a tree not far from the pond in case we ever needed it for such an emergency. Until now we had never had occasion to use it. I tied the rope around our neighbor's waist, and he started to crawl out onto the ice toward his dog. He didn't get far before the ice was too thin and cracked, dropping him into the water. He managed to crawl back on the ice and then farther out where it was stronger and could support him. He finally reached his dog and, grabbing him by the collar, called for us to haul them both to the shore.

We knew if we did not get our neighbor out of the water quickly, he was going to be in serious trouble. Peggy and I continued pulling on the rope while our neighbor held tightly to his dog, and soon he was able to wade to shore. Our children and the neighbor's children stood around, watching and excitedly giving advice. As our neighbor walked out of the water with his dog, the fire department arrived across the pond with a boat. I told Laurie to run to the fire truck, tell the firemen we had the man and his dog out of the water, and thank them for their prompt response. One of the neighbor's children had run home to tell his mother about the efforts to rescue their dog from the icy pond. She arrived as her husband waded ashore carrying the dog. Almost in tears she asked if he was all right. He said he was, but wanted her to immediately take the dog to the veterinarian.

As she left with the dog, Peggy told her we would take care of her husband. We walked him back to our home, where Peggy told him to go upstairs. She knew that to prevent shock, he needed to get into a warm, not hot, shower. I went to our bedroom for a heavy robe and slippers. When I returned, I found Peggy and our neighbor in a lively debate. Peggy told him to peel off his cold wet clothes and get into the shower; otherwise he could go into shock. He refused to take off his clothes in front of her. Peggy insisted on staying in case he passed out. She reminded him she was a nurse and had seen a lot of naked men in her professional career. He must have realized he could not win the argument, so he undressed and got into the warm shower. When he came out, Peggy and I toweled him dry and he put on the robe and slippers.

Through chattering teeth our neighbor asked for some brandy. Peggy responded she would fix him some hot tea, but not brandy. As a nurse, she knew alcohol lowered the core temperature of the body and could lead to hypothermia and shock. But he kept pleading and finally she relented, asking me to warm a small amount of brandy, She led our neighbor downstairs and gave him a blanket to wrap around his shoulders. A few minutes later, I joined them with a glass of warm brandy for our neighbor and one for myself. I offered to get Peggy some too, but she declined; she said that at least one of us needed to keep our senses about us. Sitting by our warm woodstove, our neighbor apologized for not listening to me about waiting for the fire department. He admitted it was poor judgment to enter the pond to try to save the dog. He said that if it had not been for Peggy and me, he and his dog might not have survived. He also asked us to thank our daughters for having the good sense to warn us about his rescue attempt. He said our children were thinking far more clearly than he.

Peggy and I tried to make every day a learning day for our children. One of the many things we taught them was safety and taking responsibility for their brothers and sisters, as well as for those needing assistance. When Victoria and Rachel recognized our neighbor was in trouble, they were wise enough to recognize his plight and come and tell us.

Scientific Conferences and Teaching in Latin America

By 1965, the development of the Anatomy Department at Tufts medical school and construction of new and expanded teaching and research space had significantly advanced. I was especially pleased with the installation of a Philips electron microscope. The electron microscope was five thousand times more powerful than a light microscope. Its acquisition advanced the research potential of the entire department. My colleagues and I used it to study the ultrastructure of cells. Within two years of my appointment as chair, two new faculty members with active research programs had joined the department. With training grant funds from the National Institutes of Health, we started a graduate program in anatomy, and soon several students were working toward their PhD or MS degrees. As the department grew and developed its teaching and research capabilities, I finally found time to turn my attention to another interest in medical education: improving the quality of anatomical teaching and research in Latin America.

I had long been concerned about the quality of health care in Latin

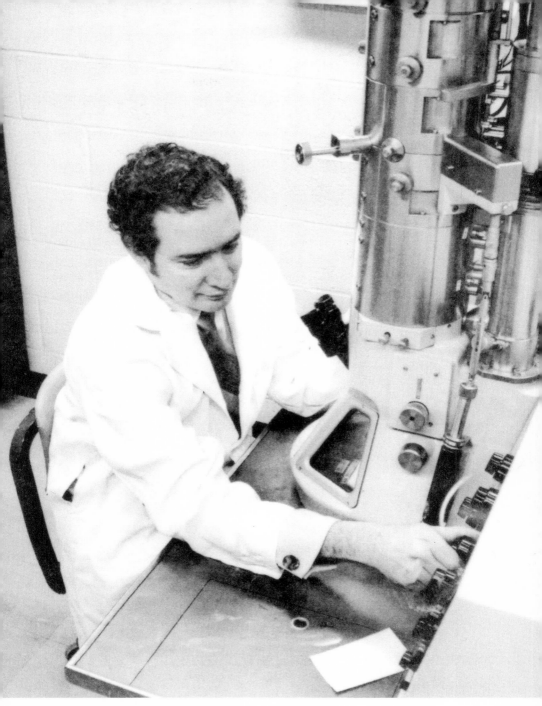

At the electron microscope, Tufts University Medical School, 1965

America. This was because I am a Hispanic and because I believed that the only long-term hope of improving health care in Latin America was through better medical education of the health-care providers. With those motivations, I made several trips to Mexico, Central America, and South America for the Pan American Health Organization (PAHO) to participate in research meetings, to teach, and to evaluate the education medical students receive.

As a result of research I published on renal tumors in hamsters, I was invited to participate in a conference on renal neoplasia in Brasilia, the capital of Brazil, held in September 1965. I welcomed the opportunity to meet with basic scientists, pathologists, and clinicians in Brazil to learn more about the pathology of renal tumors and treatment possibilities. The multidisciplinary conference included investigators from the fields of anatomy, pathology, biochemistry, immunology, virology, endocrinology, radiology, and clinical urology. I asked Peggy to go with me. She said she would like to, but hesitated leaving our nine children with a sitter. Also, we were expecting our tenth child, and she wondered whether it was safe for her to travel. When her doctor approved the trip, we asked Mother to spend a week with our children in Concord while we were away.

The conference was interesting and extended my knowledge of renal tumors. My presentation of a study of renal tumors, subsequently published in 1967 in *Renal Neoplasia*, was well received. Afterward Peggy and I toured Brasilia. Built to be the nation's capital in 1960, it was still a new city. On the last day of the conference, Brazilian president Humberto de Alencar Castelo Branco hosted an elegant reception for the conference participants in the Palàcio do Planalto, the president's palace. The next day, at the close of the conference, we flew to Rio de Janeiro where we spent two days touring the city. Finally we flew back to Boston. It had been an interesting and scientifically productive trip, and we enjoyed being together, but we were glad to be home and with our children. To our relief they were all well. Mother said the children had been no trouble, and she had even taught Laurie, Sarita, Rick, and Lisa how to play penny-ante poker. To this day, the children insist Mother cheated at poker because she won all of their pennies. I assured them she was just a good player. I still marvel how at age sixty-five she managed to deal with nine children ranging in age from one to nine. Peggy and I like to think it was because we had brought up such well-behaved and obedient children. I believe, however, she probably applied strict discipline with our children as she had done with my brothers and sisters when we were young.

The next summer, Peggy and I went to Mexico City to participate in the founding of the Pan American Association of Anatomy that was a joint meeting with the Third National Congress of the Mexican Society of Anatomy. The distinguished Mexican anatomist Professor Fernando Quiroz Pavia chaired the meeting. We became friends, and in subsequent visits to Mexico, Peggy and I made it a point to find time to meet with him. I was one of the two delegates representing the American Association of Anatomy. The other was Dr. Liberato J. A. DiDio, chair of anatomy at the Medical College of Ohio. The Pan American Association of Anatomy was formed to improve the quality of teaching and research of the morphological sciences, and to facilitate scientific exchange. The meeting was interesting and educational. I learned about new techniques to use in my research, but most importantly I met several anatomists from three continents. Some of the participants from Latin America were familiar with my research on the male reproductive tract, and we exchanged ideas and discussed our research findings. During the scientific part of the meeting I presented research on the ultrastructure of the cells of a sex accessory gland, the seminal vesicle. I gave my talk in Spanish. I stayed active in the Pan American Association of Anatomy and served as vice president at the association's third meeting in New Orleans in 1972.

After the meeting ended, Peggy and I flew from Mexico City to Acapulco, along with Fabio Rosabal, chair of the Department of Anatomy at the medical school of Costa Rica, and Stanley Jacobson, a neuroanatomist from Tufts. That afternoon, we went with Rosabal to arrange a charter fishing trip for the next morning. He insisted we shop for straw hats, reminding us that the sun would be brilliant and strong on the Pacific Ocean. In the open-air market we saw a small shop with several straw hats. Before we entered, Rosabal told us to pretend we did not understand Spanish. He said he would tell the proprietor he was the guide for these Americanos and he would bargain for our hats.

Fabio walked into the shop and selected straw hats for each of us to try on. When we were ready to pay for them, Rosabal took the shop owner aside and asked the price for the four hats. When the owner responded, Fabio, with a pained look on his face, told him the price was far too high. He insisted that even American tourists were too smart to pay that much for such poorly made straw hats. The two haggled and bargained. Then, in a low voice, Rosabal told the shop owner that he needed to lower his price even more. He told him his guiding business had been slow and that he was hoping to receive a substantial gratuity from the Americanos in addition to his usual fee. Finally, when the deal was closed and we walked away with our hats, I told Fabio I felt guilty for going along with the pretense that he was our guide. He told me not to feel bad because we probably still had paid too much for the hats.

Early the next morning our boat left the dock and we were soon out of sight of land. The Pacific Ocean swells were substantial and rolled the small fishing boat from side to side. Soon our two colleagues were seasick and had lost their appetite for the sandwiches and fruit I had brought along. Peggy had picked up some Dramamine the day before but did not have to take any. I have never been seasick and was fine. Peggy and I ate the lunch we brought on board and shared Rosabal's and Jacobson's sandwiches with the two crew members. That day, Peggy and I caught two sailfish, but my colleagues did not wet a hook.

The next year, 1967, we attended the Central American Congress of Anatomy in San Jose, Costa Rica, hosted by Rosabal. After the Pan American Congress of Anatomy in Mexico the prior year, we had exchanged letters and our friendship grew. All the anatomy departments in Central America were represented at the conference. There were also a number of us from anatomy departments in the United States, Canada, and Brazil. The first morning we attended a reception outside of the meeting room. When the president of Costa Rica, José Trejos Fernández, arrived, Rosabal's three young daughters serenaded him with the song "Born Free." I was impressed that the president made an appearance.

After President Trejos Fernández left, we assembled in a large amphitheater for the scientific lectures. The papers were to be given in Spanish, English, or Portuguese. At each desk were earphones so we could listen to instant translations provided by a translator in a booth in the back of the lecture hall. But when the time came to begin the program, Rosabal learned the translator was delayed and would not arrive until late in the morning. So he asked me to do the translations. I wanted to help my friend, but didn't think I was capable of providing instant translation of scientific papers. Fabio insisted, and took my arm and walked me to the translator's booth.

For most of the morning I sat in the booth and did my best to translate the scientific papers from Spanish to English and English to Spanish, but the stress was tremendous. I did a terrible job translating a paper given in Portuguese by a Brazilian anatomist. He spoke far too rapidly for me to follow and translate. Soon after he started his talk, I gave up. Finally, to my relief, the translator arrived and took over. Despite the failure of my attempt to translate Portuguese, I found the Costa Rica meeting rewarding. Only through the exchange of scientific knowledge can anatomy advance and flourish. This is why journal articles and professional meetings are so important. They provide medical faculties the latest scientific information to use to teach their students.

In 1968, Dr. Manuel Sigaron, of the School of Medicine at the University of El Salvador, invited me to lecture at his school on cell biology. I had known Dr. Sigaron since we attended the Pan American Association of Anatomy two years earlier. He had also visited my laboratory at Tufts on a trip to Boston. I agreed to teach a three-week course in cell biology to the medical faculty. I knew the course would help the faculty when they taught cell biology to medical students. My only concern was that participating in the program would mean being away from Peggy and the children, so I suggested to her that we go to El Salvador as a family. Although we were reluctant to pull the children out of school for three weeks, we believed the trip would be an educational experience for them.

After Emerson Hospital approved Peggy's request for a three-week leave, she met with the principals and teachers of our children. They agreed a trip to El Salvador would be a learning experience for the children. The teachers gave her a lesson plan for each of our children so Peggy could tutor them while we were away. With the lesson plans, Peggy selected textbooks, math and spelling flash cards, and school supplies, such as writing pads, tablets, pencils, and crayons, in case they were not readily available where we would be staying. She packed maps of the Americas to teach the children about the geography of our destination. She also wanted the children to gain some insight about Central American culture, so she insisted we take the children to the countryside to learn about the rural areas of the country and not just urban San Salvador.

The logistics of transporting ten children to Central America were formidable. We used a travel agent in Concord to arrange our round-trip flights, and we obtained visas for our trip. We wanted to be sure we had housing when we arrived in San Salvador, so I contacted my colleagues at the medical school and asked them for assistance. They located a small three-bedroom apartment we could afford to rent. It was crowded, but comfortable. The apartment had a high wall about it, and big trees shaded the yard.

Once we were settled in San Salvador, each weekday I went to the medical school and taught my class in cell biology to twenty-four faculty members. I conducted the classes in Spanish. Although I am fluent in the language, giving formal lectures in Spanish was challenging. Thankfully, the students understood me. We went to El Salvador to learn as well as to teach, and the three weeks spent at the School of Medicine was most instructive to me about the many problems the medical school faced in providing medical and dental education. The physical plant of the school was barely adequate and not well maintained—I'm sure because of the in-adequate funding from the state. The microscopes were old, obsolete, and therefore barely adequate. Electron microscopy did not exist. Dis-section material for gross anatomy was in short supply. It took several days before the school could provide an embalmed cadaver for my class of pathologists.

The university in San Salvador was making a valiant effort to provide the health care needed in both the city and countryside. Still, many Sal-vadorans did not receive adequate medical and dental attention. Early one morning, as a faculty member enrolled in my course was driving me to class, we passed by a hospital. People waiting to be seen in the medical clinics were lined up for a block outside the hospital. Pointing to them, the physician said many had probably been in line for hours.

At our rental home, Peggy's tutoring sessions with the children went well. Each morning and afternoon she gathered the school-age children around her under the trees in front of the apartment. She gave the older children writing assignments and checked their papers for accuracy, then drilled them in math. From where she taught her classes, they could see the volcano, San Salvador. It dominates the landscape. The city experi-enced frequent earth tremors and had survived a few tragic earthquakes. In some areas of the city, several blocks were devoid of buildings, de-stroyed by a recent earthquake. Our colleagues assured us we would feel a tremor before we left, and in fact, one morning we were awakened by a strong one.

In San Salvador, El Salvador, 1968. With four of our children in the shade of a tree in the yard of our rental house. From left to right: Victoria Maria, Daniel, me, Tom, and Veronica Maria.

We were in El Salvador during the dry summer and enjoyed magnificent weather. On the weekends, faculty members took turns giving us tours of the beautiful countryside. They drove us to parks and lakes; we saw the recently active volcano Izalco (known as the Lighthouse of the Pacific) and the hot springs and lava beds at Ahuachapán. At Tazumal we climbed the ruins of a pyramid built by the Nahuas, the indigenous inhabitants of the area. They had a civilization similar to the Aztecs. These trips to the countryside were a wonderful learning experience for our children.

In San Salvador, our children saw struggles and poverty. It was obvious to the older children that the people needed more and better health care. Peggy and I are convinced that the trip to El Salvador brought us closer as a family. There, daily life was not disrupted as in Concord by the children's many friends. Our children saw their mother in another role—"educator"—as she taught them under the trees.

Our small refrigerator made it necessary to shop every day for food, so we hired a woman to shop for us at the local outdoor market. Occasionally, some of the elder children accompanied her. Once, after one such trip, Rachel and Victoria, our two blond-headed daughters, told Peggy that people came up to them and stroked their hair. The women who accompanied the children explained that blonds were rare in San Salvador, so people wanted to touch the girls' beautiful hair. She assured Peggy they meant no harm and were just curious.

One day Peggy said the children were adjusting to the environment of San Salvador and its microbes. I asked what she meant by "microbes." Peggy said our landlady had seen our daughters with the woman who did our shopping strolling hand in hand through the marketplace eating ice cream cones. Peggy said because our two girls hadn't come down with a stomach bug, they must have adapted to the flora and fauna of San Salvador. One afternoon during our third week in El Salvador, Dr. Sigaron suggested our family join his for a late afternoon picnic in one of the parks overlooking the city. He said we had been in El Salvador long enough to develop an immunity to the bacteria in their food. He explained his wife would bring the food, including *pupusas*. Pupusas are a Salvadoran traditional food made of thick patties of masa potato cakes with shredded beef centers and fried in oil. He said they would be a real treat.

Sigaron and his wife drove us to a lovely park overlooking San Salvador. Mrs. Sigaron and Peggy laid out the picnic dinner of salad, sandwiches, fruit, juice, water, and soft drinks as well as freshly cooked pupusas. They were delicious. Peggy and I were pleased the children did not hesitate to try them. After the picnic dinner, we walked about the beautiful park enjoying the view of the city below us and the many flowers and trees. As I walked down a path, I spotted a thin, dark stone nearby. I picked it up and saw it was an arrowhead. Sigaron told me the arrowhead was probably pre-Columbian in age. He said it was rare to find a pre-Columbian artifact in El Salvador because most had been collected over the hundreds of years since the arrival of the Spaniards in the New World. When we returned to Concord, I added the arrowhead to my collection of arrowheads and spear points from South and West Texas and Mexico as a reminder of our family travels to El Salvador.

A few days before we left El Salvador, on April 4, 1968, Martin Luther King, Jr., was assassinated in Memphis. Peggy and I were shocked and saddened to learn of the death of the great civil rights leader whom we admired. My colleagues and students at the medical school in El Salvador were distressed by the news. They asked me if I thought the racial climate in the United States would ever improve and all of its citizens given their civil rights. I could not answer their questions.

I finished my teaching program, and we flew from San Salvador to New Orleans on April 9. We landed there so I could attend a three-day meeting of the American Association of Anatomists. Peggy and the children went on to Boston, stopping to change airplanes in Atlanta. As their flight neared Atlanta, one of the flight attendants told Peggy there would be assistance for her and the children in connecting to the Boston flight. When the plane landed, one of the attendants accompanied Peggy and the children down the ramp stairs of the airplane and onto the tarmac. On the tarmac was an electric cart that took them to the airplane going to Boston. Soon, they were on their way to Boston and to our home in Concord. On the flight, Peggy learned from one of the flight attendants that Dr. King was to be buried that day in Atlanta, and apparently the airline decided to transport Peggy and our children to their connecting airplane because they anticipated turmoil and confusion in the airport. At Boston's Logan Airport, Peggy was relieved to see Bill Feagans, a faculty member in the Tufts Anatomy Department, waiting to take them home to Concord.

Peggy and I thought the trip had been worthwhile because our family had seen another's country's people and culture, and especially the problems they faced regarding medical care. I felt my classes in cell biology had gone well. And Peggy had done such an outstanding job schooling our children in San Salvador that when they returned to school none of them had problems returning to their grade level.

Several years later, in early March 1974, I went to San Francisco de Quito, Ecuador, to participate in a teaching program for pathologists at the request of the Pan American Health Organization (PAHO). Ecuador was one of the countries chosen for the training program because it had an acute shortage of pathologists—there were only two board-certified pathologists in the country. I was to teach a two-week refresher course in gross anatomy, histology, and embryology to a class of ten physicians training as pathologists. Since we had only ten days of teaching time, the physicians were in class all day from 8:00 a.m. until 5:00 in the after-noon, with a short break for lunch. Only a few of my students were fluent in English, so I conducted the classes in Spanish. They were an eager lot, and soon we established a rapport. Several expressed their appreciation of my taking time from my work to travel so far to assist in their education. I explained that being there was part of my long-standing commitment to improving medical education in Latin America.

Each day, at the start of the class, I lectured on the microscopic struc-ture of cells, tissues, and organs. I had brought three boxes, each con-taining a hundred microscope slides from the microscope slide collection of the Department of Anatomy at Tufts medical school, so my students would have first-rate slides to study. It was fortunate I brought the mi-croscope slides, because the quality of those in the anatomy department in Quito was quite inferior. After the lecture, the students studied slides for the rest of the morning. I stayed with them, answering their questions and discussing the structures they saw on their slides with the light micro-scope. When I left Quito, I gave my slides to the histology professor. He was quite grateful for the contribution.

In the afternoon, I directed a gross anatomy session. The students dissected a cadaver in the autopsy room next to the histology laboratory. During these sessions, I reviewed their dissection, answered their ques-tions about the structures they exposed, and reviewed the embryology of the structures dissected. Our histology classroom and the morgue were located in the same non-air-conditioned building. The autopsy room was poorly lit. The two large windows running halfway up the wall to the ceiling provided most of the light.

One morning, walking into the autopsy room, I saw a pathologist pre-paring to autopsy a body. He welcomed me and said he would be honored if I would take time to view his work. I thanked him and told him I had only a few minutes before the histology class started again, but would stay as long as I could.

Although people could not stand on the ground outside and see into the autopsy room, I noticed several people on a small grass-covered hill immediately behind the building quietly looking directly into the autopsy room. I mentioned this to the pathologist and asked why security had not moved the observers. The pathologist said that usually the family of the deceased watched from the hill when he did an autopsy. He felt they had a right to watch, and saw no reason for security to force them away. He believed it was a matter of closure for them. He remarked that having an audience on the hill did not bother him and it shouldn't bother me. I glanced at the pathologist, the cadaver on the table, and the family looking in on their relative about to be autopsied and nodded. I felt I had learned a new perspective.

There were two autopsy tables in the morgue. One afternoon after lunch I entered the autopsy room to prepare for my gross anatomy session. On one of the tables was the body my class would dissect; on the other was a dead dog. I saw blood and fluids were dripping from the animal and pooling on the table and spilling onto the floor. I asked the morgue attendant working in the room why there was a dog on an autopsy table. He did not know; it was there when he returned from lunch. He suggested the dog might be one the residents used to practice surgery on. He asked if the dead dog bothered me. I told him I did not want my class dissecting a cadaver at the next table without knowing the cause of death of the dog. I knew rabies was quite common in Quito and certainly did not want to expose my students to the fluids and secretions of a rabid dog. The attendant nodded and left the room.

A few minutes later the attendant returned and confirmed my suspicion. He had learned that the dog had bitten two children, and a policeman had shot and killed it and brought it to the autopsy room. The veterinary pathologist was going to autopsy the dog that afternoon to determine if it was rabid. The morgue attendant advised me not to worry about the dog. My class could go ahead and dissect the cadaver, and when the veterinarian arrived later in the day he could autopsy the dog. I told him my class would not dissect the cadaver on the autopsy table until the dog had been moved to the cold box and the area thoroughly cleaned. The table and floor would have to be scrubbed of blood and fluids. I added that the autopsy of the dog would have to wait until the next morning when my students were not in the morgue. I cautioned him to wear gloves and shoe covers while he moved the dog and cleaned the area, to be careful and avoid contact with fluids and blood, and to change clothes after he finished cleaning. I asked him to hurry because I wanted to begin the dissection class promptly. He did as I asked.

The students proved appreciative and highly motivated to learn. It was a pleasure to teach them. As the students studied slides under the microscope or stood over a cadaver, they asked pertinent and thoughtful questions.

Once or twice during the week, we gathered for lunch in the histology laboratory. We ate sandwiches and had cold drinks and frequently talked about the delivery of health care in Ecuador. We discussed several strategies to enhance medical education in Ecuador. Some of the doctors said the entire educational system needed to be improved. It was not that the formal medical training was insufficient. Ecuador required potential physicians to spend six years in medical school, followed by a year's clinical rotation in a rural area, where they served people with little or no access to medical services. The problem was that there were too many formal lectures and not enough clinical work. All of the physicians in my class wanted a more hands-on practical education in health care. Some hoped to teach in the medical school and do research. Others were thinking about private practice in rural areas.

Late one afternoon, a young faculty member who had completed his initial pathology training invited me to a nightclub for a drink and dinner. He frequently attended my lectures, asking thoughtful questions and participating in the discussions following the lectures. He was not a student in the PAHO pathology program, but he wanted to learn more anatomy and pathology. I accepted his invitation.

That evening we drove to the central part of Quito. The faculty member told me he had been born in Quito, not far from where we were going—in the old city. We walked into a bar and restaurant where several of the waiters greeted him by name. We sat at a table near the stage. Soon after we ordered, the evening entertainment started. The lights were lowered, and a beautiful young woman, elegantly dressed in a classical Spanish gown and wearing a mantilla on her head and shoulders, stepped out on the stage. The woman strummed a guitar and then started to sing. Her lilting voice was soft and pleasing to hear. After a few songs, she left the stage amid applause and approached our table. We rose to meet her, and my host introduced me to his wife. He said she had been singing in this café for almost a year and had quite a number of fans. I thought to myself that her working must supplement the limited income of an academic pathologist.

The pathologist said his wife was not only beautiful but had great musical talents. The young woman laughed and said it was a pleasure to meet me. She said her husband had spoken highly of me, and had told her I was a great teacher and had an excellent reputation as a medical researcher. She told me she appreciated my teaching her husband more anatomy because it was essential to becoming a superb pathologist, which she knew he would be one day. Soon she left us to sing several more songs. I knew I had found new friends in this couple. Their love for each other was readily apparent.

At dinner I learned the pathologist had a passion for mountain climbing and loved the beauty of the Andes Mountains. I said mountain climbing was a dangerous hobby and asked if he wasn't concerned about an avalanche or a fall during a climb. With a smile, he assured me he was the most careful mountain climber in the world. He agreed there were risks climbing mountains, but the thrill of reaching the peak after a difficult climb made the risk worthwhile. He said the views from the mountaintops were exhilarating and lifted his sprits. To him, mountains presented a challenge he wanted to meet head-on. He said getting caught in an avalanche could happen to anyone; to him it was a matter of bad luck, not of the experience level of the climber. He said it was pointless to spend time worrying about dangers or what might happen while climbing.

On the way back to the hotel after dinner, the pathologist said he wanted to give me a tour of magnificent old Quito the coming Saturday afternoon. He told me he knew the back streets, churches, and parks better than most tour guides. He promised to show me some of the architectural marvels of old Quito few tourists saw. He said our tour would end at La Iglesia de la Compañia de Jesús, a colonial church simply known as "La Compañia," built by the Jesuits in the seventeenth century. So the next Saturday afternoon the young pathologist drove me to the central part of Quito. He was a knowledgeable guide, taking me up alleys and back streets, through gateways, and across yards and under arches. It was obvious the young man loved the old city and took great pride in showing its beauty to others. I'll never forget the splendor of La Compañia. Construction on the church started in 1605, and was finally finished in 1765. In this beautiful church, I saw magnificent altars, statues, and murals. The central nave of the church is covered in seven tons of gold leaf. I admired the marvelous paintings covering the walls.

The following week, after class, the pathologist told me he had received a letter informing him that he had been accepted into the pathology residency program at Tufts medical school. He said he knew studying pathology at Tufts would be a great learning experience. I congratulated him on his acceptance and asked that he let me know when he would arrive in Boston. I promised to take him and his wife on a tour of Boston and Concord, but added that the sights would not be nearly as magnificent as the ones he had shown me on my tour of Quito. He told me he expected he and his wife would be in Boston about the middle of June because his residency program started July 1.

At the conclusion of the anatomy refresher course for prospective pathologists, I returned to my work at Tufts. I looked forward to hearing from the young pathologist. Late May came, and still I had not heard from him. Then one day in June, I received a letter from Quito. When I opened the envelope I saw that it was not from the pathologist but his wife. She wrote that her husband had wanted one last climb high into the Andes Mountains before leaving for Boston. On that trip, he and his mountain climbing companion had been swept away by an avalanche. Their bodies had not been found. Now, she wrote, her beloved husband was buried and resting for eternity in the mountains he cherished. She added that this gave her some comfort, but she missed him terribly. I wrote expressing my regrets and sorrow at the loss of her husband. We lost contact after that, but I will always remember her husband for his passion for learning and for that spark that I believe can be fanned in every human under the right circumstances.

Chapter Nine :: **Manzanillo**

In 1970 the Pan American Health Organization requested that I evaluate the morphological science department at the School of Medicine of the Autonomous University of Nuevo León in Monterrey, Mexico. While there, I asked one of the professors where the faculty took their vacations in Mexico. I explained that my wife and I were looking for a place to vacation with our children in summer, someplace where there were not too many tourists. The professor said a number of the faculty vacationed at a small town on the west coast named Manzanillo. He described it as a resort town, but quite isolated, so that not many tourists went there for holidays. According to him, the beaches of Manzanillo were beautiful, and the town was not crowded. The professor said there were no scheduled flights, so we would have to take the train from Guadalajara to Manzanillo. He suggested taking the sleeper car, because the day train ride was long and tiring.

That July, Peggy and I took all ten of our children to Manzanillo. We wanted to continue their education into their Hispanic heritage and show them another part of Mexico. We also took along three of Peggy's nieces, Tammy, Tessie, and Tria Ince. From Boston we flew to the Dallas–Fort Worth airport, picked up our nieces, and flew on to Guadalajara. We wanted to see the countryside, so we decided to take the day train from Guadalajara to Manzanillo. We booked the sleeper train for our return.

The train trip turned out to be an interesting journey. Our aged train did not have air-conditioning, so we opened the passenger car's windows. Unfortunately, clouds of dust flew in. So we opted to keep them closed despite the heat. After we left Guadalajara, the conductor came through the car checking tickets. As he punched our tickets, he said we were wise to take the day train because we would pass through spectacular isolated country. First, he said, came the desert; then the train would ascend the mountains and cross the jungle. Next, we would descend toward the coast and enter the beautiful tropical rain forest area of Mexico. The conductor assured us we would enjoy the ride.

Before leaving Guadalajara, Peggy and I talked about food for the trip. She suggested taking sandwiches and drinks. It would be a long day and the train did not arrive in Manzanillo until early evening. I said we could eat in the dining car. Shortly after the train departed I asked the conductor directions to the dining car. He said there wasn't one. Fortunately, though, the train made frequent stops during which food peddlers boarded to sell soft drinks, sandwiches, tortillas, tamales, and all sorts of other good food. With a smile, he said the food would come to us.

About four hours into our trip, Peggy told me the children were getting hungry, and asked if we should buy some food at the next stop. I thought it would be a mistake to eat the food the peddlers sold. Joking that I could see hot and cold salmonella lurking on the food, I persuaded her that it would be risky. I suggested soft drinks might be safe. I did not even trust the bottled water offered by the peddlers. On other visits to Mexico, friends had warned me not to buy plain bottled water because it might have come from the tap. They advised *aqua con gas*, or carbonated water, since one could not fake carbonation. So, we had nothing to eat for the entire day, satisfying our hunger only with soft drinks.

At each of the stops food peddlers quickly boarded the train and moved down the aisles selling food and drinks. They had phenomenal timing, and at the first lurch of the train, gathered their baskets and wares, made change if necessary, and hopped off of the train just before it left the station. Other peddlers boarded to sell curios and trinkets. Others came through offering live chickens. At each station stop, beggars got on board. Many had deformities. At some of the stops, children led blind persons through the train. They extended their palms begging for coins. Watching the vendors and beggars moving up the aisle, our children learned that many people in Mexico lived in grinding poverty and resorted to begging. The sight of so many poor people deeply affected some of the children, and I was glad to oblige when they asked for change to give out.

At one stop, we saw several armed Mexican soldiers boarding. They stayed on after it pulled out of the station. When I inquired about it, the conductor said they were taking precautions. The train was nearing a jungle zone where there had been considerable bandit activity in the countryside. The conductor said that occasionally bandits tried to stop the train and rob the passengers. He told me not to worry because somehow the bandits knew when soldiers were on board and did not attack the train if there were. I guessed they were warned by one of the food or trinket vendors at the preceding station stop.

Our train arrived in Manzanillo just as it was getting dark. One would guess every person living in the small town had come to meet the train, so crowded was the station. We had rented a house near the beach; so after unloading our bags and gathering the children, we left the station in three taxis. We spent five days in beautiful Manzanillo. It was peaceful and quiet, and twice a day we took the children to the delightful beaches. The best beach was a short walk from our house. To get there, however, we had to navigate around large rocks and follow the steep, narrow path leading to the beach. I always led the way, with Peggy at the end of the column of children. With the Pacific Ocean surging and crashing onto the shore and the rocks below us, Peggy kept telling them not to look down, to watch their step, and to stay in line.

Most mornings Peggy and I went to a taco stand nearby and picked some up for breakfast. Almost daily, Peggy, with the help of the eldest girls, Sarita and Lisa, shopped at the market in town. They bought milk, eggs, soft drinks, fruits, vegetables, sandwich meats, and ground beef for spaghetti and meat loaf. Fish and shrimp were plentiful and inexpensive, so they were often the main dish in the evening. Bollos (Mexican buns or rolls) made excellent sandwiches. For desert, there was fruit, ice cream, and Mexican cookies. In order to avoid food that would make us ill, Peggy shopped at places recommended by our landlord. For the most part, the shops were required to follow heating and refrigeration rules similar to those in the United States. Peggy was careful to thoroughly wash and cook the vegetables and meat. We kept food that might spoil in the refrigerator.

At the end of the week we left Manzanillo for Guadalajara on the sleeper night train. Before departing, the station master asked if he could take a picture of our beautiful family. He said he wanted to pin it to a wall of the depot to show other passengers an example of the fine families coming to Manzanillo for their vacation. We agreed. Less than a decade after our trip there, Manzanillo became a major tourist attraction. Large, modern hotels and elegant shops were built. The small airport was expanded, and now there are jet flights to there. Peggy and I hope the little town has retained some of its charm.

From Guadalajara we went to Mexico City. I arranged for a guide to show us some of its magnificent museums and historic sites. Our tour included the Cathedral Santuario de la Virgen de Guadalupe, the site of the appearance of La Virgen de Guadalupe, whom Pope Benedict XIV named the patroness of Mexico. When we entered the cathedral, we saw it was packed with people. Peggy told the children to hold hands, and I and our guide led the way toward the main altar while Peggy followed at the rear of our parade of children. At the front of the church, we viewed the display of the cloth with the image of La Virgen. Once we were back outside, we walked around the building and marveled and commented on the hundreds of icons, crutches, and walking sticks left by people who believed they were healed of their illness or their disabling disease after visiting the shrine and praying to La Virgen.

While at the shrine, I thought of my uncle Manuel "Tío Meme" Álvarez, a deeply religious man who lived in Kingsville, Texas. He believed La Virgen wanted him to visit the shrine. So he walked most of the way there, sometimes catching rides. At the Cathedral Shrine of the Virgin of Guadalupe he prayed, lighting candles for his relatives and friends. The trek took almost a year. After our own visit to the shrine, we toured the magnificent Chapultepec Castle. On September 12–13, 1847, during the Mexican-American War, US forces engaged the Mexican army here during the Battle of Chapultepec. The US forces were victorious.

We spent part of an afternoon at the Museo Nacional de Antropología (National Museum of Anthropology), which holds an enormous collection of ancient Mexican pieces, including the Aztec Calendar Stone known as the Sun Stone. The museum is vast, and it was impossible to see and understand what it had to teach in one day. I told the children that this trip was just an introduction; we hoped they would return on their own someday. Indeed, they have. Our eldest son, Laurie, frequently pilots a jet to Mexico City and Guadalajara carrying cargo. Our daughter Sarita spent her junior year at Tufts University studying Spanish in Mexico City, and Dan studied in Mexico while a student at Tech. Others have vacationed in Mérida, Yucatán, Oaxaca, or Monterrey.

*Chapter Ten :: * **On to Paris and Versailles**

On December 31, 1971, we flew to Paris. I had a six-month sabbatical from Tufts to work and study at a research institute in Le Kremlin Bicêtre, near Paris. There, I expected to learn research methods to use in my study of the prostate gland.

That year for Christmas, the children received presents they would find useful in France. All were given backpacks, and the older children got watches and calculators. We decided not to enroll our children in the French schools. This would allow us to travel and not be hindered by school schedules. Peggy would do as she had done in El Salvador—tutor them. Before we left Concord, she met with each of the children's teachers and received lesson plans and suggestions on topics to cover.

We knew finding housing in Paris for a family of ten children, two adults, and our dog, Nickels, would not be easy. I contacted a rental agency in Paris. They assured me they could locate housing for us and would start a search as soon as they received our deposit. Peggy and I were skeptical about sending money, but complied.

We needed a place to stay for a day or so after we arrived in Paris, so I made reservations at a small hotel on the Left Bank where one of my colleagues in the Anatomy Department had stayed the year before. He recommended it as inexpensive, yet clean.

I already had a valid passport, but Peggy would need one. The ten children could be included on hers. A few days after the passport arrived, we went to the French consulate in Boston. There we obtained visas valid for our six-month stay in France. The logistics of moving a family our size to France was multifaceted, but Peggy did a grand job organizing the trip. She selected airline flights and purchased tickets with the assistance of our travel agency in Concord. We arranged to put Nickels at a kennel until after we moved into more permanent lodging in France. We rented our home in Concord for the six months we were on sabbatical to the recently appointed dean of the Tufts dental school. Our neighbor agreed to drive us to the airport.

On Friday afternoon, December 31, we loaded the family into our neighbor's Volkswagen bus. I had checked our bags at the Air France counter the day before. The heavily loaded bus struggled climbing the hills, but we made it to the airport without incident. At the check-in counter, our ten children, ages five to fifteen, were a crowd and attracted attention. A woman waiting to check in for her own flight remarked to me that we had a lovely group of children and asked the name of our school. She added that she had been to Paris many times and that a school tour there would be highly educational. I explained that these were our children, not a school tour. She gave me a look of disbelief and asked no further questions.

Our flight left Logan Airport late that evening, New Year's Eve, and somewhere over the Atlantic Ocean we toasted in the New Year. Peggy and I had champagne and the children drank fruit juice, and soon they were asleep. At dawn, we saw Paris out of the airplane window. At Orly Airport, the inspectors stamped our passports, didn't open a bag, and waved us through customs. Although Peggy was surprised at the ease, I said we didn't fit the profile of a gang of smugglers or terrorists.

Once we were outside the terminal, I saw a line of taxicabs waiting across the street. In my best French, I told the driver of the first in line that I wanted to hire three taxis to take our family to a hotel. By the look the driver gave me, I knew my best French had not been good enough. I tried English, and he shrugged his shoulders and shook his head. In desperation, I switched to Spanish. The driver smiled; he told me he was from the Basque Country. I had found a language we both understood. While Peggy and I organized the three groups for the taxis, our daughter Sarita said she hadn't realized I was so fluent in French. I admitted that we had spoken in Spanish. With our luggage and so many children, even three cars was a tight fit. Once arrived at our small hotel, we went to our three rooms and took naps. Jet lag and differing time zones were taking their toll.

Peggy's and the children's passport photograph for our sabbatical in France, 1971. Front row, left to right: Victoria Maria, Tomas, Daniel, Rachel Maria, Veronica Maria, Roberto. Back row, left to right: Ricardo, Alicia Maria, Peggy, Sarita Maria, Lauro III.

The next morning, I tried to contact our rental agency about our housing arrangements, but no one answered the telephone. Leaving the two eldest children, Laurie and Sarita, to care for their brothers and sisters, Peggy and I went to the address of the rental agency. To our dismay, they were not open. I inquired about the firm at a nearby shop and was told they were no longer open for business. No one knew where they had moved. We realized the realtors had disappeared with our hundred-dollar deposit and that we now had no place to stay during the sabbatical. Peggy stayed upbeat, saying she was sure we would find a great place to stay the next day.

We managed the financial hardship. Later that morning I contacted the head of research at a scientific company I consulted for and got an advance of the honorarium I was to receive when I returned to Massachusetts. This more than made up for the loss of the deposit and gave us some financial cushion. Although money was tight during the sabbatical,

Peggy and I managed to stay on budget. We never discussed details of our finances with our children, and they did not ask about them. If we could not afford an item they wanted, we simply told them that, and they accepted our decision without complaint or question.

We had never been to Paris, so we knew nothing about the city, including housing. So I sought assistance from the people at the laboratory where I was to work. That afternoon, Peggy and I went to the laboratory located in Le Kremlin Bicêtre, an incorporated municipality almost three miles south of the center of Paris. The elderly couple operating our hotel told us which metro line and bus to take. Thirty minutes after leaving our hotel, we were at the laboratory.

We met the director, Etienne Beaulieu, and the scientist with whom I was to work, Charles Robel. We chatted for a few minutes about our trip, and then I explained our housing problem. Robel said he had an American working in his laboratory who could help us find a place to stay. His name was Dr. Charles Wira, a physiologist on leave from Dartmouth medical school. Wira had worked in Robel's laboratory for two years and was fluent in French.

We walked to Robel's laboratory, where Robel introduced us to Wira. A young man, perhaps in his late twenties, welcomed us into the laboratory. Wira was six feet tall, physically trim, with black hair and a ruddy complexion. I liked his friendly, relaxed manner. Robel explained our situation and asked Wira if he could assist us. Wira promised to pick up the newspapers on his way to work the next morning so we could search them for available rentals. He also offered to drive me around the city to look at some of the locations.

The next morning I returned to the laboratory, while Peggy stayed with the children in the hotel. Wira brought in the daily newspapers, and we started looking through the housing rental section. Soon we decided there were few places in Paris big enough to accommodate my family, and those that were large enough I could not afford. Wira asked if living in the suburbs was an option. He said it would mean a commute, but there was first-rate train service to Paris from many of the suburbs. I told him I had no problem commuting if we could find a decent place to live and one we could afford. After all, I had commuted by train between Concord and Boston for years. He said in that case, we should look at two apartments, one in St. Cloud and the other in Versailles.

We looked at the apartment in St. Cloud, but I did not think it would meet our needs. We met the agent for the Versailles apartment in her office in Paris, and she drove us to 26 Avenue de Paris. As soon as I stepped out of the car, it was obvious to me that the apartment was quite old and must have seen a lot of history. From the sidewalk in front of the apartment, I could see the magnificent Palace of Versailles three blocks down the street. I remarked that in 1789, the occupants of the old apartment must have had front-row seats as the French revolutionaries moved King Louis XVI, Marie Antoinette, and their family from Versailles to a prison in Paris.

The apartment was furnished, had three floors, with a small kitchen, dining room, a sitting room, two bathrooms, and several bedrooms. I liked it and the rent fit our budget, but first I needed to talk to Peggy. I told the rental agent I would let her know our decision late that day or by early the next. At the hotel, I described the apartment to Peggy. The rent was exactly the amount our home in Concord was rented for, so we could afford it. The train station was only a short walk from the apartment. The train went from Versailles to Gare Montparnasse in Paris. There I would board the Metro, taking me to Le Kremlin Bicêtre. From the metro stop, I would catch a bus that stopped near my laboratory, or I could walk to the lab from the Metro station.

Peggy asked if there was a fence around the property. She did not want the children getting in the street or Nickels running away. I told her the backyard had an attractive nine-foot wall around it, and had some beautiful trees and a small garden. The apartment faced a boulevard with grass and many trees in its broad median. I assured her the neighborhood was safe because our apartment was four buildings from a jail. There were guards and police practically next door. The convenient commute, scenery, and the layout made the Versailles apartment an ideal place to rent. So late that afternoon, I called the rental agent; I told her we wanted a six-month lease. She was fine with that and said the contents of the apartment would be inventoried by early evening, and because there were ample amounts of linens, towels, and blankets in the apartment, we could move in that night. Wira drove me to the real estate office and I signed the lease agreement and put down a deposit.

After we left the real estate office, Wira drove me to rent a Volkswagen bus for one day. He assured me the rules for driving in Paris and on the roads outside of the city were practically the same as those in the United States. There were, however, two differences. First, I could use only parking lights in the city. There was no need for headlights because Paris was well illuminated at night. Second, Wira said, the car on the right always had the right-of-way. Remember, he said, to yield to the car on the right and to keep "*la droite*" in mind as I drove.

I rented the bus and followed Wira to our hotel to pick up Peggy and the children. Stopping by some open-air markets, we chose food, soft drinks, and wine for dinner that night. By the time we finished shopping, it was almost dark and raining, not ideal conditions in which to follow Wira to Versailles. I didn't know the streets of Paris and had no idea how to get to Versailles, so I focused on keeping Wira's car in sight. My most anxious moment came when we went around the traffic circle surrounding the Arc de Triomphe. Keeping "*la droite*" in mind, I managed to keep behind Wira, and we arrived at our apartment without mishap. Shortly after we unloaded our groceries and bags, the agent arrived to inventory the contents of the apartment. After the inventory was completed, I signed off on it.

Although the apartment was ample for a small family, it was a challenge to provide sleeping space for two adults and ten children. Still, Peggy made it work. On the first floor, the living room sofa could be converted into a bed for Lisa and Victoria, and there was a small bedroom with a single bed where our eldest daughter, Sarita, could sleep. Nearby, on the same floor, Laurie and Rick would share another small bedroom. The master bedroom was on the second floor. Peggy and I could sleep there on a double bed. The third floor consisted of one long room, without furniture. We decided to make it into a coed dormitory for the five youngest children. The next day we had five cots and mattresses delivered to our apartment. Until the cots arrived, the youngest children slept on pallets on the floor.

A few days later, Peggy and I went to Paris and bought linens, sheets, pillows, and towels to supplement the ones in the apartment. In a few days, Peggy changed it into a livable and comfortable space. Although we were crowded, the children did not complain or say they wished they were back in their Concord home.

We quickly adapted to the routine of living in a small French town like Versailles. Our refrigerator was small, so daily shopping for food was a necessity. Each day by midmorning, Peggy took her shopping bags and walked to the nearby markets to buy groceries and dairy products. Usually, Sarita or Laurie went with her because they could communicate with the shopkeepers in French. They became their mother's translators and advisors on French customs. Daily, Peggy sent two or three of the other children to buy bread, croissants, and baguettes at the bakery about a block away. The children could not resist the smell of freshly baked bread and sometimes ate most of one baguette before they arrived home. For that reason, Peggy usually asked the children to buy three so that they would bring at least two home.

As soon as we were settled, Peggy started schooling the children. The schoolbooks the children had brought formed the basis for Peggy to teach them. Weekdays, she insisted they assemble to do their schoolwork. Peggy gave Laurie, Sarita, Rick, and Lisa assignments in math, history, social studies, and English composition. They were required to write essays that Peggy read and reviewed and critiqued with each child. The eldest children enjoyed reading, and Peggy had several books for them to read and then write reports on. Laurie and Sarita taught their brothers and sisters some French phrases. Peggy had purchased a tape recorder with French lessons before our departure to France. She had started playing the tapes in Concord and continued while we were in France.

Peggy concentrated on helping Victoria, Rob, Rachel, Veronica, Tom, and Daniel with math, phonics, writing, and reading and spelling. She used a number of different reading and writing aids as well as math and spelling flash cards. She worked with the children individually and on occasion as a group. In the United States, Peggy had purchased a small typewriter with colored keys and finger rings of different colors matching the keys. This typing activity seemed to improve the children's reading and spelling abilities. Peggy had a small record player, and played the records that came with the typewriter. The records had exercises explaining to the child which key to punch. She worked with the youngest children on their lessons each day, and before we left Versailles some had learned to type, while all were reading and writing at their grade level or above.

Before we left Concord for France, Peggy suspected one of our children, a fifth grader, was not reading at grade level and might be dyslexic. She went to the school counselor responsible for testing for learning disabilities and insisted that our daughter be tested. The testing confirmed

Peggy's suspicions. The school provided a tutor for our daughter. When we returned from France, Peggy took her to enroll in school. To her dismay, the administration wanted our child to repeat the fifth grade. Peggy did not agree, but the school administration refused her request to promote our child. Not to be denied, Peggy met with the principal of another school in Concord previously attended by several of our children. The principal was sympathetic and told her to enroll our daughter in his school where she would start in the sixth grade. He felt she would benefit academically by participating in their excellent tutoring program. There, despite her dyslexia and I'm sure helped by Peggy's tutoring in France, our daughter finished elementary school and graduated from high school without significant academic problems. She applied to Texas Tech University, was accepted, and earned a baccalaureate degree. Another of our daughters also had dyslexia. In Concord, Peggy insisted she be tested and tutored. With the proper diagnoses, and Peggy's devoted teaching in France, our daughter did well in school after that. Subsequently, she received two degrees from Texas Tech. Peggy and I are proud of our two daughters who overcame learning disabilities and went on to success in higher education.

A week after we settled into our apartment in Versailles, I telephoned the Palmer Kennels in Acton, Massachusetts, where we had boarded our dog, and asked Mr. Palmer to send Nickels to Paris. The children missed him and were anxious about him. Palmer said he would have the veterinarian sign Nickels's health certificate and by the end of the week he would be flown to Orly Airport. On the day Nickels was to arrive, I rented a car, and Laurie and I picked him up at the airport. As soon as we entered our apartment, Nickels jumped on the children and raced about the house, obviously pleased to see them. I told them they could let Nickels run in the backyard because it was fenced, but to be careful and keep the gate closed.

I heard a chorus of "Yes, Pop," from the children. But the next day when I returned from the laboratory, Peggy met me at the door. She said one of the children had left the front door open a bit, and Nickels had run out. When she heard the children shouting and calling his name, she came downstairs; stepping out our front door she saw Laurie and Rick chasing Nickels down the boulevard divider of the Avenue de Paris. The dog was obviously enjoying his run, staying just ahead of the boys. They

Peggy and our ten children on the Left Bank in Paris, January 2, 1973.

didn't catch him until they were almost at the gates of the Palace of Versailles.

The beautiful and magnificent park behind the Palace of Versailles became the children's playground. Laurie, Sarita, Rick, and Lisa went there several times a week. On weekends, Peggy packed a picnic basket, and all of us enjoyed lunch on the lovely wooded grounds around the palace. There are approximately 230 acres of gardens where we found a number of excellent sites for our picnics. The children showed us places in the park where they had discovered beautiful statues, elegant fountains, or buildings. They led us to the Petit Trianon and the Grand Trianon. Frequently, we toured the interior of the Palace of Versailles. Starting in 1664, the Sun King, Louis XIV, built the palace as a hunting lodge and a place to get away from Paris. Louis XV and the ill-starred Louis XVI enlarged the hunting lodge considerably and eventually transformed it into the Palace of Versailles.

On one of our tours of the palace, we visited the Royal Opera. Sarita was awed by its grandeur. I agreed, yet when I saw the furnishings, gilding, mirrors, the magnificent architecture of the buildings, and the splendor of the grounds, I understood why there had been a French Revolution. I pointed out that French royalty had this opulence while most of the people lived in poverty, and were hungry and suppressed.

Early each morning during the week, I had coffee, a piece of fruit, and a croissant with Peggy. After breakfast, I slipped out of the house before the children awakened and walked to the train station. Usually, I arrived at the laboratory by 8:00 a.m., when only the cleaning people were in the building, and concentrated on my research program. At 10:00 a.m. the others working in the laboratory arrived.

The scientists in the laboratory were skillful researchers, and I learned some new research methods from them that I subsequently applied to my studies of accessory sex glands. Soon I had many friends there. They tolerated my efforts to communicate in French but were kind enough to speak English to me most of the time. Although the laboratory research personnel arrived late in the morning, they stayed until early evening, while I left about 5:00 p.m. At least twice a week, after tea, one of the senior scientists or a visiting scientist presented a seminar on the results of their research. Eventually, my French improved and I understood the seminars. I, too, gave a seminar describing results from my research at Tufts. The senior scientists in the laboratory were fluent in English, so I gave my seminar in English.

The children quickly adapted to life in France. On weekends and holidays we rode the train to Paris. During these outings, we became tourists, taking a boat down the River Seine and ascending to the top floor of the Eiffel Tower. We walked to the western end of the Champs-Élysées to the Arc de Triomphe at the Place de l'Étoile. We saw the tombs of the unknown soldiers. We marveled at the architectural beauty of Notre-Dame Cathedral and climbed one of the towers. We visited the Basilique du Sacré-Coeur located on Montmartre, the highest land point in Paris. We went to a number of museums, toured the marvelous zoo of Paris, and spent hours in the Louvre. There we enjoyed the magnificent artworks, and Rick, quite an artist and a student of art history, explained some of the paintings and the artist's message.

At least twice a month, I invited the eldest children to meet me in Paris for a walking tour of part of the city. Laurie, Rick, and Lisa always accepted my invitation. Usually we met at the Place de la Concorde. It was here the French revolutionaries erected a guillotine and executed King Louis XVI in 1793, and subsequently Queen Marie Antoinette. The children brought a lunch Peggy packed for us. Usually it was ham and cheese on a sliced baguette, some fruit, and soft drinks. We shared a lunch on a bench in the square, and later walked about admiring the beauty of Paris. We usually ended up at the Louvre for another art history lesson from Rick.

By the time we had been in France for about two months, the eldest children knew more about Paris and how to move about the city than they did about Boston. Peggy said she worried less about them catching a train from Versailles, arriving in Gare Montparnasse, and boarding the Metro to Place de la Concorde than she did when they were going by commuter train and subway from Concord to downtown Boston to meet me at the medical school.

Three months after our arrival in France, in late March 1972, I returned to the United States for a week. I went to Boston, then to Texas, and subsequently to New Orleans to attend the third meeting of the Pan American Association of Anatomy. In 1970, I had been elected vice president of the association, so I felt an obligation to attend. I was concerned about leaving Peggy and the children in France. But Peggy believed my involvement with the anatomy organization was important to my academic career, and she assured me they would be fine. All of the children were in good health, but because there was a possibility she might need a doctor, I gave her the names and telephone numbers of two physician graduates from Tufts practicing at the American Hospital of Paris. I would also write out several checks on our bank in Paris and leave as much cash as I could gather.

Peggy gave me a list of some items to get while in the United States because they were too expensive to buy in France. First on the list were the largest jars of peanut butter and grape jelly I could buy. The children were hungry for a real peanut butter and jelly sandwich. There were several spices she needed, too, including mustard; they were so expensive in

Paris. She would also give me a list of magazines and books to purchase, including the latest issue of *Cosmopolitan* magazine. Why that magazine, I asked? Peggy laughed and said that she and Sarita had read that the actor Burt Reynolds was the centerfold. The magazine was not a priority, but she did want the spices and the peanut butter and grape jelly.

When I arrived in Boston, I spent a day in the Anatomy Department at Tufts medical school. The next day I flew to Corpus Christi, Texas. I rented a car and drove to Kingsville to see my mother. The two of us had a grand visit, during which I brought her up to date on each of her grandchildren and Peggy. The next day, she asked me to drive her on a shopping trip in Kingsville so that she could purchase clothes for each of our children and Peggy. When I left Kingsville for New Orleans, I had three large suitcases and one small bag to carry. They were filled with the items Peggy wanted me to bring back, including the issue of *Cosmopolitan* and the clothes Mother had bought.

I left the meeting in New Orleans one day early and took a flight to Paris. While in the United States, I had telephoned several times. To my relief, Peggy and the children were well. She urged me to come home as soon as I could because they all missed me. After what seemed to me an especially long night of flying, I arrived at Orly Airport and quickly cleared customs. I could not manage so many bags on the Metro, so I hired a taxi to take me to Gare Montparnasse, then caught the next train to Versailles. I thought I would surprise everyone by returning a day early.

As the train neared Versailles, I realized the struggle I would have getting the luggage to our apartment. I decided to check most of the bags at the station, carry one, and walk to our home. There I would ask the eldest boys to come back to the train station with me and help carry the remaining luggage to our apartment. At last, the train pulled into the station platform in Versailles; I managed to unload the bags and move them into the station. When I entered, I heard someone call, "Hi, Pop! Need a hand?" I turned, and to my delight I saw our three eldest sons, Laurie, Rick, and Rob, waiting for me. Later Peggy told me that that morning, they insisted on meeting every train coming to Versailles from Montparnasse. They had a feeling about my returning early, and they wanted to welcome me at the station. The boys hefted my baggage and we hurried home. There, peanut butter and jelly sandwiches were quickly prepared and enjoyed by all.

I was thankful to once again be with Peggy and the children, and thankful that they were well and safe. Our time in Versailles passed quickly, and soon Peggy and I started thinking about our return to the United States. Our visas were valid for about three and a half months longer, but they expired three days before our scheduled departure. I anticipated renewing our visas might take some time. So to be on the safe side, I asked Peggy to go to City Hall (Hôtel de Ville) in Versailles and request extensions. Laurie went with her to act as translator.

When I returned from Paris that evening I asked Peggy how her trip to City Hall had gone. She said I wouldn't believe the bureaucracy she and Laurie had encountered. They had located the clerk responsible for visa renewals. But he sat in his office behind a desk, reading, and ignored the people waiting to see him. Peggy said it was frustrating just sitting there. After two hours, the clerk rose and announced that the office was closing for the day, and suggested that those waiting come back tomorrow.

Though I regretted putting Peggy and Laurie through this ordeal, I said they would have to go back the next day and start over. Peggy said she had a better idea. During the two-hour wait, she talked to a young Canadian who had worked in France for two years and was at the hall on other business. He told her he had given up waiting for a bureaucrat to issue a new visa a year before. When his visa neared expiration, he went to Germany, had his passport stamped, and then reentered France and had his passport stamped again. This proved he had been out of the country, and the visa was automatically extended for six more months.

Peggy proposed we rent a Volkswagen bus and do the same. I thought it was a good idea. That way, in addition to getting our visas renewed, we would see some other countries in western Europe. I suggested we visit Idar-Oberstein in Germany. This town had been the center for gemstone cutting and carving for over five hundred years. As an amateur lapidary, I had read several articles about Idar-Oberstein, and I knew a trip to its museums and shops would be interesting and educational for the children. We spent a day planning and packing and rented a Volkswagen bus. Nickels would stay in a nearby kennel until we returned.

It was a beautiful and pleasant drive, the small towns we drove through picturesque and interesting. We had packed water, soft drinks, and orange juice. But around noon Peggy said the children were getting hungry and suggested stopping in the next town to buy bread and ham and cheese. In a town not far from the French border, we found a small market. Speaking in French, I asked the clerk for a "midi-kilo" (1.1 pounds) of ham and one of cheese and two baguettes. She gasped. She assumed that, as an American, I did not understand how much I had ordered. She asked me to repeat the order. I did, and told her I had ten children to feed. She smiled and explained the typical order of ham and cheese for a French family was only four or five slices. At the edge of town, we found a small park with a table and had a picnic, then resumed our trip. Approaching the French border, I saw the guards stopping cars and checking papers. I asked Peggy to get the passports ready for the border guards to check and stamp.

But to my surprise, when I extended our passports for examination and stamping, the guard ignored them. He looked into the bus, saw ten children and two adults, smiled, and waved us on. As I drove ahead toward the German border crossing, I said to Peggy that surely the Germans would stamp our passport. Yet, when I pulled up to where the border guard stood and extended our passports, he paid no attention to them, either. He spoke a few words of greetings and looked into the car packed with children. Then, with a smile, he saluted, wished us a pleasant visit to Germany, and waved us on. Our plan for renewing visas by getting our passports stamped was not working. But I reassured myself that we still had a lot of borders to cross before we returned to Versailles.

After we had driven a little way into Germany, Peggy told me the children were getting tired and that we needed to find a place to spend the night. Coming into a small town, I spotted a hotel. Walking up to the registration desk, I asked in French for three rooms to accommodate my wife and our ten children. The woman behind the desk smiled, informing me they had only three rooms in the hotel and two of them were taken for the night. She regretted not being able to accommodate our family. I asked for suggestions. The desk clerk said she would telephone the hotel in the next town, not far away, Idar-Oberstein, and inquire for us. She telephoned, and in a moment told me they had rooms and would hold them for our arrival. In French, she gave me directions to the town and to the Parkhotel. I had difficulty understanding her French. But a German man standing by the desk overheard our conversation, and, speaking to me in English, said he lived nearby and would be pleased to lead me to the hotel. When we entered Idar-Oberstein, our new friend accompanied me into the lobby of the Parkhotel, where he told the desk clerk about my reservation. She said they had three lovely rooms ready for us and hoped we found them comfortable.

When we returned to the VW bus where Peggy and the children were waiting, I thanked the German man for his assistance. Before he turned to leave, he said he hoped I would not be offended by his question, but he wondered my age. I told him I was forty-five. He looked at me, nodded, shook my hand, and walked away. I mentioned the strange question to Peggy. She agreed it was an odd question to ask a stranger. We speculated that he wanted to know my age because it would indicate whether I had served in the American armed forces during World War II. He was old enough to have served in the German military during the war, and perhaps the question and handshake was his way of acknowledging that the war was behind us and that former enemies would live in peace. We did not see him again, but I have not forgotten his question. From time to time, I still puzzle about it.

We unloaded the bus and assigned the children to their rooms. After a fine meal in the hotel dining room, we put them to bed. Tom and Daniel, the two youngest children, were crowded into our room. With extra rollaway beds, we managed to get the five girls into one room and Laurie, Rick, and Rob into the other. The next morning, after breakfast, we left the small hotel and set out to explore Idar-Oberstein. We spent several hours walking about the ancient village. I especially enjoyed looking at the fine gemstones cut there. We couldn't afford to buy any of the cut stones, but I did purchase some small mineral specimens of citrine, amethyst, and crystalline sulfur that now are in my mineral collection in Concord.

Later in the afternoon we packed the bus, loaded the children, and started our return trip to France. Peggy said she looked forward to being at our home in Versailles because the hotel in Germany had been expensive. As we neared the border, I said surely the border guards would stamp our passports. We arrived at the border and saw guards checking the papers of those leaving, and soon a customs official approached our bus and said he hoped we had had a fine and enjoyable visit to his country. He said they were glad to have American families visit them, adding that we had a large family of handsome children. I offered our passports to him, but he waved his hand, declining them. He told us he hoped we would come back soon and to have a safe journey. He ordered the gate opened and we drove into Belgium. At the Belgium border station they did not check our passports, nor even look into the car. They just waved us through. At the French border, the same thing happened. It did not occur to me to insist that the border guards stamp our passports. By that evening we were back in Versailles. Although it had been a pleasant and interesting trip, we were disappointed we had been unable to get our visas renewed.

Our visa problem concerned us. Peggy reminded me that we were scheduled to depart for Boston on July 4 and that our visas expired on June 30. I suggested it might be possible to obtain some sort of exit visa at the airport if they demanded a valid visa for departure, or we could plead our case with the visa officials and hope for the best. I assured her all would work out well and we would leave France as scheduled. I'm not sure I convinced Peggy. For some reason, I did not think to ask the people in the American embassy in Paris, or those in the laboratory where I worked, for assistance with our visa problem.

During the remainder of our stay, Peggy continued tutoring the children, and during the week I went to the laboratory to do research on the prostate gland. On weekends, we enjoyed a number of picnics on the grounds of the Palace of Versailles. We also went into Paris a number of more times, returning to the Louvre and other museums and extending our explorations of the city. I made arrangements to ship Nickels to Boston. I telephoned the Palmer Kennels in Acton and talked with Mr. Palmer, who agreed to pick up Nickels and board him until we returned on July 17. Laurie and I took Nickels to the TWA shipping area of the airport, where I purchased a dog crate and signed the necessary papers. The attendant assured us that our dog would be safe and would have a good, quality trip. The next day Palmer telephoned to say that our dog was all right and he would look after him.

These were quiet days for us, and we took pleasure in being together as a family. Toward the end of June, Peggy and I started preparing for our return to the United States. By July 1 we had done most of the packing. That afternoon, Peggy and I and all of our children took a last walk through the grounds and gardens of the Palace of Versailles. Normally, only a few of the fountains were left on all year, but for some reason, on that day every fountain was turned on and water gushed forth. It was an impressive sight. As we walked through the palace grounds one last time, we recalled the many picnics and outings we had enjoyed there as a family.

Years later, when I was secretary of education, Peggy and I returned to Versailles. We saw that our apartment, 26 Avenue de Paris, was still there, and we again toured the Palace of Versailles. Although little had changed, it just did not feel the same without the children accompanying us.

We were scheduled to leave Paris for Boston late in the morning on July 4, 1972, on a TWA flight. Our home, however, was rented until July 15. For that reason, we decided to drive to Texas and visit with Mother, returning to Concord by July 16. Three or four days before leaving, we started packing. Peggy and I were amazed at the amount of material goods we had accumulated during our six-month stay in France. We gave away cots and mattresses and blankets to the house cleaner who came to help Peggy once a week.

Although we were apprehensive about not having valid visas, we tried to keep much of our everyday routine going as we prepared to leave France. Peggy did the daily shopping for food, and the children were sent to the bakery for baguettes and croissants. On July 2, our last full day in Versailles, Peggy asked several of the children to pick up bread. Returning from the bakery, Rob told his mother the shopkeeper had taken their photograph. They told her as she packed their bread order that this would be the last time they would be in her bakery because they were leaving for the United States. Rob told her they had enjoyed the fine, tasty bread she baked. He said she looked a bit sad that we were leaving; no doubt, we were her best customers. The shopkeeper lined them up and snapped their picture and gave each of them a croissant with chocolate. In retrospect, our cost of living in France was comparable to that in Concord. Some items, such as Cokes, bread, and wine, were less expensive. Peggy was careful to stay in budget, and when we left France, we had no debts. The daily shopping for the household did not significantly increase our expenses. Later, the same day, Peggy went to the meat market to shop for the evening meal. Paying for her purchase, she told the butcher we were returning to our home in the United States. During the months we were in Versailles, the two of them had managed to communicate in a mixture of French and English. The butcher told Peggy he appreciated her business and regretted she and her nice family were leaving Versailles. Clearly, when we left Versailles, the food industry experienced an economic downturn.

We had reservations at a Hilton near Orly Airport the next night.

Before we left, though, I met with one of the Realtors for an inventory of the apartment and to turn in the keys. Any breakage or damage to the items inventoried would be charged against our deposit. I walked through the apartment with the Realtor, and to my relief he found all in order. But when we entered the backyard, the Realtor complained there were some bare spots where there had been grass. I told him I regretted the grass appeared somewhat trampled, but what could he expect with ten children playing in the yard? I added that I did not see "grass" on the inventory. The Realtor said the inventory reflected the conditions, and there were bare spots where there should be grass. According to him, some of the grass would have to be replanted and the expense would be charged against our deposit. He said he would send the money remaining in our deposit to us in the United States. I requested he send me the difference as soon as possible. Not surprisingly, we did not hear from the rental company again and never received the remaining part of our deposit. That was my lesson on the price of grass in France. On the afternoon of July 3 we left Versailles in three taxies, checking into our hotel near Orly Airport.

The next morning after breakfast we boarded the hotel shuttle to the airport terminal. When we arrived we checked our bags with TWA and were issued boarding passes for our flight to Boston. The airport monitor showed that our flight was delayed about two hours, so we sat near the customs area. We saw many heavily armed police and soldiers patrolling the airport. During the early 1970s, there was a rise in terrorist attacks across Europe and other parts of the world, including airline hijackings. Peggy and I were apprehensive about the possibility of terrorist activity, but did not let our children know of our concern. We simply kept them close to us.

Sitting near the boarding gate, Peggy worried about our expired visas, concerned we would be delayed before we could leave France. I reassured her everything would be fine. I suggested that because she and all of the children were on the same passport, they stay together when we went through customs. I would lead the way with both of our passports in hand, while she would bring up the rear, with the children between us.

Finally, we heard the announcement for our flight and moved to the customs gate. I handed the customs official our tickets and our two passports. With a quizzical look, he asked if all of those children were ours. I assured him they were and said we had had a great visit in France. I told him we wished we could stay longer, but needed to return to the United States because the children's schools were starting in a few weeks. Barely looking at the passports, he stamped them, gave a wave of his arm, and told us to go ahead and have a pleasant journey. I thanked him and urged Peggy and the children to move quickly to the boarding area. As she went by, the customs official smiled and waved at Peggy. She smiled and waved back. The customs official probably had never seen ten children on one passport. He simply counted them as they went by and did not notice the expired date on our visas. A few minutes later as we sat in the boarding area, Peggy told me quietly that it was a miracle they did not jail the lot of us for trying to leave the country with expired visas.

We heard the announcement that our flight was ready for boarding, so we moved the children toward the security area. There each of us passed through the metal detectors for screening. Laurie carried a shopping bag filled with teddy bears and other stuffed animals. Still vivid in my mind is seeing a soldier take a teddy bear from the bag and poke its belly with his pistol. He must have realized we were not a band of terrorists, because he handed Laurie the bag and waved us on board the airplane. Thankfully, Laurie did not say anything to the soldier. But I knew by the look on his face that he did not appreciate a soldier poking a pistol into his brother's bear.

We put all of the children in their assigned seats, expecting at any moment the cabin door would close and the airplane would be pushed back from the gate for departure. After a short while, we realized there was a problem. I suggested that perhaps they were waiting for tardy passengers or that our airplane had a mechanical problem. Then the flight attendant announced that all boarding passes had to be checked.

A ticket agent, followed by two armed soldiers, started down the aisle of the cabin. The agent reviewed boarding passes. When they reached us, I handed him our stack of twelve boarding passes. It took a while for him to sort through so many. After examining them, without a word, he handed the boarding passes back to me. I was relieved when I saw the ticket agent and the soldiers leave the aircraft. A few minutes later, the cabin door closed. The aircraft taxied to our runway, and soon the engines accelerated and we were on a nonstop flight to Boston. After our airplane lifted off, Peggy squeezed my hand. She said she had enjoyed her stay in France and it had been educational, but it was a relief to be on the way to Boston with all our family well and safe.

An hour into our flight, the flight attendant announced through the public address system that there would be an in-flight movie. Headsets were available for $2.50. Immediately, Laurie asked if they could buy headsets to watch the movie. Lisa and Sarita joined in the pleading. Peggy and I talked it over and decided in-flight movies were not in our budget. We would have a lot of expenses in the days ahead. When we arrived in Boston we would spend two nights in a hotel, then buy a new car and drive to Texas and back, spending several nights in motels on the road. We said "no" to the movie request, suggesting the children read a book and not run up and down the aisle of the cabin.

Some of them groaned but hid their feelings about their cheap parents. Soon, the cabin lights dimmed and the movie flickered on the screen. When I saw its title, I knew we were in luck. It was a Charlie Chaplin silent movie with subtitles. We saw this classic film at no cost. I presume the flight attendants sold headsets because the film had some musical background, and because the news, music, and current events presentations afterward required headsets. For the remaining hours of the flight, the children dozed or read. Just like during one of our car trips, they asked numerous times if we were almost there and when were we arriving in Boston.

About 4:00 p.m. the seat-belt sign came on and our aircraft started its decent into Boston. I noted to Rick, who was sitting by the window in our row, that it appeared the pilots planned to use the east-west runway, approaching the airport over the bay. Our flight swept over East Boston. Looking out the window, we saw the beautiful Boston harbor. It was good to be home. After we touched down and the aircraft started its taxi to the terminal, I remarked to Rick how the sight of East Boston, with its water, beaches, gulls, and boats, all sparkling in the afternoon sun, made for a splendid homecoming. He agreed.

When we arrived at the terminal, Laurie, Rick, and Rob helped me stack the bags on two carts and push them to the customs area. I handed the customs officer our passports. He looked at our large stack of luggage and our ten children. As he stamped our passports, he noted that we had been gone for quite a while. And he wanted to know if all of these children were ours. I responded, "Yes, I've been on sabbatical leave from Tufts University to France and took the whole family." Although we had an educational six months in France, it was wonderful to be back in the United States. I did not tell the customs officer it felt strange to not have to think to myself in English how to say something in French. I thought it might take at least an hour for us to move through customs. To our surprise not one bag was opened. When I pointed this out to Peggy, she suggested the customs inspector just wanted to get us all out of their area to reduce the confusion and diminish the noise made by our ten children.

From the terminal, a courtesy van picked us up and took us to the hotel. After checking in, I telephoned the auto dealer in Acton, asking if the station wagon I had ordered had arrived. He said it had, exactly as I wanted, and it was ready for delivery. Before leaving for our trip to France, we had traded in our old Mercury station wagon. I told the salesman we would be back by the end of June, asking him to give me credit for my car toward the largest station wagon manufactured.

The next day, Laurie and I went to Acton and picked up our new station wagon. It was a white Mercury with a luggage rack, two rows of seats at the front and midsection, and three seats facing each other at the back of the automobile. It was spacious enough to hold us all, and we drove it for ten years. Early the next morning, July 6, 1972, we loaded the car and started the four-day drive to Texas to visit my mother and family in South Texas. We enjoyed the trip, but all of us were eager to return to our home on Annursnac Hill Road. We left Texas on July 12 and arrived in Concord on July 16. We picked up Nickels the next day.

I looked forward to returning to Tufts medical school to teach and do research. I had learned a number of new scientific techniques in Professor Beaulieu's laboratory from Dr. Robel, and I planned to apply them to my research program on the prostate gland.

Just before we left Versailles, I told the children to take pleasure in the trip and to enjoy being with each other. I explained this would probably be the last time we would be together as a family for such an extended period. Soon, Laurie, Sarita, and Rick would be off to college, and before long the other children would follow. They would transition to their own lives. Some would marry and begin their own families, while jobs would scatter some of them to different parts of the country. Sure enough, our children soon became adults, and their education, jobs, and their own family led them away from home. Peggy and I are grateful they have remained close and in frequent communication and that they visit one another and with Peggy and me. On our fortieth, fiftieth, and six-tieth wedding anniversaries, and on Peggy's and my eightieth birthdays, we gathered with them to celebrate our milestones and our family. Our children had heard what I said those last few days in Versailles.

*Chapter Eleven :: **Administering a Medical School***

Before leaving on sabbatical, I accepted the job of associate dean on the condition that I retain my professorship in the Anatomy Department. Upon returning from sabbatical leave, in July 1972, I closed my office in anatomy and moved into the medical dean's administrative suite. As associate dean, I assisted the faculty in the development and implementation of the teaching and research programs. The dean, William Maloney, focused on the medical school's external relations, hospital affiliations, securing funding from the federal government, and alumni matters. He also met on medical school matters with the central administration of Tufts University and the board of trustees.

To my surprise, Maloney announced in January 1973 that he was going on sabbatical leave to Germany. He had not mentioned to me a pending six-month sabbatical. A couple of days before he left, the president of Tufts, Burton C. Hallowell, asked me to be the acting dean while Maloney was away. I told him his request was unexpected, and I had to think about it. Peggy and I discussed Hallowell's proposal, and I decided to take the job.

Then, upon returning from sabbatical leave in 1973, Maloney resigned as dean. A few days later, President Hallowell came to see me and said he wanted me to continue as acting dean until a new dean was recruited. He promised to appoint a search committee promptly to start a national search for Maloney's replacement. I agreed to stay on the job, but told President Hallowell I hoped the committee would move quickly. I explained I wanted to return to the Anatomy Department to teach and to carry on my research program. He assured me that appointing a new dean for the medical school was a high priority for him.

When I took the job of acting dean in 1973, I had twenty years of teaching experience, had chaired a basic science department, and done research at two medical schools. The dean's position gave me considerable experience in medical education and administration. The faculty and staff soon learned I did not hesitate to make decisions. I reviewed the problem, thought about it, analyzed the issues, and decided on the appropriate solution and action. I challenged the faculty to seek ways to improve the teaching programs and to expand our research activities. I kept the faculty, students, and staff informed about my expectations and aspirations for the medical school. I managed to keep the medical school expenses in budget. Unfortunately, I was too busy administering the medical school to spend significant time in the research laboratory, but I collaborated with other researchers and published two papers in scientific journals. I also wrote and published three review chapters on the male reproductive system and collaborated on a report on medical school—hospital relations.

The basic science departments—anatomy, physiology, biochemistry, microbiology, pharmacology, and pathology—were academically strong. They had considerable research funding, active graduate and postgraduate programs, and participated in the medical school teaching programs. These departments did not require as much attention from the dean's office as did some of the clinical departments.

Tufts put minimal funding into the clinical departments. We had a superb clinical faculty who did not expect significant compensation from the medical school. They felt a professional commitment to educate medical students. For most, it was pro bono work. The Tufts clinical faculty considered a faculty appointment an honor and sufficient compensation for participating in the teaching program.

Soon, I learned the former medical school administration had not spent much time meeting with the administration of our teaching hospitals and visiting with the faculty there. For that reason, I made it a point to frequently go to the hospitals. There I got together with administrators and faculty and listened to their desires and suggestions. Subsequently, I worked to address their needs and follow up on their suggestions.

As a mechanism to improve communication between the medical school and its teaching hospitals, I established a council of Tufts associated hospitals. We met to discuss the clinical teaching programs and ways to improve them. Many evenings I met with medical school alumni groups. Past deans had not worked closely with the alumni, and there was some resentment among them, a sense that the administration only wanted their financial support and would not listen to their ideas for and concerns about the medical school. I made it a major part of my administration to work with the alumni groups, keeping them informed about and connected to their medical school. Soon, alumni contributions to the medical school increased markedly.

Contrary to my expectations and despite President Hallowell's assurances, the search for a new dean went on for two years. Although I was one of the candidates for the dean's job, I did not let this long search distract me from my work leading the medical school. Finally, in 1975, after they considered a number of candidates, I emerged as the choice of the search committee, the faculty, and university administration to lead the medical school. I was appointed dean in July 1975.

After my appointment, I continued to work with the Tufts Medical Alumni Association to make the organization an important part of the medical school. In 1976, the association elected me an honorary member.

Chapter Twelve :: **Alice Williams and Our Nantucket Journeys**

One afternoon, soon after my appointment as dean of Tufts medical school, Edith Thistle, my assistant, came into my office. She told me Alice Williams was on the telephone and wanted to talk to me. Before answering the call, I asked, "Who is Alice Williams?" Edith explained that Williams was a major benefactor of Tufts who had left her Nantucket property to the medical school. She lived on Nantucket Island and was a friend of former dean William Maloney.

I picked up the telephone and heard a voice say hello and how pleased she was I had taken her call. I asked if I could be of assistance. She said she first wanted to congratulate me on my selection as dean. Then she began telling me about herself. She said she was the daughter of Dr. Harold Williams, the third dean of Tufts medical school from 1898 until 1913. She told me she had read about my appointment and thought my academic credentials impressive. She said she understood I was an "anatomist" by profession. Alice recounted that her father graduated from Harvard Medical School and often told her anatomy was one of his favorite subjects. She added that Dr. Oliver Wendell Holmes, the Boston Brahmin, great anatomist, poet, and writer, had taught her father anatomy.

Alice Williams explained that her father administered the medical school during the academic year, but in late June it closed for the summer. Once school was out, Dr. Williams moved his family from their Beacon Hill home in Boston to Nantucket Island. They did not return until almost the end of summer, just before the medical school opened for September classes. On Nantucket, Alice said her father practiced medicine. Most of the year, there was not a physician on the island, so the residents welcomed his presence during the summer months. Alice told me she was born on the island during one of those summers away from Boston. She went on, saying that over the years she had acquired quite a bit of property on Nantucket; someday, most of it was going to Tufts medical school.

I assured our benefactor that we at Tufts appreciated her generosity to the medical school and that her bequest would help many students obtain a fine medical education. Alice said she was pleased to hear her funds were advancing the education of students. Then, she told me the second reason for her call. She wanted to invite my family to Nantucket to stay at her Pleasant Street house, a lovely old whaling mansion. She said she knew we would enjoy it. I thanked her for the invitation and told her we had not yet made plans for a summer vacation. I said we usually stayed home during the summer if we didn't travel to Texas or out of the country. I added, most importantly, I needed to talk with my wife, Peggy, about her kind offer for a Nantucket visit. I cautioned her that we had ten children, five boys and five girls, ages eight to eighteen, and we needed quite a bit of living space. Alice said she was glad I didn't make all of the decisions regarding our family by myself. She assured me not to worry about the size of our family, as her house on Nantucket had enough bedrooms to easily accommodate fourteen persons. Before I could get another word in, Alice said that if we decided to come to Nantucket for a holiday, we should call her secretary, Hildegard Cassidy. Miss Williams said to give Hildegard the dates we would arrive and depart and she would make arrangements to receive us. Alice added she looked forward to meeting me and getting to know my family. With a pleasant, "Good day, sir," she ended the call.

That evening I told Peggy of Alice Williams's telephone call, her generosity to the medical school, and her offer to let us use her house on Nantucket. Although we had lived in New England for a number of years, we had not been on Nantucket Island. I suggested we take her up on the offer and go there for our summer vacation. Peggy agreed a Nantucket vacation would be a great way to end the summer. She said she would like to see the house described as a "whaling mansion" and to explore the island, and the children would enjoy the beaches.

I called Hildegard Cassidy the next day and gave her some dates for a three-day stay. With a pronounced German accent, Hildegard replied Miss Williams expected us to stay at least a week. I told Ms. Cassidy I would have to get back to her. After checking our schedules at Tufts and Emerson Hospital, Peggy and I arranged to spend five days on Nantucket. I telephoned Hildegard with the dates we could travel. She said the dates were fine, and added that Miss Williams would be pleased.

The children naturally were excited at the prospect of a summer vacation on Nantucket Island. Three weeks later, we loaded our station wagon, drove to Hyannis, Massachusetts, left our car in a nearby parking lot, and boarded the ferry for the two-hour ride to Nantucket. As soon as we walked off the ferry onto the island, I knew we were going to enjoy our stay. I felt as if I had stepped back in time to the era when Nantucket was the whaling capital of the world. Carrying our bags, we continued our walk down the main street of the island on our way to Pleasant Street. Cobblestones brought to Nantucket as ships' ballast were used to pave Main Street. As we walked, we passed many stately and magnificent homes. Three were almost identical. Later we learned they were known as the "Three Bricks." In the mid-nineteenth century, Joseph Starbuck built these graceful houses for his three sons, who were in the whaling business with him. Starbuck made millions from whaling, and it is estimated that the cost to build the homes totaled $154,000, an enormous sum of money in the 1850s. In today's dollars, this would be about $3,900,000. Though he built the homes for each of his sons as they married, Starbuck kept the title to all three of the houses to ensure the sons stayed in whaling with him.

We turned off of Main Street onto Pleasant Street and located Alice Williams's house—an impressive building. Later we learned a whaling captain, John Macy, had built the house. Most of his sons stayed in whaling, but one, Rowland Hussey Macy, gave up whaling, left the island, and in 1858 opened a store in New York City. He named it R. H. Macy & Co., better known as Macy's. A large elm tree stood in front of the three-story white wooden whaling mansion. Tall columns framed its entrance. As we approached the house, I saw a "widow's walk" at the top.

As we entered the foyer, Hildegard Cassidy was waiting in the hallway to greet us. She was tall, rather thin, with an angular, handsome but stern face, and her red hair was pulled back and pinned in a bun. Hildegard gave me the impression she ran the house and that we had best behave while we were in it. The interior of the house was elegant. When we en-

Alice Williams's home, Nantucket, 1986.

tered the hallway, I noted a sitting room to our right and across the hall a library. A beautiful curving staircase led to the bedrooms on the second floor. Later, I told Peggy I liked the house so much I would have gladly moved in and lived on the island. Peggy agreed the house was magnificent, but believed I would have a difficult time running a medical school in Boston from an island.

Hildegard directed us upstairs to our bedrooms. While showing us the bedrooms, she said Miss Williams expected Peggy and me to call on her at her home on Cliff Road the next morning at 10:00. Hildegard added it was not far, about a twenty-minute walk. She emphasized that when we arrived at the Cliff Road house, we were to knock loudly. According to Hildegard, Miss Williams was hard of hearing but refused to wear a hearing aid, and she would probably be in her upstairs office writing. If we got no response, she suggested we open the front door and shout until she came to the door. Hildegard cautioned us to watch out for Alice's little terrier dog, because he bit strangers. She said the children would be fine in the house, adding she would keep an eye on them.

Peggy said she was a little anxious about the visit to Alice Williams's home the next morning because it felt like a "command appearance." I assured her it would be a pleasant visit, as Alice had sounded so interesting on the phone. I reminded Peggy of Miss Williams's Tufts connection and her generosity in leaving her substantial estate to the medical school.

The next morning Peggy and I walked to Alice Williams's other home. It was neither as elegant nor as large as the Pleasant Street house, but it was sizable. The Cliff Road house was set back from the street. It had a large lawn and two big trees in the front. A white picket fence surrounded the front yard. We walked to the porch and I pushed the doorbell. I heard it ring, but no one opened the door. I knocked loudly. Still, no answer, but I heard a dog barking. I pushed the screen door, and found it was unlocked. Opening it, I stepped into the house. I shouted, "Hello," and announced ourselves. Still, no one responded, but we did hear someone coming down the stairs. Then, I heard a voice telling us she had heard our call, she was on her way, and assured us she wasn't deaf. She just needed time to negotiate the stairs. Alice Williams stepped into the entrance hall where we stood.

When Alice Williams walked down the stairs to greet us, it began one of the most valued and significant relationships Peggy and I have ever had with another person. Alice was about five feet six inches tall, rather heavy-set, and must have been in her early eighties. Her hair was completely white and her complexion ruddy. Thick glasses magnified her sparkling blue eyes. Alice had a smile on her face and a grace about her. Her walk, manner, and soft and precise voice in speaking suggested to me her Boston Beacon Street origins. In many ways, she and Peggy were alike. While one was raised on Beacon Street and the other on a small farm in central Texas, their values, openness, determination, outlook on life, and frankness were similar.

Alice told us she was pleased we had accepted her offer to visit and hoped we were comfortable in the Pleasant Street house. She said Hildegard had telephoned her earlier in the morning to tell her we had arrived and said our children were handsome, well behaved, and polite. She looked forward to meeting them. We thanked her for inviting us and letting us use her Pleasant Street house for a vacation home. I added that we expected to learn about Nantucket and its whaling traditions during our stay on the island. Alice told us to enjoy the house and to remember that someday it and the home on Cliff Road would go to Tufts. She informed me she liked raising money for the medical school because her father had been strongly committed to it. She told us she also owned land on Nantucket Island, on the ocean side. She guided us into the sitting room, saying we would be more comfortable there, and asked us to call her Alice, mentioning that we would learn she did not care for a lot of formality. Acknowledging her request I told her our first names were "Larry and Peggy." We followed her to the front room where she told Peggy and me where to sit so that she could hear us better. I asked Alice to tell us about herself.

Alice said the house where she was born was still there, adding with a smile that it was now a restaurant named The Mad Hatter. When she was a child, she said, there was a picket fence around the house. People visiting the Williams family home used the turnstile to enter their yard. Now, the fence was gone, but the turnstile remained. Alice resumed telling us of her early life. She said her family would leave Boston by train for Hyannis. There they took the ferry to Nantucket. Alice said she enjoyed her summers on the island, and many years ago decided to live on Nantucket permanently. She added that it had been years since she was "off-island." She said she had no reason to leave, so she stayed home and wrote. Alice had published several books and now was working on another one about the Australian outback. She said her books were not great, and unfortunately none of them a best seller. Her memoir *Thru the Turnstile: Tales of My Two Centuries*, about Nantucket and Boston's Beacon Hill, had recently been published. In it she wrote of many interesting people who had visited their home. Alice reached on the shelf beside her, picked up a book, and handed it to me. She said she had autographed a copy for me. When I opened it, I saw that she had written, "For Dean Lauro Cavazos from the daughter of a former Dean of Tufts School of Medicine! Alice Cary Williams." I thanked her for the book and said I looked forward to reading it. Alice insisted we have tea with her; she wanted Peggy to tell her about herself and our family. She left the room and returned with a tea service and cookies. We spent a pleasant hour with Alice, sipping tea and getting to know each other. She was interesting to talk to, and her sense of humor and down-to-earth attitude appealed to Peggy and me. We knew we had found a new friend. It wasn't long before Alice grew fond of Peggy, considering her an exceptional and interesting person. As the years went by, their friendship grew and strengthened.

For the rest of the hour we talked about Tufts and our families. Alice told us about her childhood on Beacon Hill and Nantucket. She had a great sense of humor and laughed as she told us about volunteering as an ambulance driver during World War I. As part of her training, she was required to change a tire in the dark. Alice failed the test because of her poor eyesight and therefore could not serve as an ambulance driver in France. Subsequently, she was assigned to drive Boston's mayor, James Curley, about town. Alice said she did not like him and tried to hit every pothole in the street to jar him around the backseat of the car. She said he fussed at her for being such a poor driver and hitting so many potholes. She told him that if he fixed the streets, there wouldn't be so many pot-holes for her to hit.

Late that morning, Peggy and I left Alice Williams's home and re-turned to Pleasant Street. We agreed we had met a remarkable person and one we would like as a friend. The rest of the week we took long walks on the island and in the center of town. I rented a car and drove Peggy and the children about Nantucket, enjoying the beautiful countryside. We took the children to a nearby beach for a swim. When the older children complained it did not have much wave action, I promised I'd locate one with surf.

We invited Alice to dinner at the Pleasant Street house. After a fine meal, Alice asked the children if they wanted her to tell them ghost stories about the Pleasant Street house and Nantucket. She added her stories were true, not fables. Several of the children wanted to hear her ghost stories. Lisa, then sixteen years old, said she knew she wouldn't be scared, but Alice had to promise her she wouldn't have nightmares. Alice assured Lisa she would sleep like a lamb. She said not all ghost stories were scary; some were happy. Alice told them one story about a ghost trapped in the cellar of the house and how a little boy, about Tom's or Dan's age, managed to free him. The children were spellbound as Alice wove her stories.

That night, Lisa did not have nightmares, but Sarita, our eldest daughter, believed a ghost walked into the room while she slept. The next morning, she told me about the ghost. I said she was too old to believe in ghosts and asked if she had seen it. She had not seen the ghost, she said, but she knew one had been in her room. She had awakened for some unknown reason. She had not seen anything because she lay facing the wall. Still, she said, she felt a "presence," and was too scared to turn over and look. To this day, she asserts a ghost came into her bedroom.

After five days on the island, we returned to Concord. Peggy and I were enamored with Nantucket and pledged to return when we could. In subsequent years, we made many trips to Nantucket, and our friendship with Alice grew each time we were on the island. Every summer while I was the dean, Alice offered us the use of the Pleasant Street house for our vacation. In addition to the summer trips to the island, Peggy and I would go in the fall. These were especially pleasant because the tourist season was over, the large crowds of visitors gone. On our trips with the children, we usually booked our car on the ferry. If we did not take our car, Alice loaned us her old Chevrolet, which she never took off-island. The first time she loaned it to us, I saw it had only about six thousand miles on the odometer. It was good basic transportation.

On our visit to Nantucket with the children the following summer, Peggy and I stopped by the Cliff Road house to see Alice. She greeted us, inviting us to sit on chairs on the porch, and we had a brief visit. After a few minutes of conversation between the three of us, Alice turned to me and suggested I go for a walk, for about an hour. Alice explained that she and Peggy needed to talk, and that I would be in the way. With a nod of my head, I left the two women on the porch and walked about the town center.

When I returned, Alice informed me that she and Peggy had had a good talk and she hoped I had enjoyed my walk. I told her it had been pleasant and enjoyable watching so many tourists and the locals wandering up and down the streets of Nantucket Center. I told them I had found a comfortable bench on Main Street and tried to blend in as a local. Alice said she was glad I had had a good walk and assured me I would have been bored to death listening to two women talk about family. Alice told me Peggy had agreed to bring all of the children over for tea the next day. She said she planned to make it a real Beacon Hill tea, using her best silver and china. She wanted our eldest daughters, Sarita, Lisa, and Victoria, to pour and serve. Alice promised to prepare cucumber sandwiches and some cookies and cake, and knew the children would enjoy the tea. And so they did. Peggy and I thought the children would be bored taking tea with an elderly woman from Boston and Nantucket. Quite the opposite, they loved it. All of them became fond of Alice, and she, in turn, took a liking to them.

Alice arranged special activities for us on each of our visits to Nantucket. On one occasion, she borrowed a four-wheel-drive Jeep and had me take the family to Caskata Pond. It is located close to the north shore of the island, off the paved roads, and is reached by a sandy road. Alice wanted us to see the abundance of wild flowers growing near the pond. Another time, she organized a boat ride and clam digging outing for Peggy, our children, and me to Tuckernuck, an island west of Nantucket and east of Muskeget Island. Alice waited back on Nantucket. As the guide she had hired steered the boat to Tuckernuck, he told us about the island we were going to visit. He said many years ago Tuckernuck was part of Nantucket, but a hurricane had cut the channel we were running in, and it became a separate island. He explained that over the years hurricanes and major storms had shaped Nantucket Sound in odd ways, creating shoals, splitting off islands, and building sandbars. All of the islands in Nantucket Sound and Martha's Vineyard had been connected at one time. He said that if one knew the way, one could walk through the shallows from Nantucket to the island of Martha's Vineyard.

The guide said we were going to Tuckernuck because there were plenty of clams on the beach and in the shallows. Alice owned a small cabin on the island and in it were shovels and burlap sacks. The guide said Alice wanted him to show us where and how to dig the best clams. He told us after we had a couple of sacks full of clams, we would return to Nantucket. Alice planned to meet us later at the Pleasant Street house. He understood that Alice wanted to teach Peggy how to prepare real clam chowder, Nantucket style.

He pulled up to the small dock on Tuckernuck, jumped off the boat onto the dock, and tied up. We walked to Alice's cabin and found the shovels and burlap sacks. The guide directed the clam digging, and quickly we filled two burlap sacks with clams. He took us back to Nantucket and on the deck shucked the clams.

Soon after we returned to the Pleasant Street house with the shucked clams, Alice arrived. She asked me to go to the fish market on Main Street and pick up the cooked lobster she had ordered. One lobster would hardly feed a family our size, I thought to myself. Still, Laurie and I walked to the market and asked the clerk for Miss Williams's lobster. When he came back with it, Laurie and I gasped, and I asked how much the lobster weighed. The clerk said a bit over fourteen pounds. According to the clerk, Alice had wanted a bigger one, but he didn't have anything larger in the pound that day. He said the lobster would feed an army, would be sweet as honey, and wouldn't be tough. He told me to use a hammer to crack the claws and said I would need a pair of pliers, too. I looked at the enormous lobster and just nodded, knowing I had a demanding job before me just shelling it.

Laurie and I lugged the lobster back to the house. It caused quite a stir when the children saw it. They all had to look it over and touch the claws and the tail. Tom said he didn't know lobsters grew that big, Lisa doubted I could crack the claws, and Rob wished for two lobsters that size. I searched the garage and basement and found a hammer and pliers. The lobster claws gave in to my pounding, and when I had finished shelling it, we had a formidable mound of lobster meat for our dinner. Alice was right—it was enough to feed all of us. It was an outstanding dinner, with the clam chowder Peggy had cooked under Alice's direction turning out excellently. After dinner, Peggy, Sarita, and Lisa started cleaning the kitchen and washing dishes and pans. Alice told Peggy she was not any good at house chores, especially washing dishes, and asked to be excused. Before she left the kitchen, Alice told me to help Peggy clean up. She asked Sarita, Lisa, and the other children to gather in the parlor for another session of ghost stories.

In 1972, I was still the associate dean when Laurie turned sixteen. He was a good student in high school and held a part-time job working in the photography laboratory at the high school. He saved enough money to buy a used Fiat car, but shortly after Peggy and I decided he was spending far too much time driving about Concord with his friends. We knew we had to find other ways to keep him busy. Laurie was interested in airplanes, so Peggy and I suggested he go to nearby Hanscom Field and take flying lessons. We told him we would pay for them. We made it a condition, however, that as soon as he received his private pilot's license, he would earn his instrument rating. The weather in New England can be quite unforgiving for small (as well as large) airplanes. Within a few months, Laurie had his certification as a single-engine pilot, and several months later became instrument-rated.

The Christmas after he received his pilot's license, Laurie left a note for me under our Christmas tree. It stated that the bearer was entitled to an airplane ride with his son. A few days after Christmas, he and I went to Hanscom Field, where he rented a single-engine airplane. I watched as he checked it over, doing the "walk around" to assure himself all was in order and it was safe to fly. Once he was satisfied, he told me to board and fasten my seat belt. The cockpit was configured so that the pilot sat in the left seat and the passenger in the right. Laurie closed the hatch to the airplane and, using the microphone, asked the air traffic controller in the tower for permission to taxi to the runway. The controller told him to taxi to the runway and hold. Then the controller cleared us for takeoff, and soon we were airborne. As he flew the airplane, Laurie's professional demeanor impressed me. When we reached cruising altitude, he turned the airplane and we flew up the north shore of Massachusetts.

Laurie asked if I wanted to fly the airplane. He knew I had taken a few flying lessons when I was in high school. I told him it had been decades since I had flown a craft, but would be glad to take the controls. Laurie took his hands off of the wheel and told me I had the airplane. He asked me to continue flying up the north shore until I saw the Merrimack River emptying into the Atlantic Ocean. With somewhat sweaty palms, I flew the aircraft and managed to keep it level and on course. Soon the Merrimack River came into view, and Laurie told me to bank the aircraft and follow the river inland. It was a magnificent sight and then, to my relief, Laurie took back control of the plane. He said I had done a good job flying it, keeping it level and making turns. I explained I had no trouble flying the aircraft as long as I could see the turn and bank indicator and the altimeter indicating if I was flying it level, climbing, or losing altitude. Since then I have flown with Laurie many times in single- and twin-engine airplanes, but I will never forget the splendor of that Christmas present—my first flight with our eldest son.

In 1975, the year I became dean of the medical school, Laurie graduated from high school. He and Sarita were in the senior class. Laurie had lost part of the school year because of six months in France, so he finished high school at midyear and enrolled at Tufts University. When Sarita finished high school at the end of the school year, she, too, was accepted to Tufts. Sarita moved into a dormitory at Tufts, but Laurie lived at home and commuted to the university. He continued flying as much as we could afford. After a year and a half at Tufts, he transferred to Nathaniel Hawthorne College in Antrim, New Hampshire, because in addition to providing an academic experience, it had a flying program, and Laurie wanted to continue his education while logging flying time. At Nathaniel Hawthorne College he received his commercial pilot's license and became a certified flight instructor. He obtained a part-time job giving flight instruction to students in the flying program and earned enough money to pay for twin-engine flying time and became certified as an air transport pilot. The licenses signified he was a highly qualified pilot.

Laurie constantly worked on improving his flying skills. One evening he flew Peggy and me to Hanscom Field from Nathaniel Hawthorne College. Earlier in the day, we had driven Laurie's car from Concord, where he had left it for repairs, to the college at Antrim. We had earlier dropped off our own car at the airport as we knew Laurie would fly us back to Hanscom. Soon after we arrived he borrowed a single-engine airplane, and we were on our way to Hanscom Field. Peggy sat in the backseat of the airplane and I in the copilot's seat. It was a clear night, with shining stars and a bright moon; we marveled at the beauty of the many lights below us.

Shortly before our arrival at Hanscom Field, Laurie told us he wanted to practice using an instrument approach for the landing. He called the control tower and asked for authorization to do an instrument approach and landing. The flight controller granted him permission and said they would guide him in under the instrument flight rules. Laurie asked his mother to hand him a plastic hood from the backseat and put it on. It allowed him to see the instruments, but it blocked his view through the front windscreen of the airplane. Laurie asked me to keep a sharp eye for other air traffic. He said there should be none, but I was to constantly search for other aircraft nearby.

Laurie said that at an altitude of three hundred feet, he should just be passing over the outer perimeter marker of Hanscom Field on a final glide for a landing. At that point he would take off the hood and land the aircraft visually. Although a bit nervous about being part of an instrument landing exercise, I had confidence in Laurie's flying ability. I asked Peggy in the backseat to join me in looking for other aircraft flying nearby. She assured me she was already scanning the sky. I watched the altimeter, and when it indicated an altitude of three hundred feet, Laurie removed the hood. I looked out my window and saw we were passing over the outer perimeter marker lights of the field. The runway lights were ahead of us, and I felt the airplane touch down to a smooth landing. I breathed a sigh of relief, and complimented Laurie on his excellent approach and landing.

One afternoon, during his last year in college, Laurie telephoned us to say he was flying to Hanscom Field that afternoon. He said he would be flying a single-engine airplane he needed to return to New Hampshire the next morning. I told him we looked forward to seeing him, that we'd feed him a fine meal, and assured him we would take him back out to Hanscom Field early the next morning. Peggy and I hurried to Hanscom Field, arriving as he landed. Laurie taxied in, went into the operations office, did the required paperwork, and made arrangements for an overnight tie-down of his airplane. After dinner, we stayed up late listening to his stories about flying.

The next morning we were up before dawn. After breakfast, the three of us left for the airport. It was a cold, clear morning following a light rain during the night that had frozen on the surface of our car. We scraped ice from the windshield and ran the defroster, and soon we left for the airport. At the Hanscom terminal, Laurie asked Peggy and me to follow him to his airplane parked nearby on the apron. He told us he needed some help before he could fly that morning. I asked how we could be of assistance, and he said there was probably ice on the surfaces of the tail and wings of the airplane. He examined them, and it was obvious—even to me—that ice coated them.

Laurie told us it was not safe to fly an airplane when it had a coating of ice. He showed us how to pound on the wing and tail surfaces with our fist to loosen and knock off the ice. Between the three of us, we soon de-iced Laurie's airplane. He said good-bye, did his walk around the airplane to make sure all was in order, climbed on board, and gave a wave. Peggy and I walked back to the fence by the terminal, where we watched as he started the aircraft and taxied out to the runway. Peggy said she hoped we had removed sufficient ice so that the airplane would fly. I told her not to worry; Laurie took no risks flying. Still, I must admit I was a bit anxious watching his takeoff that morning. Happily, Laurie's airplane quickly gained altitude, turned north toward New Hampshire, and soon was out of sight.

In May 1979, Laurie received a BS in business administration and an AS in professional pilot and aviation administration from Nathaniel Hawthorne College. Now, Laurie is a professional pilot, a captain, and flies jet airplanes nationally and internationally. Each year I fly many miles on commercial aircraft. In the winter, especially in the Northeast and in the Midwest, I usually have two or three delays because our airplane has to be de-iced before takeoff. I am never impatient with the procedure or mind the delay. On those occasions, I'm reminded of pounding on Laurie's plane to get the ice off, and am thankful that larger commercial jets can use a chemical spray.

The vacations on Nantucket provided Laurie with the opportunity to log flying hours. Once, when he and Sarita were enrolled in college and could not join the family on the island, they flew over to deliver a forgotten coffeepot from our home in Concord for Peggy. We met them at the small airport on the island. Sarita said she was sure we were less worried about her safety flying with her brother than we were about the coffeepot making it safely to the island. As she handed Peggy the coffeepot she assured her mother it had not been traumatized by the flight.

On one occasion, Laurie took several of the elder children and me for a flight around the island. It was a beautiful day, and from the air the island sparkled. After two trips around the island, Laurie said it was time for him to fly back to the mainland because he had to return the airplane to New Hampshire that afternoon. Tom, at that time ten years old, was disappointed when Laurie told him there was not enough time to take him on an airplane ride. I should have insisted Tom take my place on the flight around Nantucket. But Tom had his day of flying. When he was in high school, Laurie taught him how to fly. Soon, Tom earned his pilot's license, and after he graduated from Texas Tech University he chose a career in aviation as well. Now he is a captain and flies jet airplanes for a major airline.

During the summers on Nantucket, we took the children to the beach almost every day. There are some magnificent beaches there. Initially, we took them to a beach near the ferry landing, but this was quite shallow and they wanted more wave action. I promised them we would check on the other beaches and find a safe one with waves. We explored the island looking for beaches and found several, but most, Peggy and I decided, were not safe for our children because they had large waves and the surf appeared treacherous. Then we discovered Surfside Beach. I asked Alice about it. She said it was a beautiful beach with fine sand. It had a gradual slope into the water, and the waves were not too large. She said, though, we needed to be watchful of the children, because not too far out, there could be a strong riptide.

Alice said her father told her that one warm night, while returning from a house call on one of his patients, he decided to go for a swim at Surfside. A strong and excellent swimmer, he went a ways out from the shore. Suddenly, he felt himself pulled by a riptide. He didn't panic, Alice recounted. He knew he could not swim to shore, so he swam with the current, and it carried him parallel to the beach. Soon, it pushed him close to the shore, and he managed to swim to the beach. If he had tried to swim against the riptide, Alice concluded, he wouldn't have survived.

In the summer of 1978, on a warm and sunny day, several of the children pleaded with us to take them to the beach. On that occasion, only seven were with us. The three eldest were on the mainland in college. Peggy and I decided it was a fine day for a swim, so we agreed to take them to Surfside. After our arrival, we unloaded the cooler containing soft drinks and water and arranged our towels and mats. We noticed a lifeguard on duty. Peggy told me to keep an eye on the children, reminding me that

Our fourth son, Tom, in
Austin, TX, 1982.

she couldn't swim and couldn't help me if one of them got into trouble.

I asked Peggy if she wanted to get into the water and wade. She said she
would rather stretch out on a mat and catch up on reading her nutrition
and health journals. She said she would face away from the water so she
would not be anxious watching the children playing in the surf.

I sat close to the water, keeping an eye on the children. I had been out
in the surf and felt a strong current as the waves receded from shore. I
told the children to be careful and not go out too far because of the pull
of the waves as they rolled back from shore. To their credit, they did as I
asked and played in the surf,

As I sat on the beach, I noticed a short, obese, middle-aged man approach the surf. He stepped into the water up to his knees. A large wave
struck him, and he fell backward, and then turned sideways as he struggled to regain his footing. The incoming waves continuously washed over
him, and I saw a panicked look on his face. I realized the man might

drown if he didn't get out of the surf. I shouted to Peggy that I was going to help a man regain his footing. Then I ran to where the children sat on the beach. In a stern voice, I told them not to move from there; I was going to help a man get out of the water. As I ran to the man, I saw that my teenage sons, Rob and Tom, were running beside me. Rob assured me I would need help because the man in trouble was so big.

I told Rob and Tom not to let him grab them because he might pull them under. I said we would grab his feet and pull him out of the surf by his legs, staying away from his arms and hands. The man was spinning like a barrel in the water, thrashing, gasping for air, and unable to regain his footing. Rob and Tom grabbed one foot and his ankle and I the other ankle, and together we managed to pull him out of the surf. Once we had him on the beach, several onlookers came rushing to help us. We stretched the exhausted man out on the sand. He was gasping for breath and couldn't speak. I feared he might go into shock, but soon I saw his color return. The lifeguard had wandered away from the beach and missed all of the action, but now came rushing up. He told those standing around the man to stay back and he would take charge.

The boys and I left the man surrounded by several people offering assistance. Fortunately, he did not need medical attention. The other children had watched our rescue efforts. Lisa ran to Peggy shouting that I had rescued a man from drowning and Rob and Tom had helped me. She said we were heroes. Startled, Peggy sat up and asked Lisa what she meant by a drowning man. She asked if the children were safe. I told her they were fine. Because her back had been turned to the surf, she did not know of our rescue efforts. She said she was glad that she hadn't been aware of the commotion or seen me and the boys struggling to save a man from drowning. If she had, she said, surely she would have fainted or had a heart attack. Then she announced that there had been enough action and heroics for one day and it was time to head to the Pleasant Street house.

Off-Island

On a winter day in early 1977, my assistant, Edith Thistle, told me that Hildegard was calling and wanted to talk to me about Alice. When Hildegard came on the line she said Miss Williams wanted to come to the Tufts hospital that day, and asked that I please make arrangements for her admission and that I make appointments with doctors to examine her. I inquired if Alice had seen a doctor on the island, and if she had been referred to Boston for medical care. Hildegard said that Alice had not seen a doctor, but she did not feel well and wanted a checkup. She said Alice had packed her bag and was determined to fly to Boston that day and go to the Tufts hospital. I asked Hildegard a few more questions about Alice's condition, and then said I would call back as soon as I made the arrangements to admit her. Hanging up the telephone, I knew I had a problem.

I told Edith the reason for Hildegard's call and explained that in a meeting earlier that day Dave Everhart, the director of the New England Medical Center, had mentioned that the hospital was full of patients—not a bed was open. This, I told Edith, posed a quandary. I telephoned Everhart and told him I needed his help. I explained that one of the major benefactors of Tufts medical school and a friend of mine, from Nantucket, needed to come to the hospital for a medical problem and some diagnostic tests. I asked Everhart to find a nice private room for Alice and arrange for doctors to see her the next day. I told Everhart I would check her in late in the afternoon. Everhart was doubtful there would be an available bed. Still, he said he would try. He promised to call as soon as he looked into the matter.

When my call to Everhart ended, Edith said Hildegard was on the telephone for me again and sounded stressed. When I picked up the telephone, Hildegard asked if the preparations had been made for Alice's admission to the hospital. She said Alice was getting impatient, expecting to leave for the airport immediately. At Alice's insistence, Hildegard had booked her on an afternoon flight. Sounding almost desperate, Hildegard wanted to know what she should tell her. I said that preparations were being made for Alice to enter the hospital and that I would call back in a few minutes. Fortunately, I'd no sooner hung up when Edith came in and told me Everhart had called. He had a room for Alice, and it would be ready when she arrived at the hospital that afternoon. Also, he'd arranged for two doctors to give her a checkup the next day. With a sigh of relief, I asked Edith to call Hildegard and tell her all was ready for Alice to be admitted to the New England Medical Center that afternoon. Edith was to ask Hildegard the flight number and arrival time of Alice's airplane at the airport, and I would pick her up and check her into the hospital.

Later that day, I drove to Logan Airport to meet Alice's flight. I arranged for a wheelchair to move her from the airplane to the terminal. Soon the small twin-engine airplane from Nantucket arrived. The porter with the wheelchair and I walked out to meet it. Five passengers disembarked, and then we boarded and helped Alice off of the plane and into the wheelchair. When she saw the wheelchair, she fussed at me and told me she wasn't old and feeble and didn't need a wheelchair—she could walk to the terminal. I told her I knew she was not old and feeble, but the wheelchair made it easier for me to get her through the terminal and into my car. I asked her if she had enjoyed her flight. She told me she had not, and said as the airplane took off, she remembered she hated flying. She said that if she had not been so worried about her health, she would not have left the island, especially on an airplane. When I asked about the last time she had been in Boston, she informed me her last trip off-island was in 1974 to attend Marie Byrd's funeral. Alice had been friends with the wife of Admiral Richard Byrd, the polar explorer. As we moved Alice through the terminal and to the parking area, I said that someone would meet us at the emergency room entrance of the hospital with a wheelchair to take her to her room.

I went to the hospital to visit Alice later that afternoon. She was happy with the room, the nurses, and the doctors. Diagnostic tests were scheduled for early the next morning, and then they would prepare a treatment plan. Alice hoped the tests would find nothing serious and that her doctors would not want her to stay in Boston for several days. She told me she missed the island already and needed to get back. Late the next afternoon, Peggy and I went to see Alice. We stopped by a florist and picked up a bromeliad plant with an attractive bloom. Alice was pleased to see Peggy and thought the plant was beautiful. Moreover she had good news. The doctors had found nothing serious; they prescribed some medicines and told her they would release her the next day. Again, she expressed her appreciation for my making the arrangements for her to enter the hospital and for the medical checkup. Then Alice said she had one more request of me. She did not want to fly to Nantucket. She said the flight to Boston had been the last one of her life. She explained she wanted to take the ferry back to the island and wanted me to arrange her return trip.

I told Alice I could book her trip to the island by ferry, but I would not let her travel alone. I encouraged her to rest, teasing her that she should behave and not give the nurses and doctors a difficult time. Back in my office, I checked my calendar for the next day and found I could not take her to Hyannis to arrange her trip to the island by ferry. I telephoned Peggy at Emerson Hospital to see if she could take a day off. After she had checked with the nursing supervisor, she called to confirm that she couldn't get away from the hospital on such short notice. She asked me what we were going to do about getting Alice to Nantucket. I told her I'd think about possibilities, and we could decide when we were home from work.

By the time I got home, I had an idea. I suggested to Peggy that perhaps Laurie, home from college for a few days, might drive Alice to Hyannis. Peggy agreed that might work. He could ride the ferry with her to the island and would enjoy the trip. She said Laurie was fond of Alice, and Alice had told her he was a fine and polite young man.

When we asked Laurie, he agreed readily. He asked me to call and make arrangements for her to be met when they arrived on the island. I gave him the ferry schedule, money for tickets, and asked that he help Alice on board and get her seated. I told him I would call Hildegard Cassidy and tell her the time the ferry was due to dock in Nantucket so she could meet them. After that, he could catch the next ferry back to Hyannis. Peggy and I knew he would take good care of Alice, and I told him how much his mother and I appreciated his willingness to help.

The next morning, Laurie and I went to check Alice out of the hospital. I told her she was grounded, no more flying for her. I explained that because of our schedules, neither Peggy nor I could take her to the ferry. Laurie, however, would be pleased to drive her to Hyannis and ride with her on the ferry. I said I'd call Hildegard and that she would be there to meet the ferry.

Though Alice considered herself somewhat of a stoic, I saw her eyes well up as she told us, with a somewhat husky voice, how much she appreciated our efforts on her behalf, that we had stepped in and become her family. Alice told Laurie it would be a pleasure for "this old woman to be seen in the company of such a handsome young man." Then she asked me to check her out of the hospital so she could be on her way home. Alice added she was taking her beautiful plant with her because she was sure the sea air and Nantucket would agree with it.

Off-Island Two

A few years later, Alice made another trip "off-island." She telephoned saying she needed a cataract operation and her doctor wanted her to go to the New England Medical Center. Hildegard had made the necessary

arrangements for her. I verified Alice's status at the hospital and confirmed that everything was set for her admission. I called Alice and told
her all was in order to admit her and that she had an appointment with
the ophthalmologist. I joked to Alice that I knew how much she loved
flying, but suggested this time she take the ferry. Hildegard would give me
Alice's arrival time in Hyannis, and I would meet her at the dock. Hildegard was to take Alice and her bags on board and get her seated. When the
ferry arrived in Hyannis she was to stay seated and wait for Peggy and me
to come aboard and help her off of the ferry. Then we would return to
Boston and check her into the hospital that afternoon.

On the telephone, Alice told me I worried too much about her. She
said just because she was over eighty years old, she was not a feeble old
woman. However, she promised to stay in her seat aboard the ferry until
we arrived. She added her appreciation for our meeting her at the dock
and how much she looked forward to seeing Peggy.

When the ferry from Nantucket docked in Hyannis, Peggy and I went
on board and met Alice. We helped her off the ferry, and I drove to Boston and checked her into the New England Medical Center. To our surprise, she had the same room as during her first visit to the Tufts hospital.

The next day, early in the morning, Alice underwent cataract surgery.
Late in the morning I called her surgeon, and he told me the operation
had gone well. After she came out of recovery, I went to visit Alice in her
room. She was sitting in bed with a patch covering one eye. I told Alice
she looked great, but the black patch didn't do much for her; I said she
looked like a pirate.

Alice said she felt well and that her doctor had told her he would check
her eye early in the morning the next day, and then, if all was as he expected, she could go home. He told her it was important to return for a
follow-up examination the following week. Alice said she hated the idea
of returning to the island for only a few days and regretted again imposing
on me to pick her up in Hyannis. I said that it was no trouble. I told her
that I had talked to her doctor before coming by and that he had said she
was going to be fine but needed to return in one week for a follow-up
visit with him. I suggested to Alice more travel during this winter weather
would do her no good and that she should not be out in the cold. She
might slip on some ice and fall getting on or off of the ferry or out of our
car. I said I had a great plan and that she could not refuse.

I told Alice that when she was discharged from the hospital the next day she could stay with us in Concord. I informed her we had a spare bedroom with a private bath, and she could stay there until her checkup visit with the ophthalmologist. I said the children could put her medication in her eye when they got home from school. In a week, I would take her to the hospital for her examination by her doctor. If the ophthalmologist said there were no complications and she was healing as expected, Peggy and I would drive her to Hyannis later that day, go aboard the ferry with her, and see her to her Cliff Road home. I told Alice she couldn't talk me out of taking her to Concord. I informed her it would be our pleasure to have her in our home; to us this was partial payback for letting us use her Pleasant Street house. Alice protested, saying it would be an imposition on the two of us to house an old woman, but she accepted our offer, calling it "most generous." Also, she said it would give her some private time with our children while Peggy and I were at work.

The next day, Alice had her checkup. All was progressing as expected. I checked her out of the hospital and drove her to our home. The children were excited about her visit and looked forward to seeing her. During the week, Peggy and I were gone most of the day. All of the children were in school and Peggy always left them an after-school snack. That first day they shared their snack with Alice. Victoria offered Alice Toll House cookies Peggy had baked, and asked her what she wanted to drink. Alice tried the cookies and agreed they were quite delicious. As for a drink, she told her she would like tomato juice. Veronica told Alice she shouldn't drink tomato juice with Toll House cookies; instead, she suggested a Coke and offered to get one. Alice said she had never had a Coca-Cola, but had seen it advertised. She asked if it had a good flavor. Rachel assured her that Cokes were good to drink, tasty, and said she couldn't believe she had never had one. She told Alice she would like it, and Cokes went well with these cookies. Rob told Alice that as soon as she finished her snack it was time for him to put drops in her eye.

Every evening after dinner, the children begged Alice to tell them more ghost stories. She seemed to have an endless supply of them, and I suspect she made them up as she told them to the children. At the end of the week, I took Alice to the ophthalmologist for follow-up on her eye surgery. The doctor told her he saw no signs of infection and that she was progressing as expected. She told her doctor she had received the best nursing care possible: the Cavazos children had put drops in her eyes, fed her homemade cookies, and given her her first Coca-Cola. She declared her vision improved because of the superb care provided by our children. Alice also acknowledged her doctor was an excellent surgeon. The ophthalmologist told Alice she could go back to her island and that there was no need to return for another year. At that time he would evaluate the growth of the cataract in her other eye and decide if it needed to be removed.

From Boston, Peggy and I drove Alice to Hyannis to catch the ferry to Nantucket. The evening before, she persuaded us to stay on the island overnight and then to depart for the mainland the next morning. We agreed, and I asked her for suggestions on where I should call for reservations. Alice said that wasn't necessary. In anticipation we would spend the night on the island, she had telephoned Hildegard and asked her to make a reservation for us at the Gerard Coffin House. Alice said it was one of the best inns on the island; the rooms were nice and the food satisfactory. She added there would be no expense for us; the bill was to be sent to her.

When we arrived in Nantucket, we took Alice to her home on Cliff Road. As we said good-bye she told us to be sure and thank the children for the wonderful care they had given her. Alice said she would never forget our kindness and support and the generosity of taking her into our home and making her feel like part of our family.

Peggy and I checked into the elegant Gerard Coffin House. After dinner I suggested we walk about Nantucket Center. We'd not been on the island in the winter, and I said the Christmas decorations and the snow and ice should be a striking scene. Arm in arm, we braved the cold and the blowing wind as we walked out onto the main street of Nantucket. There was not another person out. We had Nantucket Center to ourselves. It was late January, and with the wind chill, it must have been below zero. Still, it was a magnificent setting for a winter walk, and the snow seemed to make the Christmas lights even brighter.

The next morning I telephoned Alice, thanked her for her generosity, checked out, and we walked the few blocks to the ferry landing. We saw people milling about the dock. To our surprise, the ferry from Hyannis had not arrived. I told Peggy obviously something had delayed it. We soon found out. Nantucket harbor was frozen from Great Point to the light at the entrance of the harbor and to the ferry landing. The ice was so thick the ferry could not enter the harbor. I went to the ticket office and asked when we might expect a ferry to take us to the mainland.

The clerk behind the counter said he wished he could tell me, but with the harbor frozen as tight as it was, everything depended on when an icebreaker could clear a channel through Nantucket Sound. He doubted we would make it out that day, but early the next day was a possibility. The clerk told me to relax and enjoy the island, but it was too cold to be out and about. I found Peggy in the waiting room. I told her I didn't think we were going to make it out of the harbor that day. She asked what I was going to do about the Tufts Board of Trustees meeting the next day where I was to present the medical school's upcoming annual budget proposal. I said I had been thinking about how to get off the island. I suggested we call Laurie at Nathaniel Hawthorne College and ask him if he could charter an airplane, pick us up on Nantucket, and drop us off at Logan Airport in Boston. I would pay for the charter of the airplane. It was imperative I attend the trustee meeting the next morning, and flying out of Nantucket appeared to be the only way to do so.

Peggy liked my idea. She enjoyed flying with Laurie and felt safe with him. Peggy urged me to telephone right away, suggesting I call the airport at Hawthorne College first. Laurie worked at the airport, part-time, as a flight instructor while going to college. Peggy dug through her purse and found the book with our children's telephone numbers. I telephoned, and to my relief, Laurie answered. I asked if he could arrange a charter flight to the island and fly us to Boston. He said it was possible. He was free the rest of the day and could be on the island in a couple of hours. He asked me to hold while he checked the weather for the trip. A few minutes later, he came on the telephone saying he didn't expect delays. The weather was clear and sunny in New Hampshire, as well as on Nantucket and in Boston. He asked us to meet him at the airport on the island around noon, and he would have us back in Boston by early afternoon. With this arrangement, I could be in my office by midafternoon. This would give me time to meet with the business manager to finish the budget presentation for the trustee meeting the next morning.

From the harbor Peggy and I took a taxi to the airport and waited. Shortly after noon we saw a single-engine plane taxiing on the runway, headed for the terminal. It was Laurie. He parked near the terminal gate and, after refueling and doing his walkaround, he asked us to board. The air traffic controller cleared him to taxi to the departure runway, and soon we were on our way to Boston. It was a glorious sight as the small airplane lifted off and turned north. We flew across Nantucket and the harbor. We saw a sheet of ice shimmering in the bright noon sun. The ice extended completely across Nantucket Sound. Looking at the ice, Laurie said it would be a while before a boat could get in or out of the harbor. I agreed with his assessment and thanked him for flying down to transport his parents.

In the 1970s single-engine airplanes could land at Logan Airport without paying an enormous fee. I sat beside Laurie and watched as he concentrated on his landing approach to Logan. Soon we were on our final approach, and air traffic control gave us permission to land. Laurie pointed out a big Eastern Airlines jet on the taxi strip waiting for us to touch down. He said air traffic control had instructed the pilots of the Eastern jet to hold for incoming traffic—namely, our plane. Laurie guided the plane to a perfect and smooth touchdown.

After we landed, and as our airplane taxied to the terminal, Peggy asked Laurie if it made him nervous to have the professional airline pilots and many airline passengers watch him land. He assured us it did not bother him at all.

Edith Thistle came into my office about noon on February 5, 1978, and asked if I planned to send faculty, students, and staff home early. I asked why I should, and she said it was starting to snow and the weather bureau predicted a blizzard by early evening. After fourteen years on the Tufts faculty, I knew weather forecasting in Massachusetts could be challenging and sometimes erroneous. Still, after I considered the risks of and problems caused by not closing the school because of snow, I told Edith to cancel classes. I asked her to inform the faculty, students, and staff to leave the medical school as early as possible because of the incoming blizzard. It did not take long for my staff to vacate their offices because they knew the difficulties and hazards of driving in a snowstorm in the greater Boston area. Soon I was alone in my fifth-floor office. I decided to catch up on paperwork, write some memos, and read reports without the usual interruptions. I planned to work until about 5:00 p.m. and then go home.

At about two in the afternoon, my telephone rang. It was Jean Mayer, the president of Tufts University, calling from the main campus in Medford, eight miles away. Mayer wanted to know if I planned to cancel classes at the medical school the next day. When I asked Mayer why I should cancel classes, he told me to look out of the window. I did. Although it was midafternoon, it was almost dark. I had never seen it snowing so heavily. I told Mayer the next day's classes at the medical school would be cancelled. He said it was a wise decision. Mayer told me he had already cancelled classes for the next day on the main campus.

After Mayer's call about the blizzard, I started to worry about the safety of Peggy and the children. I knew I couldn't get in touch with Peggy by telephone because she was at the hospital in the operating room assisting as a circulating nurse. She was not due to leave the hospital until 5:30 that evening. If the Concord schools let out early because of the storm, the children would come home by school bus and should be home long before I arrived. Peggy always prepared dinner before she left for the hospital. Usually by the time she got home from work, I would be home. The more I thought about it, the more concerned I became about their well-being. I decided to close my office as soon as I could and drive home, to look after the children. I also knew I had a big job ahead shoveling snow from our drive so that Peggy would have a place to park our station wagon when she came home.

Before leaving the office, I contacted the person responsible for informing the radio stations about school closing the next day. I took the elevator to the first floor and stepped into the medical school parking lot near the loading dock. It was snowing heavily, and I started clearing the snow off of my small hatchback. I finished as one of the maintenance men came out into the parking lot. I greeted him and made a comment about the blizzard. He said he could not recall a snow like the one we were having that day. He looked at my car. He said he had two questions of me: one, did I plan to drive that car in the snowstorm, and two, where did I live?

I told him I expected to drive this car to my home in Concord. He slowly shook his head. Looking at me, he said I would never make Concord in my small car in this snowstorm. He told me to open the hatchback, and he'd be right back. A few minutes later he reappeared with a cart that held a hundred-pound bag of salt used for ice melt. Together, we placed it over one rear wheel. Then he rolled his cart back into the building and returned with another bag that we placed over the other rear wheel. He said I would need a lot of weight in the back. Without it my car would drive like a snake; I'd be slipping and sliding on the road. I thanked him and asked if he expected to leave soon. He shook his head, saying he had to stay at the school to keep the energy and heating systems going. Wishing me luck on my trip, the maintenance man reminded me to bring back the two bags of salt after the storm; he had to account for them.

I pulled out of the Tufts parking lot and was thankful traffic was light on the normally crowded downtown Boston streets. Entering the Massachusetts Turnpike, I saw the snowplows had passed through, but only two of the four lanes were open. I made steady but slow progress. Cars were bumper to bumper. The blizzard drastically limited visibility. It was apparent the snowplows were having trouble keeping up with the rapidly falling snow. This meant driving conditions would quickly deteriorate, making the roads almost impassable.

I left the turnpike and turned onto 128/95 north. This is a major highway, with four lanes for traffic on both sides of the road, but only two lanes were open. Travel was treacherous, and many cars were barely moving or were stopped along the edge of the roadway. I knew I needed to exit as soon as possible. After an hour, having made it no farther than what normally took twenty minutes, I left 128 and took Route 2 west to Concord. At that time the four-lane highway was not divided as it is today. I continued slowly, but at least I was moving. After driving about three miles I saw a long line of traffic barely moving. Ahead of them I could see many vehicles standing still. They were having difficulty moving forward after stopping for a traffic light at the top of a hill in the town of Lincoln. I decided to avoid the hill and look for a way to get off of Route 2 before it became impassable.

On the other side of the road, I saw a two-lane road going into the woods. I knew it would eventually take me to Concord. There was no traffic moving east, so I pulled across the highway and onto the road. It had been plowed, but the heavily falling snow was accumulating again. I was thankful there was no traffic. I kept moving and went past Walden Pond and entered Concord Center. I negotiated the snow-covered roads through the town and on to our home on Annursnac Hill Road. It was dark when I arrived about 5:00 p.m. It had taken me two and a half hours to drive home. Normally, I made the drive in forty-five minutes.

I pulled the car into our driveway with a sigh of relief and turned off the engine. I stepped out of the car and with the snow up to my knees walked to our downstairs door. Brushing snow off the front stoop, I entered our home. Thankfully, our six youngest children were home from school. Victoria said the Concord schools had been dismissed at noon and the children sent home on buses. Laurie, Sarita, Rick, and Lisa were away at college, so they missed the blizzard. The children were glad when they saw me walk in the door. Rob said they worried about me driving in the blizzard.

I was anxious about Peggy's trip home. She had to drive three miles over snow-covered roads in our station wagon from the hospital. I called the hospital, and to my surprise Peggy answered. This was my first communication with her since we both left for work. I told her the roads were almost impassable and the snowplows were having trouble keeping up with the heavy snowfall. I said the children were safely home from school. Peggy said when she learned the Concord schools were cancelled, she had called and talked to Rob to be sure everyone was home and stayed in the house. Peggy told me they were just finishing a case, and she would leave soon. She promised to be extra careful driving home. After I talked to Peggy, I asked Victoria, Rob, and Tom to help me clear part of the driveway so their mother could pull into it and get our car off the road. By this time, passing snowplows had piled about two feet of snow into the entrance of the driveway. I was relieved when Peggy pulled into the driveway at 6:30 p.m. She said the streets were in terrible shape for driving, and the heavily falling snow reduced visibility to almost nothing. She insisted it was a miracle she had made it home and hadn't slid off the road and into a tree.

The next morning, it was still snowing and our two cars were large mounds of snow. The director of nursing at Emerson Hospital telephoned Peggy asking if she could come to work early because so many nurses had called saying they could not get to the hospital. Peggy explained it would be a while before she could even get out of her driveway. The nursing director said the Concord police would come to the house and drive her to the hospital. That evening they would drive her home. Peggy said she would call the police after we cleared our driveway and she was ready to leave. The police did pick her up. But when her shift ended, she called me to drive her home. As she got into the car, I asked why the police didn't give her a ride. She explained she preferred me to be her driver.

After Peggy left for the hospital, I turned on the radio. I heard that because of the snow emergency Michael Dukakis, the governor of Massachusetts, had closed Boston to commuting traffic. That day, the elder children and I shoveled the drive several times. Although I couldn't go into Boston, I wanted to keep the drive passable so I could take Peggy to Emerson Hospital and pick her up after work. When not shoveling snow, I spent considerable time on the telephone talking to the maintenance people and staff at the medical school. A few, who lived in the city,

Peggy on duty as a circulating surgical nurse at Emerson Hospital, Concord, MA, 1979.

had driven to the medical school, but several walked or skied there. Many of the New England Medical Center personnel were unable to reach the hospital because of the blizzard. In order to help out, some medical students living in Posner Hall, a dormitory across the street on the medical school campus, were mobilized to work in the hospital.

For the next three days I operated the medical school by telephone. Classes for first- and second-year medical students remained cancelled, but I stayed in contact with the maintenance and security people. They were doing a great job keeping water and heating systems operating and the building secure. On the fourth day after the blizzard, buses were permitted to go into Boston, although the commuter trains were still not running. Private automobiles were not allowed to enter the city. I drove to Concord Center, took one of the buses into Boston, and walked to the medical school from the bus station. I spent most of the day solving problems brought on by the blizzard. Later in the day, I took the bus back to Concord and picked Peggy up after work.

As soon as the blizzard slowed, the National Guard flew into Boston's

Logan Airport. They unloaded large trucks and tractors. Plows were not effective because of the enormous snow accumulation. Snow had to be moved to make room for plowing. The National Guard troops loaded snow into trucks, which dumped it into Boston harbor. Today, because of environmental concerns and laws, it would not be possible to unload snow into the harbor. I wonder what we would do with the massive amounts of snow on the streets if we had another snowstorm as ferocious as the blizzard of 1978.

The blizzard that year resulted in the greatest accumulation of snow in the New England area in over a hundred years. There were massive amounts of snow on the streets of the city. Snow fell primarily between the morning of February 6 and the evening of the 7th. It broke up on February 8. Massachusetts, Rhode Island, and Connecticut were inundated with snow. Northern Rhode Island reported up to 55 inches. Boston had 27 inches. About 34 inches fell on Concord before the blizzard was over. Although many working in Boston were sent home by early afternoon of the first day of the storm, thousands of people were stranded in town. For many it was hours before they got home. Some people did not make it home for several days, and the downtown hotels were filled with guests unable to drive home. Some people had difficulty leaving their homes or offices because snow drifts up to fifteen feet high blocked exits. Many people were trapped in their cars along the highways, and several people died of carbon monoxide poisoning when snow blocked their exhausts. Thousands of cars were abandoned and buried on the roads by the passing snowplows. They stayed buried for several days until the cleanup effort was well under way.

Over the years, Peggy and I frequently took the children to Nantucket. We enjoyed Alice Williams's hospitality and spent time with her on each trip. In 1980, when I became president of Texas Tech University, I told Peggy I did not look forward to calling Alice and telling her I was leaving the job as dean of Tufts medical school. Peggy said she would understand, but naturally would be disappointed by the news of our move to Texas.

A few days later, I telephoned Alice and told her about my appointment in Texas as a university president. Alice said she was sad to learn I would be leaving Tufts and Boston. She told me she knew being president of a large university was an excellent opportunity for me in my academic career and certainly of great economic benefit to our family. Alice asked about Peggy's reaction to the Texas move because she knew how much Peggy loved our home in Concord. I said Peggy was supportive. I promised Alice that Peggy and I would visit with her in the summer. Alice said to take care of my lovely family and myself. She added that she knew I would do a good job as president. She told me to not forget my promise to be back on the island in the summer. I assured her we would be by to visit her probably in July.

By late June 1980 our family was settled in Lubbock. But in July Peggy and I went back to Nantucket. We stayed at the Pleasant Street house and walked to Alice's Cliff Road house. We spent an hour talking about West Texas and the future. It was apparent to us that Alice was sad about our move to Lubbock. Finally, I told her that the family had missed her greatly since our move and we wanted her to come live with us in Texas. We wanted her to be even more a part of our family. If she moved to our

Waiting for Peggy on Main Street, Nantucket, 1986.

home in Lubbock, we would be able take care of her. I said we knew how much she loved Nantucket, but we were sure she would eventually adapt to West Texas. I said I knew she disliked flying, so Peggy and I would come to Nantucket, help her pack, close the house, and together we'd take the train from Boston to Lubbock.

Alice's eyes glistened with tears. She was somber and thoughtful and in a somewhat husky voice said the two of us were kind to "this old woman." She added that her health was failing, and she hesitated leaving her doctor on the island. She reminded us how much she loved the island where she was born and said she could never leave it. Alice suggested that instead of her going to Texas, we should bring the family to Nantucket often to visit her. We promised we would return to the island to see her as frequently as possible.

We had guessed she would turn down our proposal. But I said if she changed her mind to let us know, and Peggy and I would be back to whisk her to Texas on the next train. Alice nodded. Peggy said if we couldn't persuade her to move with us to Texas, the two of them needed to arrange how to communicate regularly. Peggy admitted her procrastination as a correspondent. She suggested she call Alice the last Thursday of each month, late in the afternoon. Alice said she liked the idea and agreed to Peggy's proposal.

During the following years, Peggy faithfully telephoned on the last Thursday of each month. Most of the time, Alice answered. On occasion Peggy had to call several times before Alice picked up. Then one day in late spring 1983, Peggy told me she was worried because she had called several times and Alice had not answered her telephone.

I told Peggy not to worry, and urged her to keep trying. That day, Peggy tried several times to telephone Alice, and finally a man's voice answered. Peggy said she was calling for Alice Williams. The man, Gary Colyer, was Alice's tenant who also took care of the place. He reminded Peggy that they had met when we visited the island during the summer. Gary said he was sorry to tell her that Alice had died the month before. They had buried her on the island.

Peggy was taken aback. Alice had not told her she was ill. She asked if Alice had had a heart attack or a stroke. Gary said it was neither. Alice had been sick quite a while with cancer of the stomach. It had been a long illness, and she had been in a lot of pain. Gary suggested that Alice was glad when the end came and that she went quietly.

With tears in her eyes, Peggy told me of her telephone conversation with Gary. She said Alice probably knew about her illness when we invited her to Texas and didn't want to be a burden to us. I'm sure Peggy would have gone to Nantucket the next day if Alice had told her about her illness. That summer, Peggy and I returned to Nantucket. This time we did not stay at the Pleasant Street house but found a bed-and-breakfast inn near the Cliff Road house. The next morning, we stopped by Alice's house and found Gary finishing a sketch of roses clinging to a trellis by Alice's side porch. It was beautiful. When Peggy admired the sketch, Gary handed it to her. He said that Alice had often told him stories about the Cavazos family. He was sure she would want Peggy to have the sketch. We had it framed, and each time I see it I think of Alice Williams.

During our years with Alice, she taught us many lessons. She told me stories about nineteenth-century Boston medicine and her father's work as dean of the Tufts University School of Medicine. From Alice, Peggy and I learned about aging gracefully, being patient, keeping a sense of humor, being optimistic, and enjoying life. By giving to Tufts financially, Alice taught us to be generous and support institutions that enhanced the well-being of society. She advised us not to take ourselves too seriously, and to accept what life gives us. To this day our children remember Alice Williams fondly and, like Peggy and me, miss her. Since Alice's death, Peggy and I have visited Nantucket several times. We've always enjoyed our visits, but somehow they've never seemed the same without Alice and our children.

Chapter Fifteen :: **Reflecting on Faith and Divine Guidance**

The Trappists Have a Visitor

Back in the spring of 1949, during my senior year at Texas Tech, I read Thomas Merton's very popular autobiography *The Seven Storey Mountain,* in which he describes his conversion to Roman Catholicism and entrance into the monastic life as a Trappist (Cistercian). I found the book interesting and thought provoking. Soon after I read it, one of the priests at Lubbock's St. Elizabeth Catholic Church told me about the newly opened Trappist monastery in nearby New Mexico. He had recently attended a spiritual retreat there.

I asked if Trappists allowed visitors who were not priests or members of a religious order. He said they did and that guests could come and stay for a few days. So I decided to visit the monastery between the end of spring semester and the start of summer school. I wanted to learn more about the Trappists and their way of life. The Cistercian order dates back to the Cîteaux Abbey in France and was founded in 1098. As I learned from Merton's book, the monks follow the Rule of Saint Benedict, living in poverty, seclusion, and prayer. I thought experiencing the monastery might help me to deepen my commitment to the Catholic Church. As a student at Tech I attended Mass regularly at Saint Elizabeth's on Sunday and frequently went during the week as well. Still, I sought more insight about my life and time to think about the future. I decided a monastery, where there were no worldly distractions, would be the place to contemplate my past and ponder my future life. I also knew it would be a place to learn more about Catholicism.

Our Lady of Guadalupe Abbey, near Pecos, New Mexico, opened in April 1948. The Cistercian monks living there were devoted to a life of contemplation in a cloistered atmosphere. Prayer, work, spiritual study, and reflection filled their day. I telephoned the monastery and told the guest master I was a senior in college at Texas Tech and sought more information about the Trappists and their commitment to such an ascetic life. I asked if I could spend a few days with them. He said I would be welcome.

The guest master inquired how I planned to arrive at the monastery. I told him I didn't have a car, so I would take a bus. The monk gave me information about the route to take, noting that the bus stopped briefly in Santa Fe and then went on to Pecos. He said he would pick me up at a road crossing near a general store located west of Pecos. I was to ask the bus driver to let me off there. He ended the conversation by saying he looked forward to meeting me.

On the day for my visit, I packed a small bag and walked downtown to the Lubbock bus station, where I bought a round-trip ticket. After paying for it, I had only about five dollars left. I wasn't concerned because I didn't think I would have many bills at a monastery. It is a beautiful trip from Albuquerque to Santa Fe, and I enjoyed the scenery. There were only a few passengers on the bus. When we arrived in Santa Fe, some people got off, others boarded, and soon we were on our way to Pecos. When I asked the driver to drop me off near the Trappist monastery, he nodded, saying he knew exactly where my ride would meet me, just a few miles outside of Pecos.

It was getting dark by the time we left Santa Fe, and before long we were in the mountains. As the bus climbed slowly up them, I saw thickening clouds and a thunderstorm building ahead of us. Occasional flashes of lightning illuminated the landscape. The bus stopped at a crossroads less than an hour outside of Santa Fe. The driver opened the door and said that if I was going to the monastery, this was the place to get off. The bus departed, and I stood alone at the edge of the crossroads. Darkness had set in. When lightning flashed, I saw a one-story general store and a gas pump nearby. It was obvious the store was closed. There was not another person in sight. Thunder rumbled and lightning flashes continued. I decided that if it started raining before my ride to the monastery arrived, I would stand on the porch of the store to keep dry. To my relief, a few minutes later I saw the lights of a truck approaching. It slowed and stopped. The driver lowered his window and called out to me. I walked to the driver's side of the aged pickup. At that moment, there was a flash of lightning that illuminated the face and upper body of the driver. For a moment I thought I saw a monk from the eleventh century. The driver had a short dark beard, a cowl covered his head, and he wore a monk's habit.

The monk introduced himself as the guest master. He asked if I was the person from Lubbock who wanted to stay a few days at the monastery. When I answered yes, he told me to put my bag in the back of the truck, urging me to get in quickly before the storm broke and I got wet. I boarded. The monk put the truck in gear, and we started to climb higher up the mountain. On the way to the monastery, I thanked the guest master for the opportunity to spend a few days at the monastery. He said I was welcome and hoped I had a pensive and rewarding visit. It was about 8:00 in the evening when we arrived at the monastery and parked in front of the guesthouse. He hefted my bag and said to follow him.

We entered the guesthouse, and the monk led me to my room. He asked if I had eaten dinner, and I told him I had not. With a nod of his head, he said he would prepare a dinner for me while I washed up from my journey. He told me he would be in the kitchen and to come there when I was ready to eat. A few minutes later, I walked into the kitchen. There, on a small table, was a plate with a serving of steak, potatoes, and some vegetables. He set a glass of water and a plate with bread in front of me, saying he hoped I would enjoy my meal. He took a chair across the table from me. I pointed to the steak and said I didn't expect to be served a steak at a monastery on a Friday (at that time, Catholics were obligated to abstain from eating meat on Friday). He informed me that because I was in New Mexico I could eat meat on that day. He explained that centuries before, one of the popes had lifted the Friday meat abstinence rule in gratitude for the missionary efforts of those in what is now New Mexico.

During dinner, he asked my expectations for the next few days. As I ate, I told him I wanted time to read, walk, and to think about my future as well as to reflect on my past life. I added I would like to learn about the Cistercians and try to understand why they choose to lead such an austere life. He chuckled and said a few days were not enough to understand much about myself or about life in a monastery. He said there would be plenty of time for the two of us to talk, and he promised to answer my questions, if possible. He said a monk's life at the abbey is devoted to prayer, reading, and manual work, and suggested I spend my days there in similar activities.

I agreed, and asked him to make a schedule for me. I knew the monks led a contemplative life of prayer and penance and spoke only when necessary. The guest master said I might want to attend some of the recitations of the Divine Office. He explained that the Liturgy of the Hours is a set of prayers, readings, songs, and responsorial psalms required of priests and members of religious orders. He went on to say that the portion of the Divine Office appointed by canon law is called a canonical hour and that the whole of the prayers take the names of the canonical hours. The service of the Divine Office consists of responsorials and psalms that are sung. He said I probably did not want to go to matins, the first service at 3:00 in the morning. He said, though, that he would awaken me near dawn so I could attend lauds. He encouraged me to be present at 6:00 p.m. vespers and compline at 9:00 p.m. These are the prayers at the end of the day.

The next morning, as dawn broke, I sat in the chapel near the altar with eight or ten other attendees who lived near the monastery. Candlelight bathed the chapel. I could not see the monks because they were in the main part of the chapel, in front of the altar, with a separating screen between us. The service consisted of recitation of certain prayers from the Breviary and responses and psalms. I listened to the chanting of the prayers and psalms. Smelling the burning incense, I felt transported across time to a monastery in Europe during the eleventh century. Hearing the canonical hours chanted in Latin by the Trappists was a magnificent experience, and one I will never forget.

I spent part of the first day reading in the small library in the guesthouse and in prayer and contemplation. Later, I took a walk in the nearby woods. I came upon a small stream running cool and clear over rocks. I stopped to rest on a boulder overlooking the stream, and it wasn't long before I spotted a large trout swimming near a log. I enjoy fishing, and for a moment I had a yearning for a fishing rod. I knew I'd catch the trout with the first cast. But as I thought about it, I decided the guest master wouldn't be pleased if I returned from my contemplative walk with a trout for him to prepare for dinner. As I watched, the trout swam on, and I continued my walk.

The next day, leaving the guesthouse on my way to the woods, the monastery's abbot stopped to talk to me. He knew of my recent arrival as a guest, and we discussed my expectations and aspirations in life. He seemed a thoughtful and understanding person. We spoke of difficulties and essentials in one's life, and the need to keep a positive outlook. Then he said one should not spend all of one's time thinking about and contemplating life. He told me physical labor should be part of a person's day and asked if I wanted a task to go along with my prayers and thoughts. When I nodded and told him I would, he asked me to follow him.

As we walked, we passed a grave marked with a simple wooden cross. I asked the abbot about it, and he told me it was the grave of the first monk to die after the monastery opened. He was a young man who died shortly after joining the order. I remarked that it was sad the monk died so young and so soon after becoming a Trappist. The abbot said I should be glad for the man because he did not have to suffer long on this earth. Now, he said, the young monk was in a happier place, near God.

The abbot led me to a small, newly painted building and, pointing to paint on some of the windowpanes, asked me to scrape the paint and clean the windows. There were only three windows. I thought of how the monks had been so kind to take me into their community, counseling me and giving me a bed and sustenance—and did not ask for payment. I told the abbot I would be pleased to help out. He left me, and I went to work scraping paint off of the panes and cleaning them.

An hour later the abbot returned, asking how the job was coming along. I told him the windows were clean, but I had one corner of one more window to scrape and clean. He examined the pane, shook his head slowly, and told me not to be concerned with a bit of paint or with trivial matters. He said, "Perfectionists never have peace of soul." I've never forgotten that lesson about living from the abbot that day.

I spent one more day with the Trappists, and early the next morning the guest master drove me down the mountain to the crossroads where he had picked me up. It seemed to me that the few days spent at the monastery offered months' worth of insight about my life. I had learned some lessons there about living and understood a bit more why a person might choose a religious life. There at the monastery, I came to understand the significance of planning and balancing the day's activities so I would have time to meditate about the direction of my life. I learned about the pitfalls of being a perfectionist and the need to keep a positive outlook about life, that one could live a life without possessions or wealth, about the need to be patient with others, and the importance of daily prayer. I realized the need to accept God's will.

The guest master stood by the road with me until the bus arrived. He waved to the driver, who stopped the bus and opened the door. As I boarded, I turned to the monk—who had given me so much of his time, counseled me, and had shared his wisdom about life with me—and said good-bye. I told him I could not thank him enough for the many lessons about living he had taught me, and that I appreciated the kindness and hospitality he had extended to me. The monk said he hoped someday I might return for another visit. I boarded the bus, finding it hard to leave the peace and tranquility I had enjoyed for a few days among the Trappists.

As the bus moved down the highway, the beautiful New Mexico scenery and subsequently the West Texas landscape passed before my eyes. I knew soon I would be back to my busy schedule of study and research at Tech, but I promised myself to return some day for another visit with the Trappists. Unfortunately, I never made it back. But the lessons from those few days in New Mexico have stayed with me throughout my life.

Dinner with the Cardinals

In 1970, Humberto Sousa Medeiros became archbishop of Boston. He was born in Portugal and grew up in Fall River, Massachusetts. Less than three years after being named archbishop, he became a cardinal. That year, as the acting dean of Tufts medical school, I had my initial meeting with Cardinal Medeiros. During our meeting we conversed in English and Spanish. Before coming to Boston, the cardinal was the bishop of Brownsville, Texas, from 1966 to 1970. I told him of my South Texas roots, and we discussed the difficult life Hispanics led in the Rio Grande Valley.

In Brownsville, the cardinal had been a strong advocate for farmworkers, most of whom were Mexican Americans. He had supported their demands for a $1.25 per hour minimum wage during the 1966 Minimum Wage March, and he went into the fields during the harvest season to celebrate Mass for them.

At Boston, the cardinal insisted he wanted strong academic health programs in the archdiocese's teaching hospitals. Soon, I became aware of the academic expectations of those operating the Catholic hospital system. They wanted the Tufts Faculty Appointments and Promotions Committee and the administration of the medical school to acknowledge the excellence of their faculty's clinical and teaching skills and the high quality of their research effort. Once I understood their academic needs and desires, I worked diligently to promote further collaboration between Tufts and the Catholic hospital system in the greater Boston area.

I made sure the credentials of our faculty in the Catholic hospitals as well as in our other associated teaching hospitals were appreciated and properly evaluated. I took time to serve on faculty search committees at St. Elizabeth's Hospital, attended and participated in their faculty meetings, and met frequently with the hospital directors of the Catholic hospitals associated with Tufts.

Our mutual commitment to improving the academic programs of the Catholic teaching hospitals resulted in strong ties between St. Elizabeth's Hospital and Tufts. As a consequence, the cardinal invited Peggy and me to many hospital and church functions. At one dinner, although we both sat at the head table, we were not seated together. Peggy sat with Cardinal Medeiros on her right side and two other cardinals on her left. Afterward, driving home, I told Peggy I'd never seen so many cardinals in one room, and there she was, right in the middle of them. I asked her if she had enjoyed her dinner with three cardinals. She said she had been a nervous wreck, not because of the cardinals but because she was unsure how to eat the shrimp cocktail. The shrimp were jumbos, with the tails hanging over the dish. Peggy said she didn't know whether to use a fork or pick them up with her fingers. Then she'd watched as Cardinal Medeiros picked up a shrimp by the tail, and figured if that was the way a cardinal ate shrimp, then it must be okay for a country girl. We laughed at her "divine guidance."

In October 1, 1979, Peggy and I were invited by the archdiocese to hear Pope John Paul II celebrate Mass on the Boston Common. John Paul II's visit to Boston was the first and only visit of a pope to the city to date, and it was the first Mass he celebrated on his visit to the United States. Knowing it would be difficult to drive to the Boston Common because of the enormous crowds and security, Peggy and I took the train from Concord to Boston's North Station. From there, we rode the subway to a stop near the Boston Common. We had seats a few rows from the front center, near the altar. It rained steadily during the Mass, but there were about four hundred thousand faithful who attended the service. It was a wonderful and fulfilling evening for the two of us. After the Mass, Peggy and I walked in the rain to North Station and caught the train to Concord. When I sat down in my seat, I took off my shoes and poured water from them. Still, it had been an evening that we will not forget.

I think about how differently my life might have turned out had I returned to the monastery back in 1949, or if I had joined a religious order, or become a priest. Looking back, I feel that my faith has been interwoven with my life's work as a teacher. Our university system is based on the old European monastic tradition, stressing service to others, and many of our first educational institutions were established to train children in the faith. While we are far removed from those times, there is still a strong tradition among educators to dedicate themselves to serve, train, and prepare future generations. Likewise, the students I taught in the health professions have continued to "pay it forward" by serving and treating many people. I think my efforts in higher education and as secretary of education to improve the life of minorities though better education might be viewed as missionary efforts. While I made a decision not to enter the religious life, my family's faith has remained very important to us. We raised our children as Catholics, and some have stayed in the Church while others have left. Today, Peggy and I would be considered "lapsed Catholics," but we still pray daily and consider ourselves Catholic.

Epilogue :: **A Life Well Led**

My life has focused on family, education, and public service. As a young person growing up on Lauro's Hill on the King Ranch and going to school there and in Kingsville, Texas, I never dreamed it would be as exciting and fulfilling as it has been. My parents and the other Kineños were my first teachers. Mother and Dad and the people on the ranch prepared me for a life of attainments in learning and public service. My marriage to Peggy is the other key to my well-led life. How fortunate I was to have married her. Still vivid in my mind is the evening I proposed to her on the Iowa State campus. Then, I did not know asking her to marry me would be the wisest and most important decision I would ever make. Peggy has been the one and only love of my life, and daily I think about my good fortune to have found her. She bore our ten marvelous children. What a joy it has been to raise, nurture, educate, and watch them as they became adults, entered their professions, and had their own families. It has been wonderful to see how each of them has achieved so much in their lives. We are proud of each of them and will love them forever.

Now, many decades after leaving the King Ranch, I still remember my father's expectations of me. They were about education, service to country, and the admonition that I never disgrace the Cavazos name. Dad's commandments were not earthshaking, but looking back I believe I have met them.

I have received three earned degrees from two universities and twenty-four honorary degrees. Not bad for a youngster who started his education in a two-room schoolhouse on a ranch.

Most of our family at a gathering in Concord, MA, 2014.

I have served my country. Following graduation from high school, I enlisted in the US Army. I know it pleased Dad I enlisted and did not wait to be drafted for service in World War II. I have served my country in other ways as well. President Jimmy Carter appointed me to the board of regents of the Uniformed Services University for the Health Sciences, where I served from 1980 until 1985, the last three years as vice chairman of the board. I was US secretary of education under Presidents Ronald Reagan and George H. W. Bush from September 20, 1988, until December 15, 1990. I was a member of the US Army War College Board of Visitors from 1997 until 2003.

Looking back on my achievements in education and public service, and how I have led my life, I do not believe I have ever disgraced the Cavazos name.

With Peggy on the summit of Mount Washington, NH (6,288 feet), August 20, 2012. It is the highest peak in the northeastern United States.

Appendix :: **A Kineño's Journey: A Historical Assessment**

Gene B. Preuss, PhD

Lauro Cavazos's memoirs provide a unique insight into the personal life of a public figure. This book is his second collection of memoirs. His first book, *A Kineño Remembers: From the King Ranch to the White House*, focused on his professional journey, from growing up in South Texas to serving as secretary of education under Presidents Ronald Reagan and George H. W. Bush. Yet, Cavazos has never been interested in writing a political behind-the-scenes tell-all as some former presidential cabinet members have done, nor is he trying to criticize the educational policy of any particular administration. The present book, rather, is a collection of stories that revolve around three important facets of Larry Cavazos's life: his education, his commitment to service, and his family. In fact, family is the prevailing theme. At the heart of the book is the story of a man who tried to follow his father's advice about what is important in life: education, service, and your family. The stories herein focus on the experiences that shaped Larry Cavazos, and how despite the politics, successes, and disappointments, he remained committed to his father's counsel.

Yet, more than just a collection of memories and stories, Cavazos's story is important on many levels. Cavazos doesn't hesitate to share the challenges and disappointments he faced, or the fact that his life might have been radically different had he made other choices. While his first book was a chronological autobiography detailing his life experiences, this book is a retrospective—a reflection on a lifetime of learning that informed his life, attitudes, and relationships.

Yet, since history will remember Lauro Cavazos as a secretary of education during the Reagan and George H. W. Bush administrations, it makes sense to begin the story in Washington. There, Cavazos experienced some of the most frustrating incidents in his professional life. Reagan appointed Cavazos to the cabinet position at the end of his second administration. After a unanimous Senate confirmation, on August 9, 1988, Vice President George Bush swore in Cavazos.[1] At the ceremony, Reagan said that Cavazos's "commitment to the profession of teaching and to excellence in education, his belief in getting back to basics and things like homework, and above all his emphasis on education's special importance to America's minorities are messages I hope that he will sound far and wide across the Nation."[2] It was a much different message from that which Reagan had made almost eight years earlier when he campaigned for the presidency with the promise to eliminate the position.

In early May 1980, candidate Ronald Reagan denounced the recent elevation of the Education Department to a cabinet-level position, calling it "President Carter's new bureaucratic boondoggle." Reagan explained that education was one of many federal programs that belonged in the hands of the states, and not the national government:

> There are undoubtedly many other programs, which should similarly be returned to their proper levels of government. The sources of revenue to fund these programs should also return to local government. Such a return both would eliminate an unneeded level of bureaucracy and give the people more control over these important and expensive programs.[3]

Reagan's call for smaller, less expensive government resonated among the American public at a time the nation was reeling from "stagflation" and a retreating from New Deal and Great Society—era programs. During Reagan's two terms in office, his administration slashed away at the federal education budget, although Congress pushed back by approving more funds to education than the administration requested. For example, in 1981, Reagan requested $13.5 billion, while Congress appropriated an additional $1.3 billion; in 1983, he asked for $9.95 billion, while Congress increased the amount to $15.4 billion.[4]

Reagan's first appointment as education secretary, Terrel Bell, led a campaign to renew public concern about the nation's commitment to education with the report *A Nation at Risk*. "I tried to convince the president and his people of the bonds that tie together education, the economy, and military strength," he wrote in his memoir, *The Thirteenth Man*. "But notwithstanding the fact that I had been a teacher for much of my adult life," he admitted, "I never succeeded in getting this lesson across to them."[5] Reagan's next appointee, William Bennett, used the office as a "bully pulpit" to push values education in American schools. Compared to his predecessors, Cavazos's two years in office seemed rather quiet.

Although some have suggested that Cavazos did too little as secretary of education, a careful analysis of his term in the cabinet reveals the important part he played in the development of the federal role in public education. First, Cavazos was instrumental in the development of the early national standards movement that began in 1989 at the National Governors Association National Education Summit in Charlottesville, Virginia. Second, as secretary of education, Cavazos further assisted in the shift in Republican attitudes from opposing a federal presence in education policy toward a position that education was an important national issue. Educational reform transitioned from a Democratic issue to a national issue, as the Republican Party took up the call. Finally, Larry Cavazos recognized the importance of educating minority students just as the nation was beginning to realize that minority students would eventually make up a majority of public school children.

The suggestion that Republicans defined educational reform in the last part of the twentieth century is not new, nor is the claim that they were behind the standards and accountability movement. Historians have made these claims for years, pointing to the results of the education summit with the governors in late September 1989. George H. W. Bush's campaign promise to be the "education president" stands in stark contrast to candidate Ronald Reagan's promise to kill the Education Department. As vice president, Bush was certainly aware that education had become a national issue thanks to *A Nation at Risk* and the growing attention in the national discussion over the quality of America's public schools. A 1989 Gallup poll on public attitudes toward education showed that Americans believed that more attention should be paid to minority and low-income schools, and that there should be a national curriculum. The survey also showed that in addition to drugs and a lack of discipline, one of the biggest challenges in public education was a lack of funding for public schools.[6]

Despite the increased public concern about education, and a general feeling that more money should be allocated to public schools, Bush's education budgets, like Reagan's before him, were modest. Bush administration officials were hesitant to budget more funds to what they and more conservative elements believed was a state and local issue, not one for the federal government.

As one observer noted, "As a Republican who believed in a limited role for the federal government . . . [George H. W. Bush's] goals and the desires of the nation were incompatible."[7]

The 1989 education summit, however, was the high point of Bush's education agenda. The goal of the summit was to establish a national dialogue about the importance of education in the wake of *A Nation at Risk*. It was at once both a federal and a local response to the challenge of negotiating a national education agenda, and establishing a set of nationally recognized standards led by the governors. As one education scholar has noted, "the summit was a powerful signal that education was a national concern in the wake of a crisis in international economic competition."[8]

The summit itself has received scholarly treatment. Most commentators agree, however, that most attention has been focused on the first goal—that children would attend school ready to learn—largely as a result of the national standards movement that emerged from the summit. As Cavazos points out in this memoir, Bush's America 2000 goals that developed from the summit were adopted and changed by the Clinton administration for Goals 2000. As governor of Arkansas, Bill Clinton was a noted leader during the Charlottesville education summit. As president, he therefore had a vested interest in continuing Bush's America 2000 goals, and expanding on them. His administration also worked to get Bush's stalled education bill through Congress. On March 31, 1994, Clinton signed the Goals 2000: Educate America Act. The act provided additional funds for states to improve their schools, but allowed them instead of the federal government to set their own standards. Former president Bush's son, George W. Bush, as governor of Texas, used the funds to revamp the Texas school system, which subsequently was often referred to as the "Texas miracle."

When the younger Bush was elected to the nation's highest office in 2000, he wanted to carry his father's guidon as the "education president," and signed the No Child Left Behind Act (NCLB) of 2001, a reauthorization of the Elementary and Secondary Education Act of 1965, and signaled the end of Goals 2000. Despite the criticism that NCLB drew in subsequent years, it emerged from the standards milieu and outcome-based education models that attracted bipartisan support on Capitol Hill and the nation. By 2010 the popularity of charter schools evidenced the American public's serious doubts—not only about the standardized testing that went along with NCLB but about the future of public education in general. Many Americans continued to look toward charter schools such as those portrayed as successes in films like the 2010 documentary *Waiting for Superman*. Indeed, a 2008 article on presidental candidate Obama's views on education made it clear that the idea of education reform was no longer isolated to one particular party, nor easily defined into conservative or liberal categories.[9] While observers have noted the change in ownership of the educational reform agenda from the Democrats to the Republicans, and some have also traced the development of No Child Left Behind from the Charlottesville Education summit, the growing role of Hispanic education in the latter part of the twentieth century has largely been overlooked by historians.

The July 11, 1988, edition of *Time* magazine was a special issue featuring Hispanic culture in the United States. The cover photo was of a young girl on a bicycle in front of a mural of actor Edward James Olmos, who had played Los Angeles high school teacher Jaime Escalante in the 1988 film *Stand and Deliver*. The magazine's featured articles explored Hispanic influence in the arts, media, music, and language. It was a harbinger of the nation's growing attention to the Hispanic population. Whereas most Spanish-speaking Americans lived in Texas and California in the early and mid-twentieth century, by 1980 the Hispanic population had spread across the country. It was predicted that the Hispanic population would nearly double between 1980 and 2000, from 6.4 percent to 12 percent.[10]

By 1980, San Antonio had grown to become the ninth-largest city in the United States, and over half (53 percent) of its population was Hispanic. In 1981, Henry Cisneros became San Antonio's first Hispanic mayor. Texas Mexican-American activists had fought for greater political participation for decades. In the 1960s, farmworkers in Texas joined agricultural laborers in California in similar strikes. Largely Hispanic South Texas was one of the poorest regions in the United States. In 1966, Texas farm laborers marched from Rio Grande City to the state capitol in Austin to get the state to increase the minimum wage for farmworkers to $1.25 per hour and adopt the eight-hour workday. Most South Texas farm laborers at that time earned about 40 cents an hour and worked fourteen-hour days. A few years earlier other demonstrations in South Texas at Crystal City had increased Mexican American representation on the town's school board and city council and even among the high school cheerleaders.

In the early 1970s, as Texas politics was reeling from a scandal that exposed lawmakers who were taking bribes from a Houston-area developer, Hispanics launched the La Raza Unida Party and ran a candidate for governor. Although ultimately unsuccessful, the increased power Mexican Americans found in the ballot box translated into more Hispanic officials. In 1974 Hispanic leaders in San Antonio formed Communities Organized for Public Service (COPS); Henry Cisneros was elected to the city council in 1975. By 1977, Mexican Americans had captured a majority of the city council seats.[11] This success was reflected in other areas, even those with fewer Hispanic residents. In 1983, Federico Peña became the first Hispanic mayor of Denver, which had a Hispanic population of only 18 percent.[12]

In addition to the increase in Hispanic political power, the Hispanic population continued to grow. Between April and October 1980, over 100,000 Cubans arrived in South Florida during the so-called Mariel boatlift. In the wake of increasing tension on the island nation, President Fidel Castro allowed free passage to anyone who wanted to migrate elsewhere. Media reports that some of the refugees had criminal backgrounds, or may have been released from mental institutions and prisons, increased the frustration many Americans felt about increasing immigration. Thousands of Haitian refugees were arriving annually in addition to an estimated one-half to one million immigrants from Mexico, many who came in illegally. In 1983, Kevin McCarthy, a demographer for the RAND Corporation, called Los Angeles "the new Ellis Island," as he estimated that the city had become home for ninety thousand immigrants in 1982 and two million since 1970.[13] Growing concern over immigration, illegal and legal, and calls for stricter control over the border led the Reagan administration to propose stricter penalties on businesses found to be employing illegal aliens and more money for the Border Patrol of the Immigration and Naturalization Service.[14]

Moreover, despite their growth in population, Hispanics were declining in terms of education attainment. At the end of 1985, *Time* magazine reported that "minorities in general are shockingly underrepresented at all levels, from the top of the faculty down to the lowliest freshman." Despite accounting for 20 percent of the college-age population, minorities earned only 8 percent of the PhDs granted in 1983.[15] If this trend continued, the Center on Budget and Policy Priorities warned in 1986, Hispanics would soon become the nation's poorest minority group due to high unemployment, low-paying jobs, and large families.[16] Indeed, in July 1990, National Council of La Raza president Raul Yzaguirre observed that "not only are we the most under-educated minority in this country, but the gap between the educational standards of Hispanics and the educational attainment of the rest of the nation is increasing rather than decreasing."[17]

It was in this environment that Cavazos became president of Texas Tech University in mid-April 1980. At the time, the Lubbock Independent School District had been embroiled in a decade-long desegregation struggle with the federal courts, and just before Cavazos's installation as president, a group of Hispanic students at the TTU School of Law brought charges of discrimination against the university. The students and other groups were concerned about the absence of African American law students, and that women and minorities accounted for only 87 of the 445 faculty members at the university. "We're not slinging mud at Tech," Victoria Galvan, president of the Chicano Law Student Association, said. "There's just not been enough attention to affirmative action." The administration had not replaced the campus affirmative action director who resigned in 1979. History professor Lawrence Graves, who served as interim president prior to Cavazos's arrival, stated that the administration wanted to wait until Cavazos was hired before selecting a new director.[18] With the increased attention to the Hispanic population in the United States, concerns about their educational future, and concerns over a lack of minority representation among the faculty at the West Texas university, it's not surprising that Larry Cavazos devoted much of his energy to increasing opportunities for minority students at Texas Tech, and that he wanted to continue to close the educational gap among Hispanic, African American, and Native American students.

Furthermore, just prior to Cavazos's selection as the primary candidate in the Texas Tech presidential search, Texas higher education institutions received an unexpected criticism from the agency charged with overseeing colleges and universities within the state. In early February 1980, the chair of the Texas College and University System Coordinating Board (after 1987 known as the Texas Higher Education Coordinating Board), Beryl Milburn, complained about the lack of quality in Texas's colleges and universities. "A&M is getting better and competing with UT-Austin," she allowed after stating that the Texas flagship university ranked only among the nation's top twenty universities, not even in the top ten. As far as the state's other institutions, she said, "I don't think they approach quality." Her comments were met with a sharp response from West Texas board member Marshall Formby and his nephew, Clint Formby, a member of the Texas Tech Board of Regents.[19] Texas governor William Clements had appointed Milburn to the Coordinating Board after she had directed his recent gubernatorial campaign, as well as campaigns for other prominent Republican candidates, but she had long had an interest in educational issues. The governor soon supported Milburn's comments, adding, "We have let some of our degree granting universities turn into nothing more than degree factories."[20] So in addition to having to confront the challenges that Hispanics faced educationally, Cavazos became the president of a Texas university whose quality was in question. While he worked to improve Texas Tech's reputation, others were working to improve the educational pipeline for Hispanic students that would take them beyond public schools into colleges and universities. He held the presidency at Texas Tech until 1988, when he joined the Reagan administration as secretary of education.

On March 22, 1989, US Representative Albert Bustamante, a San Antonio Democrat and protégé of Henry B. Gonzalez, introduced H.R. 156, the Hispanic-Serving Institutions of Higher Education Act of 1989. US senator Lloyd Bentsen later sponsored the bill's Senate version. Bustamante stated that Laredo was the nation's most Hispanic area, as the group made up almost 98 percent of the city's population. "Knowledge of this population density will have a profound effect on how we address the needs of the Hispanic-American community," Bustamante stated. "And how these needs are addressed will do more to determine the future health of the United States than most can imagine." The bill, he explained, "will create a pipeline between high school and college for young Hispanic students. Through this legislation a network would be formed of colleges and universities with at least a 25 percent Hispanic student population. This network will then be given funding to help member schools recruit and retain young Hispanic men and women."[21]

In October 1989, the Congressional Hispanic Caucus asked the president "to support legislation that the caucus has introduced to enhance Hispanic educational achievement at the postsecondary level." As the Census Bureau noted, the Hispanic population in the United States had reached twenty million, making the United States the sixth-largest Hispanic nation. The Hispanic Caucus letter read: "Mr. President, on several occasions you have said that you want to reach out to the Hispanic community and that you support minority education because you want to be the Education President. You can lend credence to both those lofty goals by supporting the Hispanic Caucus' education initiative."[22]

In mid-January 1990, the Hispanic Coalition on Higher Education, made up of the Aspira Association, Inc., the Hispanic Association of Colleges and Universities, the Mexican American Legal Defense and Educational Fund, the National Association of Latino Elected Officials, the National Council of La

Raza, and the National Puerto Rican Coalition, sent a letter to E. "Kika" de la Garza, chair of the Congressional Hispanic Caucus, urging the congressman to bring up several "issues of concern affecting the Hispanic community," especially education.[23] The coalition stressed the importance of the renewal of the 1965 Higher Education Act. "Hispanics are slipping through the cracks of the educational pipeline," the letter read. The coalition explained how the six TRIO programs under Title IV of the act (Upward Bound, Talent Search, Student Support Services, Educational Opportunity Centers, McNair Post-Baccalaureate Achievement Programs, and TRIO staff training programs) are "designed to identify qualified individuals from disadvantaged backgrounds, to prepare them for a program of postsecondary education, to provide support services for such students who are pursuing programs of post-secondary education, to motivate and prepare students for doctoral programs, and to train individuals serving or preparing for service in programs and projects so designed" (Higher Education Act, subpart 2, ch. 1, sec. 402A). The coalition asked de la Garza to encourage Cavazos to increase TRIO program funding, begin collecting statistics on the number of minority students served by TRIO programs, and to encourage Hispanic-serving institutions and community-based organizations to participate in the provisions of TRIO programs. The coalition also wanted Cavazos to increase funding for college work study opportunities, Pell grants, state student incentive grants, Perkins loans, Stafford loans, and other Title IV student financial aid opportunities to assist Hispanic and other minority students who were often dependent on financial aid for higher education. They wanted Cavazos to ensure that Hispanic-serving institutions were receiving their share of Title III funds for minority institutions. Moreover, the coalition urged administrative support of H.R. 1561, sponsored by Congressman Albert Bustamante, and Senator Edward Kennedy's Excellence in Teaching Act (S. 1675), which contained provisions to recruit more minority educators.

In late February, Cavazos sent President Bush a memo regarding a Task Force on Hispanic Education (Bush asked Cavazos to convene the task force in early December 1989). The membership of the task force came from the White House Domestic Policy Council Education Policy Working Group, which included representatives from the Departments of Defense, Interior, Agriculture, Labor, and Health and Human Services, as well as the Office of Management and Budget, the Domestic Policy Council, and the White House Office of Public Liaison. The task force was charged with uncovering information about the extent of Hispanics participating in and benefiting from federal education programs, what obstacles Hispanics faced in participating in those programs, and what efforts could increase Hispanic participation in federal education programs.[24] Cavazos planned a series of five meetings for spring 1990 to solicit concerns about Hispanic education in San Antonio, Boston, Los Angeles, Chicago, and Miami.

In early March 1990, Cavazos announced the creation of a Department of Education committee that would create a national agenda for combating ethnic and racial discrimination on college campuses.[25] A few days later, however, Cavazos ran into trouble when he told a joint session of the Texas legislature that more money would not solve educational inequality. "Money is not the only answer," he said. "It is clearly not the answer to the education deficit." Cavazos's speech angered many. (See "Address to a Joint Session of the Texas Legislature" in the appendix for excerpts from the speech.) Democratic state representative Eddie Cavazos (no relation) of Corpus Christi, and chair of the House Mexican American caucus, said Cavazos's appearance resulted in "a sad and shameful day for all Hispanics in the state of Texas." The speech came during a special session of the legislature in the wake of a state supreme court decision that the inequality between rich and poor districts was unconstitutional. Cavazos's statements led three Democratic legislators to walk out in protest: state senator Hector Uribe of Brownsville and state representatives Paul Moreno of El Paso and Gregory Luna of San Antonio. Uribe was later quoted as saying, "I am angry at what Cavazos had to say. He has wound up being a mouthpiece for the Bush administration and nothing more." Cavazos tried to explain that he was not referring to the current problems in the state educational funding plan but to education spending nationwide. "I didn't say there were areas and people that don't need additional money," he noted. "I did say overall I thought there was sufficient spending nationwide already in terms of education."[26] The next month, in April 1990, Cavazos aroused more controversy when his remarks in San Antonio seemed to place the blame for the nation's high Hispanic dropout rate on parents.[27]

Soon after these two flaps that seemed to erode Cavazos's standing with the Hispanic community, his political clout seemed to decline. In August 1990, *U.S. News and World Report* delivered a sharp criticism of the first half of Bush's presidency. According to the article, the "administration's record on education has been largely one of superficial rhetoric, halfhearted initiatives and a devastating deficiency of leadership at the U.S. Department of Education."[28] Cavazos himself does not believe that the incidents affected his standing with the administration, as he points out in his first memoir.[29]

We might be led to believe that Cavazos's comments angered Hispanics, whom the Republicans were courting in the midterm elections and that this led to his forced resignation. The conservative *National Review* observed, however, that Cavazos "was not dumped until the President had brought another Hispanic, Bob Martinez, aboard as drug czar."[30] More pointedly, President Bush sent Cavazos a note just after the Austin speech commending him on his comments: "Our message and policies may not always be popular, but I am confident we are doing the right things to reform our educational system."[31] Indeed, Cavazos continued to stress the importance of parental involvement in children's education, including teaching children English, and emphasize that more money, poorly spent, would not improve education. These were issues Cavazos had raised while as president at Texas Tech in numerous speeches on improving minority educational opportunities. He made these same comments the next few months at a League of United Latin American Citizens (LULAC) convention as well as at the National Council of La Raza annual meeting without any resulting conflict.[32]

What had caused Texas Hispanic representatives to walk out of Cavazos's Austin speech was bad timing. Cavazos appeared before Texas lawmakers at a time when school spending was being cut at the state level. Cavazos, who stated that more money would not cure the needs of poor schoolchildren, was not well received in that context. But more vexing to Bush's education program was the pushback from conservative Republicans who had never abandoned Ronald Reagan's desire to defund the Education Department. Moreover, Cavazos drew national attention to the need for more federal encouragement of minority education, actions that were opposed by more conservative elements within the Republican Party. This was problematic to the administration since Bush was poised for a challenge from within his own party by Patrick Buchanan at midterm. Indeed, as more attention was drawn to the growing Hispanic population around the nation, it led to a backlash. Some came to believe that a cultural war existed, and there was growing hostility to affirmative action policies and bilingualism. E. D. Hirsch Jr.'s book *Cultural Literacy: What Every American Needs to Know* and Allan Bloom's *The Closing of the American Mind: How Higher Education Has Failed Democracy and Impoverished the Souls of Today's Students* charged that American education had declined because of a decline in cultural literacy. Education Secretary William Bennett joined the chorus of those applauding these salvos in the "culture wars," stating, "too many schools ignore the great minds and instead try to teach kids how to make a living."[33] As secretary of education, Bennett stated, "Our students know too little, and their command of essential skills is too slight. Our schools still teach curricula of widely varying quality. Good schools for disadvantaged and minority children are much too rare, and the dropout rate among black and Hispanic youth in many of our inner cities is perilously high."[34]

Just a few days after Cavazos's resignation, Michael Williams, an African American attorney and the Department of Education's assistant secretary for civil rights, declared that minority scholarships were unconstitutional. A *Newsweek* article stated that while it seemed that the ruling would have little actual impact upon minority students, it appeared to many that the Bush administration "was no longer reaching out to black America, and that some form of Willie Hortonism was back." (Horton was a convicted Massachusetts felon who committed further violent crimes when released as part of a weekend furlough program that Massachusetts governor Michael Dukakis had supported. Bush capitalized on the incident during his 1988 campaign against presidential candidate Dukakis.)[35] "The announcement outraged civil rights, education, and business groups, emboldened Democrats, and forced Bush to order a speedy retreat from the position," *Business Week* reported.[36] When Lamar Alexander became the next secretary of education, he reversed Williams's ruling.

The history of education is an overlooked field. Although there are a good number of historians who study, research, and write about educational topics, the history of education is generally overlooked by the public. Larry Cavazos helps remind us of the daily behind-the-scenes role education plays in American politics, as well as how one person's educational quest influenced the lives of every member of his family, as well as countless others in colleges and universities around the nation in his role as an educator, college professor and administrator, university president, and ultimately as secretary of education.

As a nation, we believe in supporting some basic education for our children. A smaller percentage will continue their formal education beyond graduation, but generally that is left up to them to decide. Although our founding fathers did not include anything about education in the charter documents of the nation, the important role education would eventually play in our developing nation certainly filled their thoughts. Lauro Cavazos Jr. certainly shared in that vision of the importance of education. He likes to quote Thomas Jefferson, who stated, "If a nation expects to be ignorant and free in a state of civilization, it expects what never was and never will be. If we are to guard against ignorance and remain free, it is the responsibility of every American to be informed." Cavazos believes this responsibility compels our nation to provide a quality education for all American children. His educational beliefs are rooted deep in his own personal and professional experiences, and he continues to be a staunch advocate of the rallying cry that he so frequently stated as secretary of education, and which was reflected in America 2000 and Goals 2000, that every child should be able to come to school ready to learn.

Appendix :: **Two Speeches by Lauro Cavazos**

The following speeches reflect Lauro Cavazos's long-term interest in greater educational opportunities for minority students. They have been edited to remove introductory remarks, repetition, and concluding remarks.

The first speech, "Hispanics and Education," was made during his first semester as president of Texas Tech University. He traveled to Southwest Texas State University in San Marcos (now Texas State University—San Marcos) to stress the importance education has played in the Hispanic community, and the problems they faced in the late 1970s and early 1980s.

The second speech was delivered a decade later when Cavazos was secretary of education. The speech angered several South Texas legislators who were in special session to address educational funding issues. In this speech, Cavazos points out the lingering problems that have continued to plague Hispanics and stressed the importance of continuing the struggle for educational success.

Full copies of both speeches can be found in the Lauro F. Cavazos Papers, 1943–1991, at the Southwest Collection/Special Collections Libraries at Texas Tech University.

"Hispanics and Education"

Education is an issue of primary significance to the survival of our democracy. Lack of education among any of our citizens threatens us all. . . .

I remember my father saying, "Son, educate yourself. It is the one thing that no one can ever take away from you." Your parents did the same for you; or, if not your parents, a teacher, a counselor, or a friend.

What kind of gift have those heroes bestowed upon us?

For one thing, they have given us a tool by which free men govern themselves. Our forefathers in the United States recognized this tool.

The media frequently quote Thomas Jefferson in their defense of freedom of the press. One of their favorite quotations is from a Jefferson letter in which he said, "Were it left to me to decide whether we should have government without newspapers, or newspapers without a government, I should not hesitate a moment to prefer the latter." What they usually fail to quote is what Jefferson said after that. He said, "But I should mean that every man should receive those papers, and be capable of reading them." Jefferson believed in the common sense of the well-informed common man.

We of Spanish descent have reason to be proud of the Hispanic tradition in education. . . . We have had scholars of note throughout the ages, but we have, I think you agree, a more dismal record when it comes to educating masses of people.

Even today the figures are frightening. In the United States, 17 percent of Hispanics who are twenty-five years old or older have less than five years of schooling; 19 percent of those between the ages of fourteen and nineteen are high school dropouts; 40 percent of all Hispanics between the ages of eighteen and twenty-four did not graduate from high school. . . .

I would like to dwell for a moment on just the economic impact of these statistics. We talk about the high cost of education, but we cannot overlook the benefits.

> For every one dollar invested in a child's elementary education, we can look for a return of between 23.7 and 155 percent per year in that child's eventual income.

> For every one dollar we invest in a child's secondary education, there will be an annual return of between 4 and 28 percent in his or her income as an adult.

> For every one dollar invested in a college education, there will be annual income return of between 9.6 and 17.5 percent.

It does, indeed, pay to educate. We all benefit from the rewards of economic development made possible by the increased income of educated individuals.

So it is not a question of, "Can we afford to educate our children?" It is a question of, "Can we afford not to educate every child?"

Economically then, education is a sound investment. But what about the social value of education? I believe it is imperative that people who want to live in a democracy have the education to make that democracy work. Consider the emphasis our forefathers placed upon public education. Democracy, in their view, could not succeed without an educated electorate. . . .

Too few minority students—the black and the Hispanic students—are enrolling in colleges. Too many drop out of high school—or drop out even before they reach high school. It is true, of course, that the number of Hispanics attending colleges and universities is increasing, but the greatest numbers are concentrated in undergraduate programs, particularly in two-year colleges. Black student enrollment in higher education is tapering off, and many of those enrolled are part-time students. . . .

I ask you today to use your native intellect to achieve your vision—to make liberty work for all of us. I ask you to look upon your heritage and your future as one road. . . . Opportunities for public education are not enough. To ensure our liberty, to enjoy our independence, we must take advantage of our opportunities and persuade others to do the same. To drop out, to turn our backs on our opportunities, is to turn our backs on those who died for our freedom.

To the presidents of every Texas college and university I speak also, urging each of you to personally take on a special burden in regard to education. . . .

The harvest we reap tomorrow depends upon the effort we spend in planting seeds today. We will serve neither the institutions we head nor the state we live in if we turn our backs on any child in Texas.

"Address to a Joint Session of the Texas Legislature"

Many people tend to take our school system for granted. The buildings and buses are much the same as when we were young, and the process doesn't seem to have changed much, so we assume the schools work just about as well as they always have. Well, you know as well as I do that this is not the case. There are schools in America, and in Texas, that are failing to prepare an entire generation of young people for the challenges of the twenty-first century. I believe there is no more vital subject for reasoned debate today than how to improve America's schools, and I urge you to use this special session to give education in Texas the attention it deserves. You must act soon. To delay, to wait, will only cause this great state to fall further behind on its commitment to educational excellence for all of its citizens. . . .

We are suffering from an education deficit, which I believe is far more threatening to the economic health and well-being of America than the more publicized budget and trade deficits. And just as the accountants in Washington can track each drop of red ink, I can quantitate for you in grim detail the magnitude of the education deficit:

> There are approximately 27 million Americans who lack basic literacy skills, and an estimated 45–50 million more who are functionally illiterate, or unable to read well enough to perform effectively in the workplace. Texas ranks next to last in literacy amongst the states.

> 600,000–700,000 young people drop out of school each year. In Texas, 92,000 of the students entering ninth grade in 1983–84 had not received their high school diploma four years later.

> The average graduation rate after four years of high school was 71.1 percent for the nation in 1987. In Texas, the graduation rate was 65.1 percent in the same year, low enough to rank Texas forty-third out of the fifty states.

> The national SAT score average fell thirty-three points from 1972 to 1988. The SAT average in Texas fell by forty-two points during the same period. In 1988, Texas ranked seventeenth of the twenty-two states that use the SAT, or fifth from the bottom.

> The latest results of the Texas Education Assessment of Minimal Skills confirm what the national data suggest. Only 62 percent of ninth graders demonstrated mastery of all subjects tested in the 1988–89 assessments. That means four out of ten students failed to meet the minimal standards set by the state for reading, writing, and mathematics.

This litany of failure quantitates our education deficit. I could go on and on, but the picture is clear. Texas is a full partner in the decline that has produced America's education deficit. . . .

Allow me to suggest some principles and parameters of reform to guide you in your deliberations. First, money is clearly not the answer to the education deficit. Since 1981, aggregate US spending on elementary and secondary education has grown from $157 to $199 billion, an increase of 27 percent after inflation. Yet student test scores improved little during that same period. . . .

Now, I don't mean to deny that some schools in some districts might need additional resources, but the real answer lies in better utilization of existing resources. It is estimated, for example, that almost 60 percent of the dollars spent on education go to administration, and not to the classroom. Clearly the most important question that faces all of us is accountability: What are we getting for our money? Quite frankly, we are not getting what we're paying for. And the best way to change this is to inject some competition into our school systems, to give parents and children the option of choosing a quality school that meets their particular needs. . . .

The idea of competition in education may frighten some people. I will not deny that we need to be careful in reforming our schools, particularly in view of the failure of past efforts. But I am convinced that some of the major barriers to educational improvement include fear of change, a desire to preserve the status quo, lack of vision, and an unwillingness to give up authority or accept responsibility.

Some in Texas are concerned that choice will resegregate our schools. This is one criticism that frankly mystifies me. First, let me state that I have spent my entire life fighting racial, gender, and ethnic discrimination, and one of my strongest commitments as secretary of education is to minority advancement. President Bush and I would never advocate any education reform that threatened minority achievement. . . .

Minorities in Texas are usually limited to the schools that serve them so poorly. Because programs involving academic choice can change this, they hold great promise for the advancement of minorities and other educationally disadvantaged groups. Early choice experiments, such as magnet schools and the controlled choice model employed in Massachusetts, were designated specifically to desegregate schools. At the heart of academic choice, emphasis is on equity, among both students and schools. . . .

Furthermore, choice plans extend to the economically disadvantaged a privilege previously enjoyed only by the affluent, who can afford to move anywhere. Financial constraints have heretofore limited the options, and thereby the opportunities, available to even the most gifted children in less affluent districts. Open enrollment plans change all this, providing minorities with the same opportunities as other members of society. With academic choice, minorities can leave second-rate schools and pursue excellence in education. I am convinced that those who will benefit the most from a well-designed choice plan are those who need it most.

Those suffering the greatest education deficits include persons with disabilities, the economically disadvantaged, and minorities. Virtually every indicator of educational progress shows that these groups are being left behind.

This cannot be if the nation, and the State of Texas, is to advance. We cannot waste the potential that goes untapped every time a person drops out of school, or graduates without the skills necessary to lead a productive life. . . .

The future of Texas rests with the children sitting in its classrooms now—children that too often are being shortchanged by an obsolete educational system. Unless we act soon, we will discover the terrible penalty of failing to prepare large numbers of our young people to meet the challenges of our complex world. . . . With so many children at-risk, the future of Texas is also at-risk. The only solution is for Texas to pursue educational restructuring with the same vigor and purpose it devotes to economic restructuring. . . .

Notes

1. Ronald W. Reagan, "Remarks at the Swearing-in Ceremony for Lauro F. Cavazos as Secretary of Education," September 20, 1988, Public Papers of the President: Ronald Reagan, 1981–1989, https://reaganlibrary.archives.gov/archives/speeches/1988/092088c.htm.

2. Dr. Lauro F. Cavazos, "Speech to the Employees of the Department of Education," September 21, 1988, folder 6, "Department of Education, Speeches (September 1988)," box 40, Lauro F. Cavazos Papers, 1943–1991, Southwest Collection/Special Collections Libraries, Texas Tech University, Lubbock, Texas.

3. Lauro F. Cavazos, "Statement before the Senate Committee on Labor and Human Resources," January 27, 1989, folder 3, box 34, Lauro F. Cavazos Papers, 1943–1991, Southwest Collection/Special Collections Libraries, Texas Tech University, Lubbock, Texas. Also found in US Senate Committee on Labor and Human Resources, *The Labor Shortage—Poverty and Educational Aspects: Hearings before the Committee on Labor and Human Resources, United States Senate, One Hundred First Congress, First Session, January 26 and 27, 1989* (Washington, DC: US GPO, 1989).

4. George H. W. Bush, "Remarks at the University of Virginia Convocation in Charlottesville," September 28, 1989, Public Papers of the President George H. W. Bush, George Bush Presidential Library and Museum, https://bush41library.tamu.edu/archives/public-papers/969, accessed March 18, 2016.

5. Office of the Press Secretary, "National Goals for Education," February 26, 1990, White House, Washington, DC. Available at ERIC ED 319143, http://files.eric.ed.gov/fulltext/ED319143.pdf, accessed March 18, 2016.

6. National Education Goals Panel, *National Education Goals: Lessons Learned, Challenges Ahead* (Washington, DC: National Education Goals Panel, 1999), http://govinfo.library.unt.edu/negp/reports/negp31.pdf, accessed March 18, 2016.

7. David Q. Bates, memo to Lauro Cavazos, n.d., folder 1, "Hispanic Education, 1987–1990," box 38, Lauro F. Cavazos Papers, 1943–1991, Southwest Collection/Special Collections Libraries, Texas Tech University, Lubbock, Texas.

8. George H. W. Bush, "Remarks on Signing the National Hispanic Heritage Month Proclamation and the Educational Excellence for Hispanic Americans Executive Order," September 24, 1990, Public Papers of the President George H. W. Bush, George Bush Presidential Library and Museum, https://bush41library.tamu.edu/archives/public-papers/2249, accessed March 18, 2016.

9. Indian Nations at Risk Task Force, *Indian Nations at Risk: An Educational Strategy for Action* (Washington, DC: US Department of Education, October 1991), 6–7.

10. William Demmert, Peggy McCardle, Joan Mele-McCarthy, and Kathleen Leos, "Preparing Native American Children for Academic Success: A Blueprint for Research," *Journal of American Indian Education* 45.3 (2006): 93.

11. Lauro F. Cavazos, "Emphasizing Performance Goals and High-Quality Education for All Students," *Phi Delta Kappan* 83 (May 2002): 697.

12. Arne Duncan, "No Child Left Behind: Early Lessons from State Flexibility Waivers," Testimony of Secretary of Education Arne Duncan to the US Senate Committee on Health, Education, Labor, and Pensions, February 7, 2013, http://www.ed.gov/news/speeches/no-child-left-behind-early-lessons-state-flexibility-waivers, accessed March 18, 2016.

Notes from essay by Gene B. Preuss, PhD

1. "Cavazos Takes the Oath as Education Secretary," *New York Times*, September 21, 1988.

2. Ronald W. Reagan, "Remarks Announcing the Resignation of William J. Bennett as Secretary of Education and the Nomination of Lauro F. Cavazos," *Public Papers of President Ronald W. Reagan*, Ronald Reagan Presidential Library, http://www.reagan.utexas.edu/archives/speeches/1988/080988c.htm (accessed February 16, 2008).

3. Ronald W. Reagan, speech, "Reagan Calls Department of Education 'Bureaucratic Boondoggle,'" May 4, 1980, *NBC News*, New York: NBC Universal, https://highered.nbclearn.com/portal/site/HigherEd/browse/?cue card=3552 (accessed March 18, 2012).

4. Deborah A. Verstegen and David L. Clark, "The Diminution in Federal Expenditures for Education during the Reagan Administration," *Phi Delta Kappan* 70 (October 1988): 134–35.

5. Terrel H. Bell, *The Thirteenth Man: A Reagan Cabinet Memoir* (New York: Free Press, 1988), 163.

6. Stanley M. Elam and Alec M. Gallup, "The 21st Annual Gallup Poll of the Public's Attitude toward the Public Schools," *Phi Delta Kappan* 71 (September 1989): 42.

7. Holly G. McIntush, "Political Truancy: George Bush's Claim to the Mantle of 'Education President,'" in *The Rhetorical Presidency of George H. W. Bush*, edited by Martin J. Medhurst (College Station: Texas A&M University Press, 2006), 102.

8. Maurie R. Berube, *American Presidents and Education* (New York: Greenwood Press, 1991), 129.

9. Josh Patashnik, "Reform School: The Education (on Education) of Barack Obama," *New Republic* 238 (March 26, 2008): 12–13; See also Diane Ravitch, *The Death and Life of the Great American School System: How Testing and Choice Are Undermining Education* (New York: Basic Books, 2010), 15–30; Lawrence J. McAndrews, *The Era of Education: The Presidents and the Schools, 1965–2001* (Urbana: University of Illinois Press, 2006), 135–66; and William J. Reese, *America's Public Schools: From the Common School to "No Child Left Behind"* (Baltimore: Johns Hopkins University Press, 2011), 323–33.

10. George J. Church, "Hispanics a Melding of Cultures," *Time*, July 8, 1985.

11. Russ Hoyle, "Now Is the Time, Compadres," *Time*, April 13, 1991.

12. "A Mile High," *Time*, July 4, 1983.

13. Kurt Anderson, "The New Ellis Island," *Time*, June 13, 1983.

14. "Controls for an Alien Invasion," *Time*, August 3, 1981.

15. Ezra Bowen, "Dramatic Drops for Minorities," *Time*, November 11, 1985.

16. "American Notes Minorities," *Time*, September 15, 1986.

17. Peter Schmidt, "Hispanics' Achievement Is Declining as Population Grows, La Raza Warns," *Education Week*, August 1, 1990, 19.

18. Lisa Paikowski, "Prolonged Battles Fought by Schools, Feds during 1970s," *Lubbock Avalanche-Journal*, January 3, 1980; "Tech Petition to Spur Discrimination Inquiry," *Dallas Morning News*, April 17, 1980; Doug Nurse, "Complaints Filed against Tech," *University Daily*, April 17, 1980; Doug Nurse, "Affirmative Action: A Lengthy and Complex Problem for Tech," *University Daily*, April 29, 1980.

19. "Regent Sees Class Outside of the 'Top 2,'" *Dallas Morning News*, February 9, 1980.

20. Lee Jones, "Overall Strength of Texas College System Questioned," *Dallas Morning News*, February 13, 1980.

21. *Congressional Record*, June 23, 1989, p. H3125.

22. *Congressional Record*, October 12, 1989, p. H6987.

23. Hispanic Coalition on Higher Education, letter to E. Kika de la Garza, January 17, 1990, folder 1, "Hispanic Education, 1987–1990," box 38, Lauro F. Cavazos Papers, 1943–1991, Southwest Collection/Special Collections Libraries, Texas Tech University, Lubbock, Texas.

24. David Q. Bates, memo to Lauro Cavazos, n.d., folder 1, "Hispanic Education, 1987–1990," box 38, Lauro F. Cavazos Papers, 1943–1991, Southwest Collection/Special Collections Libraries, Texas Tech University, Lubbock, Texas.

25. "Washington Update," *Chronicle of Higher Education*, March 7, 1990, A29.

26. Cindy Rugeley, "Cavazos Sparks Furor in Austin," *Houston Chronicle*, March 7, 1990.

27. Roberto Suro, "Cavazos Criticizes Hispanic Parents on Schooling," *New York Times*, April 11, 1990; "Hispanics Lash Out at Cavazos' Remarks," *Houston Post*, April 12, 1990.

28. Thomas Toch, Kenneth T. Walsh, and Ted Slafsky, "The President's Worst Subject," *U.S. News and World Report*, August 6, 1990, 46.

29. Lauro F. Cavazos, *A Kineño Remembers: From the King Ranch to the White House* (College Station: Texas A&M University Press, 2006), 253–56.

30. William McGurn, "Bennett's Surprise," *National Review*, January 28, 1991, 49.

31. George H. W. Bush, letter to Secretary Cavazos, March 13, 1990, folder 2, "Department of Education Correspondence, Professional, 1990," box 28, Lauro F. Cavazos Papers, 1943–1991, Southwest Collection/Special Collections Libraries, Texas Tech University, Lubbock, Texas.

32. Lauro Cavazos, "LULAC Convention, Tucson, Arizona," May 31, 1990, "Department of Education, Speeches (May 1990) [Continued]," folder 5, box 42, Lauro F. Cavazos Papers, 1943–1991, Southwest Collection/Special Collections Libraries, Texas Tech University, Lubbock, Texas; Lauro Cavazos, "Remarks Prepared for the National Council of La Raza Annual Conference," July 17, 1990, "Department of Education, Speeches (July 1990)," folder 7, box 42, Lauro F. Cavazos Papers, 1943–1991, Southwest Collection/Special Collections Libraries, Texas Tech University, Lubbock, Texas.

33. Ezra Bowen, "Are Student Heads Full of Emptiness?" *Time*, August 17, 1987.

34. William J. Bennett, *American Education: Making It Work: A Report to the President and the People, April 1988* (Washington, DC: US Department of Education, 1988), 2.

35. Tom Morganthau and Ann McDaniel, "Dropping a Hot Potato," *Newsweek*, December 24, 1990.

36. Douglas Harbrecht, "A Bull in the President's China Shop," *Business Week*, December 31, 1990 / January 7, 1991, 43.

Index